The Quest for Sustainable Business
An Epic Journey in Search of Corporate Responsibility

THE QUEST FOR SUSTAINABLE BUSINESS

An Epic Journey in Search of Corporate Responsibility

Wayne Visser

Routledge
Taylor & Francis Group

LONDON AND NEW YORK

First published 2012 by Greenleaf Publishing Limited

Published 2017 by Routledge
2 Park Square, Milton Park, Abingdon, Oxon OX14 4RN
711 Third Avenue, New York, NY 10017, USA

Routledge is an imprint of the Taylor & Francis Group, an informa business

Cover by LaliAbril.com

British Library Cataloguing in Publication Data:
A catalogue record for this book is available from the British Library.

ISBN-13: 978-1-906093-76-1 (pbk)

Contents

Author's introduction

This book takes you on a journey, both around the world and through time: a journey of discovery and of ideas. In the pages that follow, I tell the story of my quest for sustainable business, a search that has taken me to over 50 countries in the past 20 years. The path begins in Africa and winds its way through Asia, North America, Europe, Australasia and Latin America. Along the way, I share what I have learned in my encounters with mega-corporations and small farmers, and conversations with CEOs and social entrepreneurs. There are facts and figures about world trends, and interviews with thought leaders and activists. This is a tale that consciously weaves the personal and the professional, mixing anecdotes and case studies. It looks outwards and reflects inwards, and is both autobiography and the life story of a global movement.

My inspiration for the book came when I decided, in 2010, to leave the security of the University of Cambridge – where I had been developing a Master's in Sustainability Leadership – and set out on a 'Corporate Social Responsibility (CSR) quest world tour', which took me to 20 countries on five continents, travelling continuously for nine months. It was one of those great ironies of my life that I had to leave one of the world's premier educational institutions in order to advance my learning. I had an itch and I needed to scratch it. I wanted to reconnect with what was happening on the ground in countries around the world; and I was excited by the prospect of making new friends, seeing new lands, soaking up diverse cultures and discovering fresh case studies. More than anything, I needed to rekindle the passion that had started me on this career in sustainable business 20 years before.

My intention was always to capture my insights along the journey and share them with a wider sustainable business audience. One of the ways I did this was to conduct nearly 100 video interviews, all of which are shared on the CSR International channel on YouTube, and referred to throughout this text. The other way was to keep a diary and to write a book about my travel experiences – the book you are now reading. However, when I started to write, I repeatedly found myself referring to earlier parts of my career. Gradually, I began to wonder if there was a bigger story to be told. After all, my journey began in the lead-up to the Rio Earth Summit in 1992, and here we were, 20 years later, preparing for Rio+20.

In the interim, I had been lucky to work, study, teach and research in the field of sustainable business, tracking its path as it emerged from a fringe concern to a mainstream movement and a global profession. There were stories to tell that ranged from hippie-like adventures in eco-villages and community enterprises to hard-nosed consulting assignments for big global brands. I had worked as a strategy analyst for Capgemini and set up and ran KPMG's Sustainability Services in South Africa. I had studied human ecology in Edinburgh and corporate social responsibility in Nottingham; established an economics NGO (non-governmental organisation) and a CSR social enterprise; lectured to students in countries around the world, from Germany and the United States to India and China; and had given keynote speeches to countless audiences, from Australia and Singapore to Hungary and Nigeria.

These had all given me invaluable exposure to people working in sustainable business. But besides these pragmatic experiences, I had also been on a remarkable intellectual journey. I wrote *Beyond Reasonable Greed* just at the moment when the world was shaken by Enron's collapse, and had tried to advance a neglected area of scholarship with *Corporate Citizenship in Africa*, capturing my own PhD research on what motivates sustainability professionals in *Making a Difference*. In *Landmarks for Sustainability* I had traced the events and initiatives that changed the world, and I interviewed some of the world's leading thinkers for *The Top 50 Sustainability Books* project. I had corralled over 100 experts for *The A to Z of Corporate Social Responsibility* and profiled 58 countries in *The World Guide to CSR*. Finally, frustrated by the apparent failure of sustainable business practices to reverse our most serious social and environmental trends, I had written *The Age of Responsibility*, calling for CSR 2.0 as a new DNA for business.

This book, therefore, is an attempt to bring all of these experiences and insights together in one place – to tell a story of personal, professional and intellectual development, which occurred on an epic journey in search of corporate responsibility. I began writing the story chronologically, but quickly found that grouping it into regions and countries made more sense. The consequence is that there is a fair bit of time travelling in the chapters that follow, as I hop backwards and forwards in time. I hope that this is not too dizzying for you as a reader.

I should also caution that I have not tried to present a comprehensive profile of sustainable business in the countries that I have visited – if you are looking for this, I recommend *The World Guide to CSR*. Rather, I share anecdotes and lessons from experiences I have had and people I have met, where the context happens to be a particular country or region. I have tried to mention many of the individuals who either looked after me, or informed and inspired me along the way. But I am sure there are many I have left out, for which I apologise in advance. I am no less grateful.

Finally, I am conscious that this book represents only one perspective on the evolution of sustainable business. It is my story and my path of learning, seen through my eyes. I am sure that many of you will have been on your own quest for sustainable business. I only hope that my story will inspire you to share your own. And if you are still near the beginning of your journey, I hope it will encourage you to be bold in choosing the way ahead, so that you can echo the words of Robert Frost when you look back in 20 years, saying 'two roads diverged in a wood, and I – I took the one less travelled by'.[1]

1 'The Road Not Taken', by Robert Frost (1874–1963).

Roots and shoots

Early days (Zimbabwe: 1970–1978)

A child of Africa

Do our childhood experiences shape our future careers? To a greater or lesser extent, I believe they do. In my case, they certainly had an indirect influence. I was born an African, in the country known today as Zimbabwe, then still Rhodesia and named after the colonialist Cecil Rhodes in the late 1800s. Today, despite having travelled to over 50 countries during the course of my life and work, and despite living in the United Kingdom as I write this, I retain a strong and proud African identity.

Growing up in Africa, basking in her sunshine and breathing her dust, I cannot help but be acutely and painfully aware of the injustices and suffering that the land and its people have endured for centuries – exploitation by colonial conquerors, mercenary slave traders, corrupt politicians, military dictators and unhinged megalomaniacs. Could my immersion in the continent's struggles have planted the seed for my own subsequent struggle against the injustices that communities and nature have endured at the hands of business?

Unbeknown to me while growing up, my country and hometown are both classic examples of the longstanding abuse of corporate power in the pursuit of wealth. I was born in what was then a small town, Bulawayo, a name that comes from the Ndebele word Gubuluwayo and which has the rather ominous meaning: 'a place of killing'. This is thought to be a reference to the struggle of Prince Lobengula to claim the throne of his father, King Mzilikazi, who founded Bulawayo in around 1840. But the town turned out to be part of a much bigger struggle – the so-called 'scramble for Africa' – the rush by colonial empires to grab and control the continent's mineral riches.

At the heart of this imperial quest in Africa was Cecil John Rhodes, English-born explorer turned entrepreneur and business magnate, who founded De Beers, the mining company which at one time controlled 90% of the world's diamond trade. It all began in 1871 when Rhodes joined the diamond rush and headed to Kimberley in South Africa. Financed by the private investment bank Rothschild, over the next 17 years Rhodes succeeded in buying up all the smaller diamond-mining operations in the Kimberley area. His monopoly was entrenched in 1889 through a strategic partnership with the London-based Diamond Syndicate, which agreed to control the world supply of diamonds, and thereby maintain high prices.

It was also in 1889 that Rhodes established the British South Africa Company, which was empowered under royal charter to trade with African rulers such as King Lobengula, as well as to form banks; to own, manage, grant or distribute land; and to raise a police force. In return, the company agreed to develop the territory it controlled, to respect existing African laws, to allow free trade within its territory and to respect all religions. Four years later, the very same company recruited its own army and invaded King Lobengula's territory in what became known at the 1893 Matabele War. The troops and white settlers occupied the town and Bulawayo was declared a settlement under the rule of the British South Africa Company. Rhodes ordered that a new town be built on the ruins of Lobengula's royal place.

Two years later, Rhodes used his company to hatch another dubious plot. In an attempt to bring South Africa under British rule, he planned to stimulate unrest among foreign workers (so-called *uitlanders*) and use the outbreak of open revolt as an excuse to invade and annex the territory. Unfortunately for Rhodes, what later became known as the Jameson Raid was launched prematurely in December 1895 and only managed to push within 20 miles of Johannesburg before superior Boer forces compelled Sir Leander Starr Jameson and his men to surrender. Jameson was subsequently tried in London, found guilty and sentenced to 15 months' imprisonment as a first-class misdemeanant. Rhodes managed to elude any charges of complicity.

For me, the lesson to learn from Rhodes and his British South Africa Company is clear: when companies have too much power – either political power or economic power by virtue of being a monopoly or oligopoly – they will tend to abuse that power to enrich themselves. The fusion of private economic interest with public political sanction is the ultimate toxic recipe for corporate irresponsibility. We see it in all the classic cases of business crimes against society and the environment, whether it is through the regressive political lobbying of the oil industry in the United States, or the majority ownership of Shell by Nigeria's former military dictatorship government.

We also find echoes of this same lesson in the story of Rockefeller and his Standard Oil Company, which I wrote up as a case study in *The Age of Responsibility*. Despite his latterly acquired reputation as a great philanthropist, Rockefeller was a businessman with highly dubious ethical credentials. In the process of building Standard Oil into a company that monopolised 90% of oil refining in the United States, he was involved in a variety of shady dealings, from cartel collusion and predatory pricing to excessive market aggression. For example, over a four-month period in 1872, in what was later known as the 'Cleveland Conquest' or 'Cleveland Massacre', Standard Oil performed hostile takeovers of 22 of its 26 competitors in the region.

Rhodes's use of private military forces also reminds me of the lessons learned by BP in Colombia, where the company was accused of complicity in human rights abuses in 1996. As then-CEO John Browne later recalled,

> BP entered that country … seeking a tantalising prize of rich resources amidst violent insurrection, a polarised society and dark undercurrents in politics … Clearly, security was a challenge but we assumed we had the answer – a thick barbed wire fence with security personnel and, if necessary, the help of the Colombian Army. What we hadn't realised was that a fence keeps you in as well as others out … The company's brand, its reputation, and ultimately its value, had been laid on the line because of our failure to fully appreciate our human rights responsibilities.

Growing up wild

The fact that I grew up in a country where human rights were being systematically undermined was a realisation that only came later. My childhood was spent (not unhappily) in the midst of the so-called 'Rhodesian bush war', in which the black indigenous majority were fighting for independence from white colonial minority rule, then under Prime Minister Ian Smith. I was too young to understand the true significance of what was playing out all around me. It was only belatedly, in South Africa, that I came to understand the malignancy of blind belief in white superiority and the horrors of institutionalised racism.

For me, the early character-shaping influence of growing up in Africa was something far less moralistic. If there was a defining theme, it was proximity to nature. My parents often took us to visit my grandparents' dairy farm, where we played in the haystacks. At other times, we went camping, canoeing, or on 'safari'. One of the clearest memories I have is of visiting Hwange National Park (then called Wankie), which is Zimbabwe's largest game reserve, a short plane-hop from Victoria Falls. Apart from the incredible wildlife we inevitably encountered – everything from elephants, giraffes and crocodiles to zebras, warthogs and monkeys – there was an incident early one morning that is branded in my memory. An antelope ran into the forecourt of the hotel, cut and bleeding and still entangled in a poacher's wire snare. The frightened deer was caught, the wire snare removed and the animal released back into the wild.

Little did I know at the time, but I had witnessed a potent symbol of another war that was already raging – between man and nature, conservation and development, environmental protection and community inclusion – between the value of biodiversity and the economics of greed. This was brought into even sharper contrast years later, in April 1990, when I returned to Zimbabwe for a pan-African Wildlife Management conference, organised by the student organisation AIESEC. After the conference, on board the Trans-Karoo train from Harare back to Cape Town, I vented my frustration in a letter to a friend:

> Although at times frustrating, the conference was really worthwhile because it brought together people from Zambia, Botswana, Kenya, Zimbabwe and South Africa. Also, it made one more aware of the importance (even the necessity) of conserving our environment and in particular 'our' wildlife. But frustrating

for me because 'conservation' seems to involve treating wildlife as a commodity; as something which humanity 'owns' and has the right to determine the destiny of. What am I talking about? I'm talking about wildlife managers having the audacity to decide that the life of an elephant is worth $5,000, or an impala $75 (these are the trophy fees for sporting hunters). Even the idea of culling wildlife seems wrong to me. Indeed, the concept of 'wildlife management' or 'environmental management' seems a contradiction in terms. An environment manages itself. Isn't our interference at the heart of the problem?

Only elephants should wear ivory

I'm probably not quite so purist these days. But I do remember that passions were running at fever pitch at that time. Wildlife poaching – especially of elephant and rhino – was at horrific levels, and there was growing pressure under the Convention on International Trade in Endangered Species of Wild Fauna and Flora (CITES) to restrict the sale of ivory and other wildlife commodities. In Kenya alone, the number of elephants had plummeted from 65,000 in 1979 to 17,000 in 1989. In a dramatic and controversial act, on 19 July 1989 Kenyan President Daniel Arap Moi set fire to a 12-ton, 20-foot-high pile of elephant tusks – a gesture to persuade the world to halt ivory trading. The tusks were from more than 2,000 elephants shot over the previous four years and would have fetched about $3 million on the open market. Most of these tusks were recovered by the Wildlife Conservation Department from elephants that poachers had shot but left behind.

What made tensions run high at our conference was the fact that Zimbabwe, which had been more effective in controlling poaching, was against the proposed CITES ban on ivory trading. The country had huge stockpiles of ivory from culling activities and wanted the opportunity to turn these into cash. One of the amusing incidents at the conference came at the end of proceedings. The Kenyan delegation of students told the Zimbabwean conference organisers that they had a gift to offer – a small token of gratitude to their generous hosts. And what was the gift? A set of T-shirts that read: 'Only elephants should wear ivory!'

The CITES-led international ban of ivory trade did eventually come into force in 1995, resulting in a dramatic recovery of elephant populations. In South Africa, the numbers more than doubled, rising from 8,000 to over 20,000 in the 13 years after the ban. Now the problem was overpopulation in the game reserves, with consequent damage to the environment. As a result, the pendulum swung back again and, in February 2008, the ban on the ivory trade in southern Africa (but not elsewhere) was lifted, once again sparking controversy among environmental groups.

According to the International Union for Conservation of Nature (IUCN), today there are between 470,000 and 690,000 African elephants in the wild, considerably down from an estimated 1.3 million in 1979, but by no means endangered. In fact, according to a recent analysis by IUCN experts, most major populations in eastern and southern Africa are stable or have been steadily increasing since the mid-1990s, at an average rate of 4.5% per year. This is certainly in part due to the CITES agreement, which entered into force in 1975. Today, CITES accords varying degrees of protection to more than 30,000 species of animals and plants that are traded as live specimens, fur coats or dried herbs.

The sixth mass extinction

I am convinced that these and other international regulatory frameworks are essential in trying to halt what scientists in *Nature* magazine (3 March 2011) have called the 'sixth mass extinction.' But I would not want to create the impression that the precipitous loss in biodiversity is primarily due to illegal poaching activities. By far the biggest cause of species decline – which is now happening 100 to 1,000 times more rapidly than the natural 'background' rate – is loss of habitat because of changes in land use: in other words, through converting wilderness and forests areas into farms, mines and urban areas.

According to the Global Footprint Network, the world's 'ecological footprint' – which tracks the area of biologically productive land and water required to provide the renewable resources people use – exceeded the Earth's bio-capacity (the area actually available to produce renewable resources and absorb CO_2) by 50% in 2007. Overall, humanity's ecological footprint has doubled since 1966. This ecological 'overshoot' is largely attributable to our carbon footprint, which has increased 11-fold since 1961 and by just over one-third since 1998. The 'water footprint of production' provides a second measure of human demand on renewable resources, and shows that 71 countries are currently experiencing stress on blue water sources – that is, sources of water people use and do not return – with nearly two-thirds of these experiencing moderate to severe stress.

Another measure of our catastrophic loss in biodiversity is WWF's Living Planet Index, which reflects changes in the health of the planet's ecosystems by tracking trends in nearly 8,000 populations of vertebrate species. The shocking finding is that there has been a decline of about 30% of these species between 1970 and 2007. Stop and think about that: in just over one generation, we have lost one-third of our biodiversity. Theoretically, our grandchildren will have absolutely nothing – a barren, lifeless planet. In some areas, the picture is even worse. Living Planet Indices for the tropical world and for the world's poorer countries have both fallen by 60% since 1970. Under a 'business as usual' scenario, the outlook is serious: even with modest UN projections for population growth, consumption and climate change, WWF estimates that by 2030 humanity will need the capacity of two Earths to absorb CO_2 waste and keep up with natural resource consumption.

Certainly, having protected areas (nature parks, wildlife reserves and wilderness areas), of which Hwange in Zimbabwe is one of 133,000 in the world, is part of the solution. They are crucial in creating the sort of affinity and respect for nature that I experienced growing up in Zimbabwe, and which undoubtedly played some part in inspiring my later career in sustainable business. Reflecting on my own childhood, I must confess that I worry sometimes about the new generation of urban city-raised children. Will they grow to love nature as well, or will they be alienated from it? Will the 'environment' be reduced to exhibition zoos, natural disasters and virtual reality games? When we have no personal experience of wilderness, do we lose our ability to care deeply about nature? For all our sakes, I hope not.

Part 1
Africa

1

Divided and united
Investing in change
(South Africa: 1978–1991)

Innocence lost

I moved with my family from Bulawayo to Cape Town, South Africa, in 1978, to escape the escalating Rhodesian bush war. My growing love affair with nature continued to blossom when I joined Scouting movement – first Cub Scouts and later Boy Scouts, where I eventually achieved the accolade of Springbok Scout, the highest award possible in South Africa. I have many great memories of numerous hiking and camping excursions – whether it was striding along the beach and wading over sand dunes for two days (the Rayner competition); trekking through the mountain wilderness for ten days and scuba-diving in deep rock pools (the Ceder-berg adventure); or hiking down a canyon river for five days and sleeping under the stars (the Fish River Canyon) – I ended up growing to relish spending days and nights outdoors.

I think it's fair to say I lived a privileged and sheltered life in Cape Town, attending racially segregated schools without much understanding about the immoral politics of the day, or the storm of popular discon-tent that was steadily building. My naivety was brought into sharp relief when, in my final year of school in 1987, I went on a Christian work camp to Namaqualand. This arid area, situated on the north-west coast of South

Africa, is famous for its multi-coloured carpets of daisies that erupt in the spring. Its population is mostly rural and poor, of mixed race (classified as so-called 'coloured' in South Africa at the time), with strong ancestral links to the San Bushmen of the nearby Kalahari desert. A few copper and diamond mines in the area provided what little employment opportunities were available.

Our mission was to help to build a community centre, working together with local community members. Believe it or not, the fact that people from different races were mixing 'socially' was, in 1987 South Africa, considered radical; *apartheid* was still legally in force, institutionalised through dozens of racist laws such as the Group Areas Act, which segregated living areas and public facilities. It soon became clear that years of separation and suspicion had taken their toll. At one point, the 'black' volunteers ('black' was used in South Africa as an umbrella term for all races of non-European descent, including African, Asian and Coloured) started singing political protest songs while they were working. The 'white' volunteers (myself included) promptly took offence, believing that politics and religion should not be mixed – this was a Christian work camp after all.

This just shows how naive we were as white children growing up in South Africa. After all, not only have religion and politics *always* mixed throughout the history of the world, but more specifically, the Church had been complicit in apartheid – for better and for worse – for decades. For one thing, the Nationalist government, which came to power in 1948, used the Bible to justify its racist policies. The Truth and Reconciliation Commission later reported:

> Some of the major Christian churches gave their blessing to the system of apartheid. And many of its early proponents prided themselves in being Christians. Indeed, the system of apartheid was regarded as stemming from the mission of the church.

On the other hand, it was also church groups that were among the most vociferous anti-apartheid activists, both at home – led by the likes of Anglican Archbishop Desmond Tutu – and abroad.

Ethical investment roots

Most significant for the emerging corporate responsibility movement was a campaign by African–American minister, Reverend Leon Sullivan, to hold US companies operating in South Africa accountable for their ethical practices. Sullivan had been serving on the board of General Motors (GM) since 1971 and was described by his colleagues at GM as the 'Lion of Zion' and the 'conscience of the board'. In addition to pushing for diversity within the company in America, Sullivan began campaigning to raise standards for black workers living under apartheid, since GM had significant operations in South Africa.

This led to the establishment in 1977 of what is arguably the world's first CSR code: the Sullivan Principles. The Principles called for US companies operating in South Africa to integrate corporate facilities, establish equal and fair employment practices and increase the number of black managers. It was not uncontroversial, since the banned African National Congress (ANC) and its rising star, Nelson Mandela, were already calling for disinvestment from South Africa. According to Reverend Jesse Jackson,

> When the big idea was to boycott South Africa, Reverend Sullivan's point was that when blacks emerged they had to have infrastructure. He argued that if you run [out] all the companies, when black South Africans were liberated they would take over a shell. In the end these were not conflicting positions – Mandela had a long appreciation for Sullivan, as did the rest of the African National Congress.

Eventually, Sullivan did call for full divestment from South Africa, a position that alienated some of the 100-plus US companies that had signed up to his original proposal. However, in 1999 he joined with United Nations Secretary-General Kofi Annan to relaunch the code as the new Global Sullivan Principles. The overarching objective of these principles, according to Sullivan, is 'to support economic, social and political justice by companies where they do business', including respect for human rights and equal work opportunities for all peoples. By the time of his death in April 2001, more than 250 companies, including Coca-Cola, British Airways and Texaco, had endorsed Sullivan's new principles.

Beyond contributing to the eventual dismantling of apartheid, the Sullivan Principles were significant for another reason. They added tremendous momentum to a movement that had barely just begun – the ethical investment or SRI movement. This was led by the US-based Pax World Fund, founded in 1971 by two men with a well-defined mission. Luther Tyson and Jack Corbett, who had worked on peace, housing and employment issues for the United Methodist Church, wanted to make it possible for investors to align their money with their values. At the same time, they wished to challenge corporations to establish and live up to specific standards of social and environmental responsibility.

Little could Tyson and Corbett have imagined that their fund, now called the Pax World Balanced Fund, would help give birth to the global SRI movement. Interest in the industry has expanded exponentially, with socially responsible and sustainable investment assets increasing from $639 billion in 1995 to $3.07 trillion in 2009, according to the US Social Investment Forum. In Europe, the figure is €5 trillion (more than $7 trillion), according to the European Sustainable Investment Forum (Eurosif). Hence, nearly one in every eight dollars under professional management in the United States today – 12.2% of the $25.2 trillion in total assets under management – is involved in some strategy of socially responsible and sustainable investing.

This explosive growth in SRI funds led to the establishment of the UN Principles for Responsible Investment (PRI) in 2006. The six principles reflect the view that environmental, social and corporate governance (ESG) issues can affect the performance of investment portfolios and therefore must be given appropriate consideration by investors if they are to fulfil their fiduciary duty. The PRI provides a voluntary framework by which all investors can incorporate ESG issues into their decision-making and ownership practices and so better align their objectives with those of society at large. As of April 2011 over 850 investment institutions have become signatories, with assets of approximately $25 trillion under management.

Removing the blinkers

Needless to say, when we had our little standoff about religion and politics in Namaqualand in 1987, I was ignorant of the important, positive role that Sullivan, Tyson, Corbett, Tutu and many other faith leaders were playing in nudging companies towards more socially responsible practices in South Africa and around the world. However, in a strange way, religion did play a pivotal role in my subsequent career path.

When I had to choose what to study at university, my two strong interests were commerce and comparative religion. I had started a few little business ventures when I was at school, selling chocolates and jewellery, and had also become fascinated by Eastern faiths by this time. When I sought spiritual guidance on my dilemma, I found a passage in the Bible, which said: 'Take the ark of God back into the city … there is no representative of the king … Go back to the city in peace.' (2 Samuel 15: 25-27). My interpretation was that I should pursue a business career, but try to bring spiritual values into my work. At some level, this is still what I am trying to do, although I no longer view it in religious terms.

I finally 'woke up' to the scourge of apartheid at university. As part of my Bachelor of Business Science degree, I took a course in development economics, taught by Professor Francis Wilson, who ran the Southern Africa Labour and Development Research Unit. He had written an outstanding book called *Uprooting Poverty: The South African Challenge*, together with Mamphela Ramphele – the doctor, anti-apartheid activist and former partner of the late black-consciousness activist, Stephen Biko. Wilson's lectures, along with his book, brought me face-to-face with the brutal reality of South Africa's discriminatory migrant labour system and the terrible consequences of apartheid in terms of poverty and under-development. Ignorance was no longer an excuse. Denial was no longer an option.

Even so, I was not one of those who immediately joined protest marches, threw rocks at passing cars on the highway, or confronted the police when they rolled onto campus in their armoured trucks – all of which was happening fairly frequently by this time. But I did want to make a positive difference and was fortunate to discover AIESEC, the International Association of Economics and Commerce Students, which seemed like a place where I could bring about change through business. AIESEC had many initiatives, such as the International Traineeship Exchange Programme and the Community Assistance Programme, all designed to promote intercultural understanding and develop leadership skills. So I ended up getting actively involved and serving first as Projects Director and then President of the Cape Town chapter.

Discovering sustainable development

It was AIESEC that introduced me to sustainable development and linked the concept to business. With the Brundtland Commission having launched its 1987 report, *Our Common Future*, and with all eyes firmly set on the upcoming United Nations Conference on Environment and Development (the 'Earth Summit') in Rio de Janeiro in 1992, AIESEC began organising seminars and conferences on business and sustainable development. I ended up attending two landmark events – the South African National Conference on Environment and Development, held in Johannesburg, and the World Theme Conference on Business and Sustainable Development, held in Tokyo in August 1990.

You can read more about the latter in Chapter 11 where I discuss Japan. Suffice to say, the impact on a young management student such as myself was profound. In preparation, we had to prepare local case studies to share with our international colleagues. I chose waste management and found myself meeting local recycling groups and attending a metropolitan recycling meeting chaired by the mayor of Cape Town, which included representatives from the plastics, paper and bottling industries. I made many interesting discoveries. For instance, I learned that South Africa had the third highest aluminium can recycling rate in the world, largely due to the armies of poor people that collected and returned the cans for a small fee. I also learned that there was a glut in the city's recycling system – not enough people were buying products with recycled content; hence, supply constantly exceeded demand.

I later wrote for the *International Ecological Economics Bulletin* that:

> recycling is an obvious win–win for the environment and economics. But in South Africa, it takes on a different face than the conventional concerned housewife separating her garbage. Here, much of the recycling being practiced is by poor or homeless people, who collect door-to-door, or clean up litter from the streets and parks, in order to generate a meagre income on which to survive. The tiny economic incentive provided, which probably only captures a fraction of the real environmental benefit of recycling, is sufficient to mobilise large numbers of people behind this 'worthy cause' and provide them with a basic livelihood.

Today in southern Africa, over two billion steel beverage cans are 'consumed' every year. They are 100% recyclable and the current recovery rate is around 70%. This impressive achievement is mostly thanks to Collect-A-Can, established in 1993. Annually, more than R20 million (around $3 million) is paid to an estimated 100,000 collectors, most of whom have no other source of income. Millions of school children are also introduced to the idea of caring for the environment through Collect-a-Can's schools competition, which attracts between 300 and 500 schools annually, earning cash and prizes. The scheme is creating a culture of recycling.

Other countries have also made great strides on recycling since my fledgling interest in 1990, although there is still a long way to go. In Europe, Austria leads with approximately 60% of its waste being recycled, while the United States recycles about 30% of its waste, double the rate of a decade ago. The United Kingdom is estimated to recycle less than 20%, with Ireland, Italy, Portugal and Luxembourg being not too far behind. Greece props up the league table with only 10%. Paper recycling is a little more encouraging, with both the United States and the European Union recycling more than 50%. On recycling of steel cans, Japan leads with 99% of the municipalities collecting and recycling. In 1973, the Japan Steel Can Recycling Association was established to promote the recycling of steel cans and today an impressive 90% are recycled.

Starting to change course

My growing interest in sustainable development led me to focus my final year dissertation on the subject. As my honours degree was in marketing, I chose 'green marketing' as my topic and focused on the efforts of a national retail, Pick 'n Pay. As it happened, Pick 'n Pay, led by founder and chairman, Raymond Ackerman, was one of the 50 cases included in the Business Council for Sustainable Development's book *Changing Course*, which was prepared as input to the Rio Earth Summit. The company had developed a range of 'green' products, mostly toiletries and household cleaners. It had also realised the enormous opportunity it had to educate its customers. Hence, stores were used as distribution points for environmental factsheets on everything from the destructive impacts of dragnet fishing to the benefits of recycling. The company also produced some credible glossy reports about its positive impacts on society and the environment.

In terms of the way I now characterise responsible business into five 'ages and stages of CSR' (more about this in Chapter 25), I would probably describe Pick 'n Pay's approach then as typical of promotional CSR, located firmly in the age of marketing. But at the time the company was considered, rightly, as pioneering. To its credit, it was also one of the more vocal companies pressuring the government to change its racist policies on employment. Today, looking at the four-page sustainability section in its annual report, I'd say it is well on its way to strategic CSR in the age of management, with the expected range of key performance indicators on energy, waste, employment equity and community investment. There are even little glimmers of transformative CSR, when it recognises that 'price remains a critical factor influencing customer decisions to purchase in accordance with sustainability criteria and we are striving to achieve price parity on sustainable and ethical lines'.

For me back then, as a university student and new convert to the sustainability cause, I was just pleased to gain research access to study the company's environmental practices. Pick 'n Pay was also a catalyst in another way. Its Chairman, Raymond Ackerman, personally endorsed and part-sponsored my trip to Japan for the AIESEC conference on business and sustainable development.

After finishing my Business Science degree in Marketing, the only thing I was clear about was that I did not want a career in marketing. My real passion – perhaps it was even an obsession – was to find a way to pursue my ideas of bringing values into business. Although I had been exposed to sustainable business at the AIESEC conference in Japan, and had explored it a bit more in my dissertation, I somehow felt the agenda was too narrow. My interests went deeper, even embracing questions of spirituality, but how was I to reconcile these ideals with a career in business, I wondered? Luckily, I did not need to figure that out immediately. Canada was beckoning.

Holism and hope
Towards a SANE society
(South Africa: 1993–1994, 1996–1997)

The whole is greater

After graduating, I spent a year working and travelling in Canada and the United Kingdom (more about these experiences in Chapters 16 and 21), after which I returned to South Africa. By then, I desperately wanted to focus on alternative models of business, so I began a Master's in Business Science at the University of Cape Town. My chosen topic was 'Holistic business: a study of synergy in organisations'. Through my research, I intended to apply Jan Christian Smuts's far-reaching theory of holism, as expounded in his book *Holism and Evolution*, to business. I could see a clear contrast between a holistic model of organisations and the rational model of commerce that Tom Peters and Robert Waterman criticised so effectively in their bestselling book *In Search of Excellence*.

As it turned out, I became deeply frustrated with the reductionist process of academic research and gave up on the Master's degree when I was offered a job with the international management consultancy, Capgemini. By then, however, my research had put me in touch with some of the leading thinkers on progressive business – such as Jan Backelin, founder of the Pathfinder Network in Sweden; Francis Kinsman, founder of the Business Network in London and author of *The New Agenda* and *Millennium*;

Edward Posey, founder of the Gaia Foundation; Peter Russell, author of *The Awakening Earth*; and futurist Hazel Henderson, author of *Paradigms in Progress: Life Beyond Economics*.

Before diving into the choppy waters of consulting, I wrote up my research findings in an article called 'Holistic business', which was published in *New Perspectives* in 1994. The article explores what a holistic employee and a holistic organisation might look like. I noted that we could build on the work of Douglas McGregor, who challenged the idea that 'authority is the central, indispensable means of managerial control' by introducing his Theory Y of motivation, as well as the breakthrough thinking of Abraham Maslow, whose concept of 'eupsychian management' integrated the 'being values' of his hierarchy of needs (such as self-actualisation) in a workplace context.

My conclusion was that,

> despite all the evidence and frameworks supporting the notion of the holistic individual, business has yet to respond in a meaningful way. Employees are still regarded as inputs to production and expenses in business rather than creative beings and genuine assets. People are still expected to leave their emotions, intuition, dreams, fears, family, community concerns and myriad other qualities characteristic of being fully human, outside of the workplace. And as workers, they are still expected to be motivated and inspired by monetary incentives, increased productivity and profit making, as opposed to personal development, genuine service to others, and the search for meaning in their lives. The time is long overdue for business to serve humans rather than the other way around.

At the time, I became particularly interested in the work of Dutch psychiatrist, Bernard Lievegoed, in which he conceived of the development of organisations through three phases: pioneering, differentiation and, finally, integration (i.e. the holistic model). For me, holistic business seemed to be about flattening the hierarchy and moving towards a network-type organisation. Along similar lines, Rosabeth Moss Kanter, professor of Business Administration at Harvard Business School at the time, suggested that future companies would need to 'pool their resources with others, ally to exploit an opportunity, or link systems in a partnership'. Similarly, I was recommending that companies apply Smuts's concept of 'fields' of influence and embrace a stakeholder approach.

Examples of holistic business were, at the time, few and far between. Ryuzaburo Kaku, then chairman of Canon, was one notable exception, describing that in the highest stage of corporate evolution 'a global consciousness emerges, and the corporation sees itself contributing to the whole of mankind'. This aligned to what Peter Senge, professor of Systems Thinking at MIT's Business School, had been calling 'the fifth discipline' or 'systems thinking', growing out of his earlier ideas around 'metanoic' (i.e. transformative) organisations.

I still believe that business can learn a lot from Smuts's theory of holism. He teaches us that, while the tendency in the universe is towards higher and more complex forms of organisation, degeneration also occurs. 'There are wholes that are weak, inchoate', Smuts observed. 'And these must be eliminated.' In other words, those organisations least able to transform themselves into more holistic entities will have failed to adapt and, consequently, will die. According to Smuts, this is after all the fundamental law of the universe: survival of the 'wholest'.

Fostering new economics

My baptism of fire into the real world of commerce started when I joined Capgemini as a strategy analyst in April 1994. The 18 months I worked for the global management consultancy – then ranked third in the world in terms of revenues – were at the same time exhilarating and exhausting, inspiring and dispiriting. On the one hand, the firm had a very holistic view of business. Its 'business transformation' model was designed to help companies to 'reframe, restructure, revitalise and renew.' It recognised that investment in people was just as important as investment in processes, and that soft values were as essential as hard numbers. However, in practice, the consulting life was a burn-out-track with a myopic financial focus. We were usually long gone before our business process re-engineering efforts took their full human toll. And as for environmental issues, they hardly even made it onto the agenda.

During this time, I managed to write and publish an article in *Human Resource Management* calling for a 'new paradigm in business', in which companies move beyond obsession with profits, competition and rationality. However, my growing disillusionment, fatigue and cynicism with mainstream consulting eventually got the better of me, and I headed back the United Kingdom to pursue a Master's in Human Ecology at the University of Edinburgh (more about this in Chapter 21). This turned out to be a watershed moment in my career, and since then I have been privileged to be able to focus completely on sustainable business.

Soon after arriving back in Cape Town, having completed my Master's, I joined with futures researcher, Dr Aart Roukens de Lange, and others to set up the South African New Economics (SANE) Foundation. We described ourselves loftily as 'an autonomous network to promote the creation of a humane, just, sustainable and culturally appropriate economic system in South Africa'. Our inaugural newsletter, *SANE Society*, carries my editorial, where I wrote that we had a 'strong, values-based agenda – to identify and promote economic solutions which enhance ecological sustainability, equity and social justice, decentralisation and devolution of economic power, and multi-level self-reliance with interdependence, all in an appropriately South African context'. Quite a mouthful!

A good deal of our inspiration and ideas came from the New Economics Foundation (NEF) in London, which I had contacted during my Master's to solicit support for me setting up a similar organisation in South Africa. In fact, before returning to South Africa, I had met up with Simon Zadek, who was working at NEF at that time on various projects such as social auditing and alternative indicators of progress. I share some of Zadek's insights on these and other subjects in Chapter 8.

The SANE Foundation's newsletters reflected our passionate, albeit amateurish attempt to challenge the status quo, with articles such as: Values in economics' (Johan van Zyl); Internet communities: governments of the future? (Dale Williams); Citizens' income for South Africa (Don Northcott); UNITAX for social and environmental sustainability (Aart Roukens de Lange); A new appreciation for work (Richard Combrink); National eco-accounts (Julie Havemann); How globalisation affects South Africa (Peter van Heusden); Global eco-villages (Jeremy Burnham); and Conventional economics fail to deliver on promises (Margaret Legum).

We found ourselves referencing global dissident voices such as David Korten, Robert Costanza and George Soros, and forming alliances with organisations including the Alternative Information Development Centre (AIDC), a grassroots, activist organisation that was a perfect complement to our rather more academic network. We even discovered an ally in the Anglican Church, especially in Reverend Njongonkulu Ndungane, the outspoken Archbishop of Cape Town who succeeded his rather more famous and no less feisty predecessor, Desmond Tutu.

Financial market reform

For my part, I found myself warning about effects of the 'casino economy' and calling for financial market reform. As I wrote at the time (1997),

> Each day, over $1 trillion pass through the world's financial markets, a 14-fold increase since 1980 which is mostly accounted for by the explosive growth in derivatives trading since it first began on the Philadelphia Stock Exchange in 1971. Of this, only between 2% and 5% is related to international trade in real goods, a phenomenon which US critic David Korten calls 'de-linking money from value'. The effects of speculative activity of these proportions on real trade, however, can be significant and potentially harmful.

One of the criticisms of speculative financial markets is that they divert capital away from long-term productive investment in the 'real economy' in favour of short-term speculative investment in the 'virtual economy'. Another is that these markets are becoming increasingly depersonalised and automated – high tech and high speed – operating without regard for the human or ecological consequences of their actions but simply chasing the highest profits to be made.

The worrying increase in the volatility and instability of the financial markets has numerous negative effects, from destroying the livelihoods of small traders and growers and the cultural fabric of indigenous or rural communities, to increasing the uncertainties and risks of bankruptcy for businesses, and disrupting the plans of governments and the economies of small nations. All of these effects amount to a decrease in self-reliance at national, community and individual levels.

At the time that I was writing on these issues, although we talked about the 'systemic risk' that speculative finance caused, I am not sure any of us really believed that the 'mother of all meltdowns' would ever come. The devastating domino effect following the collapse of Lehman Brothers and other banks in 2008 proved that we had been spot-on about the risks, even if we were rather less forthcoming on solutions. Mostly, we just touted the so-called 'Tobin tax'. This is a proposal which its creator, Nobel Laureate economist James Tobin, described as 'an internationally uniform tax on all spot conversions of one currency into another, proportional to the size of the transaction', suggesting a charge range of between 0.5% and 1%. Economist Rudi Dornbusch went further, suggesting a cross-border tax on all financial transactions (not only currency trades), which could be collected by national governments.

Subsequently, the United Nations Development Programme (UNDP) commissioned a report by a group of influential economists, which concluded in support of a Tobin fee of between 0.05% and 0.25%. This was later endorsed at the UN World Summit on Social Development in Copenhagen in March 1995 by some significant political leaders, including Mitterand (France), Brundtland (Norway) and Rasmussen (Denmark). Later that year at the G7 Summit in Halifax, Canadian HRs Minister Lloyd Axeworthy and UN High Commissioner for Human Rights José Ayala Lasso also expressed their solidarity, but the vast majority of the world's political leaders rejected the proposal and it was never implemented.

US policy analysts Makhijani and Brown favoured Tobin's second reform route, proposing an International Currency Unit, to be administered by a World Central Bank and based on an equivalent basket of goods in each country. The value of these baskets in domestic currency would determine relative exchange rates, which would therefore depend on real domestic economic conditions rather than short-term currency movements. As with the Tobin tax, the idea was not pursued. More is the pity, as I am not convinced that we are any closer to reducing the systemic risk of the casino economy, despite all the pain and suffering caused by the global financial crisis.

The growth debate

As co-founder of the SANE Foundation, I found myself walking a tightrope between challenging conventional economics, with all its negative impacts on social justice and the environment, and the tenets of 'new economics', which were also not beyond questioning. One of these 'sacred cows' was the contention that conventional economic growth, as measured by gross domestic product (GDP), should be opposed. Books such as *Beyond the Limits to Growth* by Donella Meadows, Dennis Meadows and Jørgen Randers, and *Beyond Growth* by former World Bank economist Herman Daly, were often cited. Later, in 2008, I had the opportunity to question these authors in person. But in 1997, using South Africa as a case in point, my position was simply: How can developing countries afford not to grow?

South Africa desperately needed to follow its much-hailed political miracle with an economic miracle, if its 'liberation' was to benefit the 40% unemployed. Realising this, the ANC government had effectively replaced its human-centred Reconstruction and Development Programme (RDP) – which formed the heart of its election manifesto – with something of an antithesis, namely the Growth, Employment and Redistribution (GEAR) macro-economic strategy. To its critics, GEAR looked disturbingly similar to a World Bank structural adjustment programme, with its promises of liberalising trade and shooting for 6% annual GDP growth.

But was it wrong for the South African government to be aiming for the highest possible growth, in order to fund better housing, health and education for the majority of its population? I tended to agree with Chilean 'barefoot economist' Manfred Max-Neef, and his 'threshold hypothesis', whereby growth and development move in parallel up to a threshold point, after which quality of life is eroded due to externalities such as the health impacts of pollution and stress.

I could see that the ANC, despite its socialist and communist proclivities, had very little choice about changing its economic philosophy if it wanted to benefit from globalisation and international reinvestment. At the same time, this new market openness had its downside. For example, the textile industry, which had traditionally been a strong employer in the Cape region, suffered great losses as business shifted offshore to take advantage of the lower labour costs in countries such as Malaysia.

Given these pressures and constraints, I found myself wrestling with the question of whether moving 'beyond growth', as Herman Daly and others proposed, could have much practical application for developing countries. South Africa had chosen the growth path because it was staring economic destitution and social bankruptcy in the face. In this instance, wasn't growth the more sustainable and responsible option? In the end, I concluded that growth is not inherently 'bad', but civil society must continually pressure both government and business to be more transparent and accountable for the social and environmental impacts of economic growth.

It is interesting that today, 15 years later, the growth-versus-development debate is still raging. Books such as Tim Jackson's *Prosperity Without Growth* (2010) have become bestsellers. Jackson restates the challenge starkly: 'Questioning growth is deemed to be the act of lunatics, idealists and revolutionaries. But question it we must.' Others, such as Jonathon Porritt in *Capitalism as if the World Matters* (2005), argue for 'smart growth' instead of 'dumb growth', which I return to in Chapter 24. Meanwhile, the global financial crisis has given Jackson's more uncompromising zero-growth position a renewed resonance.

My view still echoes what I described as 'appropriate economic growth in the Third World' in the SANE Society newsletter all those years ago. We cannot deny the benefits of economic growth. After all, it is economic growth that has allowed China, India and others to lift hundreds of millions of people out of abject poverty over the past 20 years. But we also need to be honest about the social and environmental costs of this growth: the world is getting more unequal as the gaps between rich and poor grow wider, and the impact on the environment has been catastrophic. At the same time, the recent global financial crisis has demonstrated the suffering that occurs when growth stalls and unemployment rises, as it has in much of the West.

It seems clear to me that we need economic growth. It is structurally and psychologically built into our global economic and social system. But it needs to be a qualitatively different kind of growth, in which production and consumption are totally redesigned to have zero or even positive environmental impacts, and trade and employment practices are overhauled to ensure that Mark Kramer and Michael Porter's notion of 'shared value' becomes more than just a popular new buzz word. Just how distant the goal of sustainability remains became abundantly clear when I began immersing myself in the world of big industry in South Africa.

3
Governance and greed
Accounting for impacts
(South Africa: 1997–2001)

Sustainability consulting

The concept of shared value became increasingly important for business in South Africa during the 1990s, long before it was coined by the Harvard academic duo of Porter and Kramer. Fortunately for me, I had a front-row seat. In 1997, having helped to kick-start the SANE Foundation, I then joined the global accounting firm KPMG. My mandate was to establish an Environmental Unit, which later evolved to incorporate social, economic and ethical dimensions and become KPMG Sustainability Services.

Over the next six years, I advised numerous companies, many of them multinationals, on how to improve their sustainability performance, covering areas as diverse as sustainability reporting, environmental due diligence, ISO 14001 certification, integrated auditing, environmental accounting, non-financial report verification, climate strategy, carbon trading, corporate governance, business ethics and social transformation, including black economic empowerment.

When I look back, these were incredible years and I was privileged to experience them. More often than not, I found myself out on client sites, donning safety gear (helmets and goggles), touring chemical plants and mine pits, inspecting factories and farms; even checking out sewage treatment plants and hazardous waste sites. At other times, I gazed over breathtakingly beautiful corporate-owned and managed wildlife conservation reserves, or relaxed in plush, marble-clad, colonial-era head office executive suites.

Sometimes, looking back, my experiences seem surreal. I have stood in the shadow of monstrous machines – some of them several storeys high – gouging at the earth, and seen desperate communities, sick and with failing crops as a result of industrial pollution. I have seen moonscapes where, in the wake of industrial activity, nothing will grow, and black tar pits so noxious that birds flying overhead were known to plummet to a sticky death. I have seen a dead mountainside, poisoned with arsenic (used in gold refining) and listened, gobsmacked, as a CEO told me that NGOs are 'not stakeholders; they are the enemy!' And, yet, over the same period of time, I also witnessed hundreds of examples of a commitment to improve sustainability performance and reduce impacts. Almost daily, I met industry-hardened managers who cared deeply about the environment and were working passionately for social justice.

Reflecting on these years of sustainability consulting 'at the coal face', I later wrote a poem called 'The Dragon', which begins with the following description:

> I have stalked the dragon for many a year
> Followed its trail and sought out its lair
> Seen it belch smoke and felt its hot breath
> Counted its legacy of both life and death

So, what of lessons? There are two that I want to share and both are areas in which I believe South Africa has made a significant contribution to the worldwide quest for sustainable business. The first is corporate governance and the second is economic empowerment.

Expanding directors' duties

Following the success of the UK's Cadbury Report in 1992, South Africa launched its own King Report on Corporate Governance in 1994, under the chairmanship of former High Court judge and company director, Mervyn E. King (not to be confused with Britain's Governor of the Reserve Bank).

King went much further than Cadbury in recognising the non-financial aspects of corporate governance and incorporating the concept of wider stakeholder accountability. The reasons are not hard to fathom and have to do with the operating context. At the time, London was still one of the great financial capitals of the world, while South Africa was having its first democratic elections.

In later updates, the King Report placed sustainability and responsibility at the heart of corporate governance. King II (in 2002), for instance, included a substantial section on business ethics and an entire chapter on 'integrated sustainability reporting', heavily referencing the Global Reporting Initiative (GRI) and the accountability standard AA 1000. King III (2009) goes even further. As Mervyn King puts it, 'the philosophy of King III revolves around leadership, sustainability and corporate citizenship'. Speaking to me in 2010, King reiterated his belief that directors are accountable to the company first, not to shareholders, and that a broader set of stakeholders provides a better perspective on what is good for the company in the long term. It is no coincidence – and I believe to the organisation's credit – that Mervyn King now chairs the GRI.

Although the King Report is a voluntary standard, in common with other corporate governance codes around the world, the Johannesburg Securities Exchange (JSE) made compliance with the code a listing requirement. This had a dramatic effect. At KPMG, I started doing annual sustainability reporting surveys in 1998, and in 2003 we looked specifically at the reporting requirements of the newly launched King II code. We found that 85% of South Africa's top companies were practising annual reporting on sustainability-related issues, and 77% of the companies referenced the existence of an internal code of ethics or code of corporate conduct.

There is a downside to this strong sustainability reporting trend, evident not only in South Africa but around the world. I believe it has distracted us from a related, and in some ways far more important trend, namely social and environmental accounting. This refers to financially quantifying the social and environmental impacts of business, or to use economics jargon, pricing the 'externalities'. As it happened, back in 1998 my second project at KPMG was to help a large chemical company design an environmental accounting system, which formed the basis of two research reports that we published on the subject. At the time, social and environmental accounting was a strongly emerging field, under the intellectual leadership of UK academic Rob Gray, and the pioneering efforts of companies such as BT (the former British Telecom), Baxter International and Ontario Hydro.

Unfortunately, I think GRI and its targeted corporate users realised that measuring and reporting physical impacts was far easier, not to mention less controversial and less risky, than financially quantifying corporate externalities. And, yet, the importance of doing this cannot be under-estimated. For example, a 2010 study conducted for the UN by Trucost found that the combined damage of the world's 3,000 biggest companies was equivalent to $2.2 trillion in 2008 – a figure bigger than the national economies of all but seven countries in the world that year, and equal to one-third of the average profits of those companies. I sincerely hope that, having gone through the GRI learning curve, we will once again return to full-cost accounting. Anything less amounts to a superficial and mislead-ing representation of the impacts of business on society, the environment and the economy.

Power to the people

The second lesson that I took away from my time with KPMG in South Africa has to do with the issue of black economic empowerment (BEE), which has strong resonance to later concepts of bottom-of-the-pyramid (BOP) strategies, inclusive business and corporate shared value. First, it is important to understand the context in which BEE emerged. When the new, democratically elected ANC government came to power in 1994 under the leadership of Nelson Mandela, South Africa's growth had been stalling for a decade. GDP growth was averaging less than 1% a year, around 23% of the population were unemployed and 57% were living below the poverty line.

The ANC government's response – in the form of its GEAR macr-oeconomic strategy – managed to boost South Africa's annual growth to 5.6% by 2007 when the global recession hit. However, serious concerns remained about the concentration of wealth in relatively few hands – typically, white-owned multinationals and high-net-worth individuals. As the Department of Trade and Industry put it: 'Societies characterised by entrenched gender inequality or racially or ethnically defined wealth disparities are not likely to be socially and politically stable, particularly as economic growth can easily exacerbate these inequalities.' As a direct consequence, the government introduced a new piece of legislation, the Broad-Based Black Economic Empowerment (B-BBEE) Act of 2003.

This was further entrenched by B-BBEE Codes of Good Practice in 2007 to provide a standard framework for the measurement of B-BBEE across all sectors of the economy. The B-BBEE scorecard was designed to cover seven areas, namely ownership, management control, employment equity, skills development, preferential procurement, enterprise development and socioeconomic development (including industry-specific and corporate social investment initiatives). The codes became binding on all state bodies and public companies, and the government was required to apply their criteria when making economic decisions on procurement, licensing and concessions, public–private partnerships, and the sale of state-owned assets or businesses.

Private companies were also required to apply the codes if they wanted to do business with any government enterprise or organ of state. As a result, many industry sectors have, following extensive stakeholder engagement, created their own voluntary B-BBEE Charters, also known as Sector Codes, which have subsequently become legally binding commitments. The question is: have all of these efforts been effective in creating a more inclusive economy? And what can other countries and companies learn from South Africa's experience?

Despite widespread criticism that B-BBEE has simply created a new, black elite class, the statistics show that the policy *has* been effective, albeit moderately, in growing a black middle class. Overall, the proportion of middle-class households in South Africa grew from 23% to 26% between 1998 and 2006. Among African urban households, the middle class comprised 22% in 2006 (up from 15% in 1998), as compared with 48% of Coloured households (up from 41%), 75% of Asian households (unchanged) and 85% of White households (also unchanged). Almost no rural African households had achieved a middle-class standard of living by 2006.

While there is a clear historical, racial element to these statistics for South Africa, I believe they also tell us something about how difficult it is to achieve a genuinely inclusive, equitable economy under modern capitalism. The rich and powerful tend to concentrate, reinforce and protect their wealth and influence, irrespective of race or other characteristics. Hence, I believe we will need much more than new jargon (such as 'shared value') or greater transparency (in the form of 'value-added statements') to reverse the 'trickle-up' economics that is hard-wired into our Western capitalist system. Sustainable business practices can certainly play their part in advancing the cause of improved equity but strong policy incentives, as well as sustained civil society activism, will be needed if real change is to be achieved.

Beyond Reasonable Greed

Apart from lessons learned from my time running KPMG's Sustainability Services in South Africa, of course there are also stories – anecdotes that serve to enlighten and sometimes to amuse. For example, there was the case of a company that was granted a legal licence to create an open-cast coal strip-mine on the banks of the Vaal river, except they 'forgot' to ask the local community about it. An environmental NGO took the company to South Africa's constitutional court and won on the grounds that the public had a basic human right to be consulted. Then there was the pulp and paper company that faced the challenge of its forests periodically and mysteriously burning down, until someone suggested providing access to the poor, local community, so the people could harvest mushrooms and honey. Hey presto! No more burning forests.

There's the story of members of my team visiting Nigeria to do environmental audits, and having their oil company hosts' car surrounded by an angry mob with baseball bats. After that, they flew everywhere by helicopter and were accompanied by an armed guard. I also recall a somewhat more amusing instance in which one company, like many others in South Africa, suffered at the hands of thieves. Usually, it is copper wire that is stolen, but on this particular occasion, the staff awoke one morning to find that the road outside their factory had been stolen. Literally! Someone had dug up the tarmac and taken it away.

There are many more anecdotes like this – so-called 'war stories from the field'. A desire to capture these experiences, and make some sense of them, is what led me write my first book, *Beyond Reasonable Greed*. The book, which took two years to write and which was the realisation of a 10-year-old ambition, was essentially a way of capturing a chapter of learning in my professional life. It enjoyed great success, ranking on *The*

Sunday Times bestseller list, in part due to the national celebrity status of my co-author, Clem Sunter.

Sunter had made a name for himself in business by becoming Chairman of Anglo American's Gold and Uranium Division. The wider public knew him better as a highly celebrated scenario planner and prolific author. Our book together succeeded, I believe, because it struck a healthy balance between information, metaphor, questioning, illustration and invitation to action. As someone from Sustainable Asset Management (SAM) commented: 'you managed to make the whole sustainability story very accessible and exciting'.

The title for the book was Sunter's idea, picking up on the Enron and WorldCom fiascos that were in the process of unfolding. Having 'greed' in the title certainly made for very good PR, but I am not sure it properly captured the spirit of the book and its message. I still prefer my original title – *Shapeshifting* – since the essence of the book was a call for transformation at every level. Changing the habit of greed is just one small part of the solution.

In the book we explored the tyranny of our political, economic and business systems, which may be rational and reasonable at the level of individual decisions, but add up to a collective insanity with disastrous consequences. I also wanted to make the point that it is the duty of society – all of us together – to be the nagging conscience of business, applying sufficient moral and ethical pressure to make certain behaviour socially unacceptable, be it unreasonable greed, ecological insensitivity or indifference to fundamental human needs.

4

Tears and flowers
Recreating a culture of ethics
(Kenya: 1991, 2010)

Weep for Africa

I first visited Kenya in 1991, during my final year of undergraduate studies, by which time I was serving as President of AIESEC at the University of Cape Town. In June, I attended their African Leadership Development Seminar in Nairobi, followed by a one-week study tour on the beautiful Mombasa Island. This was my first trip on the continent beyond southern Africa, and I was struck by how modern the city of Nairobi seemed. I do not recall the formal content of the seminar, but the informal learning was profound.

As I recounted in *The Age of Responsibility*, one of the first questions I was asked by my fellow African students was: 'So, are you still killing the blacks down in South Africa?' Behind that simple, arresting question lay an entangled maze of centuries of discrimination, injustice, disinformation, distrust and misunderstanding – a situation not so very different from what prevailed in Europe in the wake of World War II, when AIESEC was founded. You must remember that in 1991 the racist policies of apartheid were still in place, despite significant reforms begun by the white, nationalist President F.W. De Klerk in 1989.

Apart from these vigorous debates about justice and political reform, my memories of the trip are mostly prosaic, but no less instructive. For example, when we were staying in what could only loosely be called a 'hotel' in Mombasa, there was no running water – a useful reminder of the developmental challenges that still faced the country. I also remember being amused that the hotel security guard was armed with a bow and arrow. Also, when I politely declined to buy any carvings at the craft market (I quickly learned the word *apana*, which means 'no thank you'), a savvy trader surreptitiously offered me marijuana instead (to which my reply was, naturally, also *apana*!)

I brought back two Swahili songs from that trip – *Jambo* (a lively greeting song and something of a Kenyan tourism national anthem) and *Malaika* (a hauntingly beautiful song of romance). To this day, I still know all the words of *Jambo*:

Jambo!	Greetings!
Jambo bwana	Greetings, sir
Habari gani?	How are you?
Mzuri sana	Very fine
Wageni wakaribishwa	Visitors are welcome
Kenya yetu	[In] our Kenya
Hakuna matata	[There are] no worries
Kenya nchi nzuri	Kenya is a nice country
Nchi ya maajabu	A beautiful country
Nchi ya kupendeza	A peaceful country

I couldn't agree more. Sadly, when I returned to Kenya in 2010, the second country on my CSR quest world tour, its beautiful people were still recovering from the trauma of post-election violence that broke out in 2008. Around 1,200 died and more than 500,000 were forced to flee their homes. The lethal concoction of ethnic tribal conflict, political upheaval and heavy-handed military governments remains one of Africa's most wicked curses and deepest sorrows.

Those who are familiar with my writing on Africa, especially my poetry collection *I Am An African*, will know that I am usually very upbeat about the continent of my birth. But tragedies such as this – and countless others, from the Rwandan genocide of 1994, where 800,000 people were slaughtered in 100 days, to the Darfur conflict in Sudan, where at least 50,000 people died between 2003 and 2010 – cast dark shadows on this luminous continent. I was moved to write a poem in the wake of my trip to Kenya, called 'I Weep for Africa'. It begins with the following words:

> I weep for Africa –
> Whose valleys are lined with graves
> And whose rivers flow with blood
> Because revenge feeds on itself

> I weep for Africa –
> Whose villages are skeletons of mud
> And whose cities are phantoms of dust
> For progress leaves many homeless

The Chinese in Africa

When I visited Nairobi in January 2010 to deliver a two-day workshop on sustainable business, Mumo Kivuitu, Director of Ufadhili Trust, was my host.[2] It was wonderful to be back in the country after nearly 20 years, and to compare my impressions. The biggest changes I noted were political. In 1990, Daniel Arap Moi was still president (a post he held from 1978 to 2002) and ruled a one-party state with an iron fist. My impression back then was of relative stability, but no great sense of prosperity or advancement. I recall that it took nine hours to drive 440 kilometres on the pothole-ridden road between Nairobi and Mombasa.

Today, Kenya has a multiparty democracy under President Mwai Kibaki, although the disputed 2007 general election (and post-election violence) led to a coalition government in which Raila Odinga shared power as Prime Minister. Apart from changes in politics, the economy is stronger (despite unemployment estimated at 40%), and the roads are noticeably improved.

In fact, the roads sparked one of the first lively debates in the workshop. Why? Because they are built by Chinese contractors. The 'Chinese in Africa' topic is a real hot potato, and fascinating from a sustainable business perspective. The Chinese are bringing massive business investment to Africa (especially focused on infrastructure development), but

2 An interview with Mumo Kivuitu is available on the csrinternational channel on YouTube.

at what cost? They are accused of low standards of labour, ethics and environmental responsibility, as well as the 'sin' of taking away local employment.

I do not fully buy the 'evil China' story (and I fear a new Sino-xenophobia is taking hold around the world), for a number of reasons. First, I would far rather see investment in infrastructure than development aid going to Africa. Second, the Chinese government is starting to show concern about its tarnished reputation abroad, so I expect pressure and standards to rise in the coming decade. And third, the Chinese are not entirely concerned with low costs and poor standards. They have an incredible work ethic and high productivity level, which I believe introduce healthy competition and challenge attitudes of entitlement in countries such as Kenya.

The other theme that emerged strongly in the workshop was corruption, although there was less spirited 'fight' in this debate. I detected a pervasive feeling of resignation among most of the participants. How do you fight a disease that – like cancer – is so endemic and persistent, and invades all levels of government, business and society?

One refreshing voice in this debate was Ken Njiru, Executive Director of Uungwana Resource Institute and one of the leading proponents of business ethics in Kenya.[3] He believes that corruption needs to be rebranded in the public and business consciousness as *ushenzi*, a Swahili word which means barbaric, primitive or backward. This is contrasted with *uungwana*, which means civilised, advanced or righteous. I am not sure this rebranding will work, but it is worth a try, as ethical behaviour is all about reinforcing positive cultural norms.

Inclusive business strategies

As far as general sustainable business goes, my impression was that Kenya is still mostly stuck in the PR/philanthropy mode. However, there are inspiring examples of sustainable business practice, as I found out from Maryjka Beckmann, Executive Director of AAR Holdings Ltd, which has pioneered affordable healthcare services in East Africa; and from Equity

3 An interview with Ken Njiru is available on the csrinternational channel on YouTube.

Bank, which has successfully targeted the poorest sectors of society and now, with 4.1 million accounts, makes up over 52% of all bank accounts in Kenya.[4]

Another case that I find particularly inspiring and instructive is Safaricom's M-PESA scheme. In 2005, 80% of the Kenyan population were reportedly without a bank account. Also, more money was coming into the country through international remittances from family members living abroad than through overseas development assistance. However, these transfers were expensive, with the financial intermediary Western Union typically taking a big slice in commission. In collaboration with Safaricom, Vodafone developed and piloted a new service called M-PESA, whereby customers could use their mobile phones to perform basic financial services including depositing, withdrawing and transferring money using SMS texts.

The project was jointly funded by the UK Department for International Development's Financial Deepening Challenge Fund. The pilot ran in Kenya for over six months from October 2005, in partnership with Faulu Kenya, a local microfinance institution. Since rolling out through its national partner, Safaricom, the service has been wildly successful. For many, the service has been life changing, giving access to financial services for the first time and allowing them to receive remittance payments directly from the United Kingdom. Besides employing and empowering thousands of M-PESA agents, the scheme has also cut out a lot of corruption, since all transactions are electronic.

When Vodafone extended the M-PESA service to Tanzania in April 2008, it signed up more than 3 million customers in less than a year. In 2009, Safaricom also launched the continent's first commercial solar-powered mobile phone, the Coral-200. Building on M-PESA's success in Kenya, Tanzania and Roshan in Afghanistan (branded M-Paisa), the company announced in February 2010 that it would bring M-PESA to South Africa as well, and hence to Africa's biggest economy.

Given Vodafone's efforts, it is not surprising that Tomorrow's Value™ Rating placed the company first as a sustainable business in its Information and Communications Technology category. Building on the success of Vodafone and others, a 2010 study by Arthur D. Little estimates that

4 An interview with Maryjka Beckmann is available on the csrinternational channel on YouTube.

global transaction volume in mobile financial services will reach approximately $280 billion by 2015.

African mutual social responsibility

Beyond my brief glimpses into CSR practices in Kenya, I recommend the writings of Judy Muthuri and Kiarie Mwaura, who wrote the Kenya chapter in *The World Guide to CSR*. For instance, they emphasise that sustainable business practices form part of the sociocultural traditional heritage encapsulated in the concept of 'African mutual social responsibility', an institutionalised community development and resource mobilisation strategy popular in Kenya.

In a survey conducted by Muthuri and Gilbert,[5] among 70 companies operating in Kenya, they found that the most prominent sustainable business issues are education (61%), environment (48%), HIV/AIDS (41%) and health (35%). Most notably, companies have rallied behind the Kenyan government's 'Education for All' agenda to help meet the Millennium Development Goals' (MDGs') target on universal education.

Some of the sustainable business case studies cited by Muthuri and Mwaura include Unilever Kenya, Magadi Soda Company and Bamburi Cement. For instance, Unilever Kenya launched the 'Neighbours Against AIDS' project in 2002, a coalition of eight companies committed to developing a common approach to tackling HIV/AIDS in the workplace. Unilever Kenya also helped set up the Kenya HIV/AIDS Private Sector Business Council which encourages Kenyan companies to adopt workplace HIV/AIDS programmes by creating and building their capacity to fight the disease and share best practices.

Magadi Soda Company inadvertently adopted a social welfare approach to corporate community involvement by, for example, establishing a company town with vital social amenities including housing, water, roads, railway infrastructure, a hospital, schools, entertainment facilities and places of worship. Bamburi Cement, on the other hand, has become a leading example of land reclamation and biodiversity efforts, with its world-famous Haller Park, a quarry rehabilitation project.

5 J.N. Muthuri and V. Gilbert, 'An Institutional Analysis of Corporate Social Responsibility in Kenya', *Journal of Business Ethics* 98.3 (2011): 467-83.

The strong focus on social and environmental issues reflects, at least in part, Kenya's strategic role in agricultural markets, especially tea, coffee and cut flowers. For example, between 1963 and 1991, horticultural exports from Kenya rose by a factor of 12 in tonnage and 40 in value. By 1999, Kenya was exporting more than 245,000 tonnes of tea, 200,000 tonnes of horticultural products and 70,000 tonnes of coffee. Of particular interest is the establishment of the Horticultural Ethical Business Initiative (HEBI), which aims to work with NGOs, government and industry to tackle working conditions in the flower industry.

Responsible flower markets

Two academic experts on this subject are Catherine Dolan and Maggie Opondo, who wrote an analysis of the multi-sector processes in Kenya's cut flower industry for a special issue on Africa of the *Journal of Corporate Citizenship* that I co-edited. According to Dolan and Opondo, the seeds of the HEBI process were sown in November 1999 when local civil society organisations mounted a successful campaign against violations of workers' rights in Cirio Delmonte, one of Kenya's largest pineapple growers. The success of this campaign raised concerns in the flower industry, prompting stakeholders to develop the Kenya Standard on Social Accountability, and a Voluntary Private Initiative to oversee its implementation.

However, the real impetus for HEBI came from the pressure exerted by transnational alliances of NGOs and consumer groups. The Kenya Women Workers Organisation (KEWWO) was funded by the UK-based organisation Women Working Worldwide (WWW) to gather evidence of the Ethical Trading Initiative (ETI) Base Code violations. Its report catalogued various unacceptable conditions, from pesticide poisoning to sexual harassment and rape, and spurred a campaign dubbed 'Produce Safely or Quit'. At the same time, the Kenya Human Rights Commission issued a three-month ultimatum to flower producers to improve working conditions, stating that it would 'go international' in its campaign after that time.

When the ETI was alerted to these serious violations of labour rights in 2002, several of their corporate and NGO members visited Kenyan flower producers. In fear of losing the support of ETI's global corporate members (which have a combined turnover of over £125 billion), Kenyan stakeholders came together for the first time to lay the groundwork for the formation of HEBI. What I find particular interesting is that HEBI did not arise from a vacuum of voluntary codes. On the contrary, there were already seven different international ethical codes being applied, but they seemed to lack effectiveness and credibility.

What made HEBI both necessary and different was the need to involve all stakeholders. As Dolan and Opondo put it:

> In contrast to the Fresh Produce Exporters Association of Kenya, the Kenya Flower Council and the Voluntary Private Initiative, which were locally initiated attempts to protect the image of the industry in overseas markets, HEBI was a product of direct northern involvement. While ETI and WWW only performed a facilitative role in the process, they were nonetheless pivotal to the establishment of a 'locally owned' multi-stakeholder process.

Nearly ten years later, while there is still work to be done, according to ETI the changes to the audit process and in the purchasing practices of ETI members have led to a number of improvements for workers in Kenya. For example, there are now more permanent contracts, establishment of worker welfare and gender committees, better provision of protective equipment, stricter pesticide controls and extensive improvements in housing. Further, more women now have access to day-care facilities and there is general acceptance that pregnant women should have light duties.

Kenya's convoluted and painful journey to creating a multi-stakeholder sector code has, most encouragingly, set a benchmark that other standards – for instance the Round Table on Sustainable Palm Oil (RSPO) – could later learn from and emulate. I also think it is significant that the United Nations chose Nairobi as the headquarters for its Environment Programme (UNEP) and UN-HABITAT organisation. While I was there, I had a chance to speak to Antoine King, Director of the Programme Support Division of UN-HABITAT, who explained the sustainability challenges faced by rapidly growing cities around the world.[6] And it is to one such city that we now move. Next stop, Lagos, Nigeria.

---

6 An interview with Antoine King is available on the csrinternational channel on YouTube.

5
Friends and foes
Oil on troubled waters
(Nigeria, 2011)

Shell and the Ogoni

If you work in corporate sustainability and responsibility, as I have for 20 years now, 'Shell in Nigeria' is inevitably part of your lexicon, one of the case studies trotted out with regular monotony at conferences and cocktails around the world. In this, I am no different. As it happens, I have had a few personal encounters with the country and the company, which I will explore in this chapter. However, let me start with the infamous case itself – put some of the facts on the table, so to speak.

Shell's experiences in Nigeria show that it isn't always exclusively environmental issues that catalyse a crisis, nor is it only when the company is directly involved in an incident. In the 1990s tensions arose between Shell and the native Ogoni people of the Niger Delta. The concerns of the latter were that very little of the money earned from oil on their land was getting to the people who live there, and they were also suffering from environmental damages caused by Shell's practices.

In 1993, the Movement for the Survival of the Ogoni People (MOSOP) organised a large protest against Shell and the government. In response, Shell withdrew its operations from the Ogoni areas, but the Nigerian government raided the Ogoni villages and arrested the instigators. Some of these arrested protesters – human rights activist Ken Saro-Wiwa being the most prominent among them –were tried for murder (which they denied) and were executed in November 1995. This was despite a plea by Shell for clemency, and widespread opposition from the Commonwealth of Nations and international human rights and environmental activists.

Despite Shell's official opposition to the executions, activists around the world vilified the company in wave after wave of angry protests and damaging boycotts. In 2002 there was even a court case against Shell in the United States, led by close relatives of Ken Saro-Wiwa. One of the reasons for targeting Shell was that it was (and continues to be) 'in bed' with the government. This is a literal fact: the Shell Petroleum Development Company of Nigeria Ltd (SPDC) is the operator of a joint venture between the government-owned Nigerian National Petroleum Corporation (NNPC, 55%), Shell (30%), Total (10%) and Agip (5%). Rightly or wrongly, stakeholders believed that, given these close ties, Shell had to be complicit in the government's campaign against the human rights activists, and must have had the power and influence to stop the executions.

This somewhat incestuous relationship between Shell and the Nigerian government persists to this day. Between 2006 and 2010, the SPDC paid $31 billion in revenues and $3.5 billion in royalties and taxes to the Nigerian government. In fact, according to Shell in Nigeria, 95% of its revenue after costs goes to the Nigerian government from each barrel of oil that SPDC produces. Can a company that is so enmeshed with a government ever be truly sustainable and responsible? I believe this remains one of Shell's most serious and enduring challenges.

After 1995, under the leadership of Sir Mark Moody-Stuart, Shell began implementing extensive policy reforms, including increased stakeholder engagement (in a campaign called 'Tell Shell'), community support, environmental management systems implementation (notably ISO 14001) and reporting on social and environmental issues, both in Nigeria and internationally. It was the latter two issues – ISO 14001 and sustainability reporting – that brought my world into an overlapping orbit with Shell in Nigeria, although that was already some years after Saro-Wiwa's death.

Triple-bottom-line challenges

At the time when the Shell fiasco was in progress in 1995 and 1996, I was in the process of leaving my management consulting career at Capgemini behind and embarking on my MSc studies in Human Ecology at Edinburgh University. Looking back, I am surprised I was not more aware of the protest activity. Be that as it may, not long after, when I was running KPMG's sustainability services in South Africa, I very quickly got up to speed on the legacy and ongoing challenges of Shell in Nigeria and elsewhere, as they were a major client. In fact, KPMG's sustainability practice in the Netherlands had worked closely with Shell to pioneer its triple-bottom-line reporting approach, and the KPMG Norway practice was working with Shell in Nigeria on sustainability reporting and environmental management.

Two things stick in my mind from that time. One was being rather puzzled by the failure of Shell Nigeria's HSE (health, safety and environment) reports to mention the Ken Saro-Wiwa incident, which was still very much at the forefront of Shell protests and boycotts, both in the country and abroad. If ever there was an elephant in the room! The second recollection was a trip to Nigeria by one of my team members, Shireen Naidoo, to do an audit on Shell's ISO 14001 system. When she returned, I was aghast to learn that, at one point, the Shell vehicle had been surrounded by an angry mob threatening violence, after which the team travelled to Shell sites by helicopter and with an armed guard.

It is a grave lesson in corporate sustainability and responsibility to know not only that such hostility between Shell and the community could exist, but that it still exists to this day, more than 15 years later. And it still costs the company dearly. Shell tends to argue that the source of conflict nowadays is most often not from local communities, but from a very small group of agitators and organised criminals, who have malignant political and economic agendas of their own. Whichever version of the truth you accept, one thing is undeniable: the impacts have been catastrophic.

According to Shell's 2010 sustainability report, gangs kidnapped 26 SPDC employees and contractors in 2010 (down from 51 in 2009), and one contractor was killed in a related assault. Also in 2010, an estimated 100,000 barrels a day of oil were stolen from its pipelines, causing extensive environmental damage. The report states that sabotage and theft together accounted for more than 80% of the spill volume from SPDC facilities in 2010.

So what can we learn from all of this? How has Shell responded? The company's ongoing critics focus on three main issues – the environmental impacts of Shell's spills, the health impacts of its gas flares and the enduring lack of human development in the Niger delta, despite billions in oil revenues generated in the region. On all three issues, Shell has made progress, albeit not enough. For instance, in 2010, in order to lessen its operational spills, SPDC completed construction of a $1.1 billion replacement pipeline, the 97-kilometre Nembe Creek Trunkline; and in January 2011 it launched a public website which tracks the company's response to, and investigation and clean-up of, every spill from SPDC facilities whether operational or the result of sabotage.

Since 2002, flaring from SPDC facilities has fallen by over 50%. Nevertheless, SPDC has been unable to meet targets to end continuous flaring. It claims that militant violence has prevented safe access, and a lack of funding from its government partner has delayed progress. Now that conditions have improved, however, it has begun installing equipment that will reduce gas flaring from SPDC facilities at a cost of $2 billion, in addition to the $3 billion already spent to reduce flaring.

On the difficult issue of poverty in the delta, Shell presided over many failed and frustrated projects over the years, before changing the way in which it approached community development. In 2006, it introduced global memorandums of understanding (GMOUs), which are intended to put communities at the centre of planning and implementation. Communities identify their own needs, decide how to spend the funding provided by SPDC and its joint-venture partners, and directly implement projects. By the end of 2010, SPDC had GMOUs in 244 communities.

One example Shell cites is in Port Harcourt, where the GMOU model was used to launch the Niger Delta's first community health insurance scheme. More than 8,000 people had signed up by the end of 2010. Many have now received previously unaffordable medical treatment including vaccinations, maternal care and operations. Annual premiums are around $50, with GMOU funds subsidising half that amount. This compares, for example, to the typical fee of $300–$350 that women in the Niger Delta pay for care during pregnancy.

Sustainable business revival

With Shell in Nigeria being so much a part of my consciousness through-out my career in sustainable business – I even profiled it in one of my books, *Landmarks for Sustainability* (2009) – I am as surprised as anyone that it took me until 2011 to finally visit the country. And, as if to make up for lost time, I have since made five trips to Lagos to deliver sustain-able business training courses (hosted by Ken Egbas, Managing Director of Trucontact, in March and November 2011) and to present at confer-ences (the 1st Africa Round Table and Conference on CSR in June 2011, the International Conference on Corporate Social Responsibility in Sub-Saharan Africa in December 2011 and the International CSR Conference at Lagos Business School in February 2012).

I came away with mixed feelings about the country. Certainly, the raw vitality and aggressive ambition (or is it just survival instinct?) is palpa-ble. And as in so much of Africa, the culture and its people are colourful, hopeful and friendly. But there is also the malaise of powerlessness in the face of endemic corruption and greed among politicians, not to men-tion the inertia of crumbling state apparatus and economic injustice. The greatest hope lies in rediscovering good, public-serving leaders, although this remains something of a fantasy. The greatest source of faith is a Pen-tecostal brand of Christianity that gives its followers strength in knowing that God is on the side of the oppressed. I tried to capture the vitality and the paradox of Nigeria in my poem, 'Lagos Lives', which begins as follows:

> Lagos lives
> Seeding and sprawling
> Steaming and smoking
> Grasping at the shoreline
> Gasping at the skyline
> Clinging to its oil-slicked ropes
> And singing of its toil-stripped hopes
>
> Praise be!
> To the God who sets His people free
> To the fiery preacher on TV
> To the Sunday throng that still believe
> Praise be!
> To the beggar and the banker

To the fisher and the swanker
To the struggler and the smuggler
Praise be!

It is somewhat depressing to know that Nigeria's hardships are largely self-imposed, inflicted by the power-hungry on the opportunity-starved. The society is culturally robust, but morally and economically weakened by the cancers of raw greed and desperate need. I am not naive enough to believe that sustainable business heralds a new dawn for Nigeria. The general consensus among the people I spoke to was that most companies are stuck in the ages of Philanthropy and Marketing. Nevertheless, sustainable business has the potential to advance transparency and create a platform to discuss the ethics of business and government. It also has the potential to be corrupted, which sadly is already happening in some instances where corporate sponsorship of government 'CSR projects' is practised as an indirect form of bribery.

Legislating CSR

This is one of the reasons why I am not wildly optimistic about another recent development in Nigeria, namely the move to legislate CSR. At the time that I visited, this took the form of The Bill for an Act to Provide for the Establishment of the Corporate Social Responsibility Commission. At one level, it is highly ambitious, perhaps unrealistically so. It aims, among other things to (take a deep breath): create a CSR standard; integrate social responsibility into trade policies; conduct research into community needs; 'serve notices' of social responsibility requests to organisations; identify corporate compliance with legislation on equality and non-discrimination; implement social and environmental regulations; determine the nature of CSR expected of companies according to size and classification; publish annual sustainability reports; encourage community investment, including a requirement to spend no less than 3.5% of gross annual profits per year on CSR; promote labour standards and 'collective social governance'; ensure companies are accountable to all stakeholders; use fines and incentives to promote social responsibility; develop environmental guidelines; 'peg and monitor' local contents in terms of employment and sourcing of raw materials; and introduce social responsibility compliance labels. Phew!

My opinion is that this is an initiative set up to fail. Of course, on paper, it sounds wonderful, and the issues it is proposing to tackle are all important and laudable. But Nigeria should learn from the United Kingdom's mistakes. Britain created something similar – a Minister for CSR – in 2003, and eventually abandoned it in 2010 as a largely ineffectual strategy. The reason it failed in the United Kingdom, and will most likely fail in Nigeria, is the same reason that CSR departments often fail in companies: they are not integrated into the core functions of the organisation, and they do not have much political or economic clout. This is only exacerbated in developing countries where the capacity to monitor and enforce is severely challenged by weak, failing or corrupt governments.

Of course, there are examples of good practice, many of which are highlighted in the excellent chapter on Nigeria by Kenneth Amaeshi and Chris Ogbechie in *The World Guide to CSR*. I am particularly encouraged by the emergence of global MOUs between companies and communities, and conservation projects such as the Chevron-sponsored urban forest that I visited. Yet even here, one senses that these are fragile fortifications against a relentless tide of oil-slicked growth and car-jammed urbanisation.

Nigerians seem to take all these challenges in their stride, as if fighting the behemoth of inefficiency is as futile as cursing the manic traffic. One illustration of this biblical Job-like patience was during my June trip when an almighty tropical rainstorm descended on Lagos, flooding the city and delaying the start of the conference by two hours (and some speakers by six hours). Not only was I relieved that I was able to arrive earlier in the week, but it made me especially conscious of how vulnerable developing cities such as Lagos (population around 17 million) are to the impending ravages of climate change. At the same time, the event demonstrated the remarkable equanimity, endurance and resilience of people in developing countries.

One of the more encouraging sustainable business initiatives in Nigeria is the Social Enterprise Reporting Awards (SERA), run by Trucontact. It is refreshing to see reporting awards where a level of verification (including site visits) takes place, and where the UN MDGs are used as criteria to judge sustainable business projects. I was asked to help redesign the questionnaire for 2011 (initially, literally on the back of a serviette/napkin), so that the awards start measuring strategic CSR, rather than the historical focus on philanthropic and promotional approaches to CSR. Judging against transformative CSR (CSR 2.0) remains a little ambitious, at this stage.

Shine, Africa, shine!

I realise that I have been quite critical in this chapter, but I should be clear that the tone of the debates on sustainable business is not at all negative in the country; quite the contrary, in fact. On my visits I noticed repeated mention of the impact that sound leadership is having on improving governance and living conditions in Lagos and River State. I sensed a real can-do attitude emerging. This confirms my hunch that the most important thing is first to demonstrate that 'better is possible', whether it is in tackling poverty, corruption or unsustainable practices. Once people can see real benefits in one place, they are more willing to support reforms in another.

This spirit of possibility was wonderfully demonstrated by a theatrical group at the Thistle Praxis CSR conference, which performed a fantastically powerful and funny sketch about sustainable business, alive with singing and dancing. Nigerians have their heroes to inspire them – from the incomparable musical legend Fela to the brave martyr Ken Saro-Wiwa. They also have a powerful story – now of mythological proportions – in the form of the Shell saga, which we can all learn from. I recall Richard Boele, Managing Director of Banarra Sustainability Assurance and Advice in Melbourne, telling me about his personal encounters with Ken Saro-Wiwa in the early 1990s. He drew a fascinating parallel between the Shell Nigeria tragedy and the blockbuster movie *Avatar*, in which the indigenous tribe of Pandora struggles against the exploitation and violence of a military–industrial institution intent on extracting the planet's mineral wealth at any cost.[7]

All of this makes me think that talk of an African Century is perhaps not only premature, but also misguided. Rather, we should be focused on discovering, building and promoting Africa's distinctive contribution.

---

7 An interview with Richard Boele is available on the csrinternational channel on YouTube.

What is it that Africans do well, better than anywhere else, and how can this be leveraged? Maybe it has something to do with their hospitable culture, and their music, dance and style? Maybe Africa's distinctive gift to the world is in transforming the arts, fashion and tourism? Maybe Africa should stop trying to compete with China and India as a low-cost producer, and rather discover its source of pride, finding new, better (and commercially beneficial) ways to share its energy, colour and warmth with the world.

As for me, I was honoured to be given a Nigerian (Yoruba) name – Ebun, meaning 'the gift'. It is an enduring reminder for me that Nigeria and Africa have many gifts for the world, despite facing some of the toughest social, environmental and ethical battles in the world. Nigeria and Africa are the forge – the burning furnace – where sustainable business faces its biggest challenges, from the 'resource curse' and the continent's post-colonial legacy to the scourge of corruption and the epidemic of poverty. If sustainable business cannot help to improve the lives of people and the quality of the environment in places such as this, what purpose does it serve? After all, it is in countries like Nigeria and on continents like Africa that a small change can make a big impact. And so I wish my fellow Africans working in sustainable business all the very best. As I expressed it in my poem, it is time for Africa to shine:

> So shine, Africa, shine!
> Nourish our shared earth
> And feed our common roots;
> Green our tree of life
> And bear sweet fruits of peace.
>
> Shine, Africa, shine!
> Spark our imagination
> And confound us with your brilliance;
> Flame our deepest desires
> And dazzle us with your colours.
>
> Shine, Africa, shine!
> Fire our greatest passions
> And empower us with your stories;
> Blaze brightly on our soul quest
> And inspire us with your light.

Part 2
Europe

6

Directives and policies
Eurocrats take on CSR
(Belgium: 2010)

Early policy developments

I will use this chapter to explore European policies on CSR, which have been evolving for more than a decade now.

In 2001 the European Commission issued a Green Paper on CSR, which 'provided all interested parties with a platform for further discussion with the goal of policy generation in the CSR area in Europe'. After a year of consultation, the White Paper – entitled 'CSR – A business contribution to sustainable development' – was released, and represented the official policy intention of the European Commission in the field of CSR. Both papers were based on a broad consensus and had been debated through a multi-stakeholder process that included companies, business associations, governments, NGOs and trade unions.

After the White Paper, all seemed to go quiet on the European CSR policy front. Meanwhile, however, there was significant progress on waste management and climate change policy. In terms of waste, the 2002 WEEE Directives (2002/95/EC and 2002/96/EC) made a great leap forward on the restriction of hazardous substances in electrical and electronic equipment and the introduction of take-back schemes for waste electrical and electronic equipment (WEEE).

Under this legislation, producers are responsible for taking back and recycling electrical and electronic equipment. This provides incentives to design electrical and electronic equipment in a more environmentally efficient way, taking waste management aspects fully into account. Consumers are able to return their equipment free of charge. In order to prevent the generation of hazardous waste, Directive 2002/95/EC also required the substitution of brominated flame-retardants and various heavy metals (lead, mercury, cadmium and hexavalent chromium) in electrical and electronic equipment put on the market from 1 July 2006.

Significant progress was also made on climate change, with a 2003 Directive (2003/87/EC) laying the foundation for the EU Greenhouse Gas Emission Trading Scheme (EU ETS), which commenced operation in January 2005 as the largest multi-country, multi-sector carbon trading scheme in the world. The aim of the ETS is to help EU Member States achieve compliance with their emission reduction targets agreed under the Kyoto Protocol. Allowing participating companies to buy or sell emission allowances means that the targets can be achieved at the least cost. According to the EU ETS, if the Scheme had not been adopted, other (more costly) measures such as carbon taxes would have had to be implemented.

In the first phase (2005–2007), the EU ETS included some 12,000 installations, representing approximately 40% of EU CO_2 emissions. The trading price of carbon reached a peak of about €30 per tonne (/t) CO_2 in April 2006, but then collapsed down to €0.10 in September 2007 when it became clear that many industries had been given such generous emission caps that there was no need for them to reduce emissions.

The second phase (2008–2012) expanded the scope and tightened the rules of the scheme significantly, and saw the carbon price rise to over €20/tCO_2 in the first half of 2008, but then fall again below €10 when the recession started to bite. Despite these fluctuations, real reductions have been achieved. According to verified EU data from 2008, the ETS saw an emissions reduction of 3%, or 50 million tonnes. The UK's Climate Change Committee projects a carbon price in 2020 of around €22/tCO_2, while most market commentators project a price around or below €30/tCO_2 during phase three (2013–2020).

Back in the CSR space, momentum was maintained through the launch in 2005 of the 'European Roadmap for Businesses – 2010', an initiative led by the independent business association, CSR Europe, together with its national partner organisations around Europe. The Roadmap includes five goals: innovation and entrepreneurship; skills and competence building; equal opportunities and diversity; health and safety; and environmental protection. It also includes five strategies to achieve these goals: corporate responsibility in the mainstream of business; stakeholder engagement; leadership and governance; communication and transparency; and business-to-business cooperation and alliances.

The European Commission re-entered the fray in March 2006 by establishing the European Alliance on CSR. This is an open alliance of European enterprises, launched to further promote and encourage CSR. The alliance is a political umbrella for CSR initiatives by large companies, small and medium-sized enterprises (SMEs), and their stakeholders. In 2006 a research report was published by CSR Europe, the 'European Cartography on CSR Innovations, Gaps and Future Trends', which was based on an analysis of 545 CSR-related business solutions and 140 networking activities in 19 EU countries.

CSR trends in Europe

Things seemed to go quiet again and then, in May 2010, I was invited to make a presentation on CSR in Brussels to the EU High Level Group (HLG), comprising 27 Member State representatives. The topic of my presentation was 'CSR and the global financial crisis', and it gave me a fantastic opportunity to talk with some of the people helping to shape the EU agenda. There were a number of trends that I found interesting.

The first was that, whereas formerly CSR was discussed purely as a voluntary activity by business (this was especially clear in the EU's policy statement on CSR in 2006), there was now increasing discussion and even demand for what Susan Bird, CSR coordinator in the Directorate-General for Employment of the European Commission and part of the EU HLG on CSR, called 'a more active role', which may involve 'conditions' being introduced in the future, although this was all still up for debate.[8]

A second insight was how the competitiveness agenda has changed. The first ten-year economic strategy of the European Union – the Lisbon

---

8 An interview with Susan Bird is available on the csrinternational channel on YouTube.

Agenda, which ended in 2010 – was all about competitiveness and paid very little attention to CSR issues. However, the 2008 European Competitiveness Report dedicated an entire chapter to CSR and countries such as Denmark were claiming that responsible, green growth was central to its international reputation and hence its competitiveness. This changing emphasis is also reflected in the new Lisbon Strategy for 2020, which has as its central goal 'smart, sustainable and inclusive growth'.

The studies being commissioned by the HLG give some indication of where the direction of policy development is headed. In particular, there are research projects on business and human rights (integrating UN Special Representative John Ruggie's framework), supply chain integrity, CSR reporting, and sustainable and responsible public procurement.

On the supply chain work, I interviewed Marjon van Opijnen, a Senior Consultant with the consultancy CREM, who sees a number of trends, including water footprinting.[9] CREM's research reveals that it takes 16,000 litres of water to produce leather products, 2,700 litres to produce a T-shirt and 2,400 litres to make a hamburger. Palm oil is also high on the agenda, especially the issue of involving small palm oil farmers in the RSPO certification process in Indonesia and Malaysia. The post-consumer supply chain is another focus, such as the e-waste from Europe that ends up in Africa, especially Ghana, where it creates health hazards and environmental challenges.

Another area of research that is starting to reveal interesting results is the role of socially responsible investment (SRI) in Europe. For example, Walter Kahlenborn, Managing Director of Adelphi, which was commissioned to do research for the EU HLG on CSR, talked to me about studies the company has done in Germany. These found that German SRI funds are no better than non-SRI funds in terms of their portfolio's carbon footprint.[10] Survey results also suggest that, while inclusion in SRI funds of big companies give legitimacy to their CSR and climate activities, the impact of SRI is limited to those large companies that are included, rather than the broader market. And in Germany, the SRI mutual funds only make up around 0.5% of the total funds, while in companies with SRI

---

9 An interview with Marjon van Opijnenis available on the csrinternational channel on YouTube.

10 An interview with Walter Kahlenborn available on the csrinternational channel on YouTube.

investments, these investments only make up around 0.3% of their total investments.

Of course, the HLG faces enormous challenges, as pointed out to me by Thomas Dodd, a CSR Coordinator in the European Commission's Directorate-General on Enterprise & Business and serving member of the EU HLG on CSR.[11] How can they have a consistent policy for all Member States, bridging the leaders such as Denmark with the laggards, which tend to be the newer EU members? Another serious challenge, and a big focus of the HLG, is how to make EU policies on CSR relevant to SMEs, which make up the vast majority of businesses in the European Union. Looking to the future, the Responsible Business 2020 project of the European Alliance is worth watching. Among the trends that Susan Bird sees is a greater emphasis on social inclusion and more flexible ways of working, especially using ICT technologies to be create innovative workplace practices.

European Union strategy on CSR

After my visit to Brussels, I concluded that the sleeping giant of CSR policy in Europe was awakening and that we should 'watch this space'. As it turned out, we didn't have to wait too long. In October 2011, 'A renewed EU strategy 2011–14 for Corporate Social Responsibility' was launched. The document itself is only 15 pages long (which is a good thing!) and I recommend that everyone reads it. Here, however, I think it is worth presenting and commenting on the 17 actions that Europe intends to implement over the next four years (2011–2014). I will show the actions extracted verbatim from the strategy in *italics*, and my brief observations appear after each action.

> *Action 1: Create in 2013 multi-stakeholder CSR platforms in a number of relevant industrial sectors, for enterprises, their workers and other stakeholders to make public commitments on the CSR issues relevant to each sector and jointly monitor progress.*

11 An interview with Thomas Dodd available on the csrinternational channel on YouTube.

Applying CSR at an industry sector level makes a lot of sense and a stakeholder engagement approach is always welcome. The concern is whether this duplicates many similar initiatives that have already been undertaken by the likes of GRI, WBCSD and industry associations.

> *Action 2: Launch from 2012 onwards a European award scheme for CSR partnerships between enterprises and other stakeholders.*

I suppose having the European Union behind an awards scheme will give it some gravitas and greater PR mileage. But the world is already awash with CSR award schemes, and when I look at the sorts of companies that win these awards, I find they tend to be the 'usual suspects' who are doing little more than strategic CSR, when what we really need is more transformative approaches.

> *Action 3: Address the issue of misleading marketing related to the environmental impacts of products (so-called 'green-washing') in the context of the report on the application of the Unfair Commercial Practices Directive 18 foreseen for 2012, and consider the need for possible specific measures on this issue.*

This would be a welcome addition and follows existing best practice in Australia, Canada, Norway and the United Kingdom. In Australia, the Trade Practices Act has been modified to include punishment (of up to A$1.1 million in fines) for companies that provide misleading environmental claims. In Norway, car manufacturers are forbidden from claiming that their automobiles are environmentally friendly.

> *Action 4: Initiate an open debate with citizens, enterprises and other stakeholders on the role and potential of business in the 21st century, with the aim of encouraging common understanding and expectations, and carry out periodic surveys of citizen trust in business and attitudes towards CSR.*

Okay. Nothing to get excited about.

> *Action 5: Launch a process in 2012 with enterprises and other stakeholders to develop a code of good practice for self- and co-regulation exercises, which should improve the effectiveness of the CSR process.*

This could be interesting, if we're talking about a best-practice guideline on what makes good self-regulation. For instance, what makes the Forest Stewardship Council (FSC) a better self-regulatory mechanism than the chemical industry's Responsible Care initiative? To be honest, though, a lot of this work has already been done by AccountAbility and its suite of AA 1000 standards.

> Action 6: Facilitate the better integration of social and environmental considerations into public procurement as part of the 2011 review of the Public Procurement Directives, without introducing additional administrative burdens for contracting authorities or enterprises, and without undermining the principle of awarding contracts to the most economically advantageous tender.

How disappointing! By including that last phrase, the message is clear: the lowest price will continue to win the day. It is the get-out clause that public procurement agencies will use repeatedly, so that budgets will get precedence over responsibilities, despite the fact that externality costs (the impacts on society and the environment) are not built into tender pricing.

> Action 7: Consider a requirement on all investment funds and financial institutions to inform all their clients (citizens, enterprises, public authorities, etc.) about any ethical or responsible investment criteria they apply or any standards and codes to which they adhere.

Another extremely weak proposal. It doesn't even go as far as the well-established corporate governance principle of 'comply or explain', which the GRI is pushing for under its integrated reporting strategy. I can't see what this action is going to achieve, other than give a few more PR kudos to SRI-savvy funds.

> Action 8: Provide further financial support for education and training projects on CSR under the EU Lifelong Learning and Youth in Action Programmes, and launch an action in 2012 to raise the awareness of education professionals and enterprises on the importance of cooperation on CSR.

Fair enough. If we can't reshape young minds, we won't reshape future behaviour.

Action 9: Create with Member States in 2012 a peer review mechanism for national CSR policies.

The idea of learning from each other is hard to argue against. My view, however, is that these kinds of peer review mechanisms tend to be more about politics than performance.

Action 10: The Commission invites: Member States to develop or update by mid-2012 their own plans or national lists of priority actions to promote CSR in support of the Europe 2020 strategy, with reference to internationally recognised CSR principles and guidelines and in cooperation with enterprises and other stakeholders, taking account of the issues raised in this communication.

This is an attempt to extend the EU policy on CSR down to a national level. It will keep a few bureaucrats busy but I won't be holding my breath. I really don't believe we need more policy or legislation on CSR. What we need is to eliminate the contradictory policies (such as fossil fuel subsidies) and focus on more effective regulation of issues, including labour rights, biodiversity loss and transparency.

Action 11: Monitor the commitments made by European enterprises with more than 1,000 employees to take account of internationally recognised CSR principles and guidelines, and take account of the ISO 26000 Guidance Standard on Social Responsibility in its own operations.

Isn't this what the Organisation for European Co-operation and Development (OECD) Guidelines for Multinational Enterprises has been trying (and largely failing) to achieve over the last 50 years? For multinationals, this sort of requirement will add nothing to what they are already doing. Maybe a few medium-sized companies will be forced to take a look at ISO 26000 for the first time.

Action 12: The Commission invites: All large European enterprises to make a commitment by 2014 to take account of at least one of the following sets of principles and guidelines when developing their approach to CSR: the UN Global Compact, the OECD Guidelines for Multinational Enterprises, or the ISO 26000 Guidance Standard on Social Responsibility.

Giving companies the choice between these very different principles and guidelines is laughable. Through this action, the European Union is suggesting an equivalence between the minimal efforts required to sign up to the Global Compact's ten principles and the 100 pages or so of detailed guidance across seven core areas in ISO 26000.

> *Action 13: The Commission invites: All European-based multi-national enterprises to make a commitment by 2014 to respect the ILO Tri-partite Declaration of Principles Concerning Multi-national Enterprises and Social Policy.*

This is another action that will probably not achieve much beyond some poor CSR manager being tasked with reading the policy document and cross-referencing it to the company's existing CSR and labour practices.

> *Action 14: Work with enterprises and stakeholders in 2012 to develop human rights guidance for a limited number of relevant industrial sectors, as well as guidance for small- and medium-sized enterprises, based on the UN Guiding Principles.*

This is the first of many actions I expect will emerge from John Ruggie's 'protect, respect and remedy' UN framework on business and human rights.

> *Action 15: Publish by the end of 2012 a report on EU priorities in the implementation of the UN Guiding Principles, and thereafter to issue periodic progress reports.*

This looks like an action to keep the CSR Eurocrats in a job.

> *Action 16: The Commission also: Expects all European enterprises to meet the corporate responsibility to respect human rights, as defined in the UN Guiding Principles.*

It is a great pity that Europe wasn't a bit bolder, requiring companies to conduct human rights due diligence assessments, which was Ruggie's main recommendation to business.

> *Action 17: Invites EU Member States to develop by the end of 2012 national plans for the implementation of the UN Guiding Principles.*

The final clause simply reinforces the trickle-down approach. The European Union should learn a lesson from the United Kingdom, which, as I mentioned before, tried to politicise CSR by appointing a CSR Minister in 2003. It was by all accounts a failure, and was withdrawn as a strategy in 2010.

Europe has shown policy leadership on many issues, from labour rights and animal rights to environmental management and climate change. However, I can't help but wonder if this new wave of CSR policy development is doing more to confuse and distract than advance the agenda. Time will tell.

7

Green and growing
Re-engineering growth
(Germany, Austria: 2002, 2008, 2009)

Proud pioneering traditions

Europe's recent CSR policy experiments are a relatively recent phenomenon, but they build on a long and rich tradition of responsibility in its member states, and this is especially true for Germany. My first visit to Germany was in 2002 when I was still Director of Sustainability Services at KPMG in South Africa. We were conducting a safety, health and environmental (SHE) corporate governance audit for a multinational chemical company and had site visits in Germany, Italy, the Netherlands, United States and South Africa. I have two enduring impressions from that visit. First was the number of wind turbines I saw as we drove from Frankfurt to the chemical plant; and the second was how systems-driven the SHE team was – there were models and spreadsheets and management systems for everything. It was hard not to be impressed.

Since then, I have visited Germany numerous times over the years, in my capacity as Visiting Professor of CSR at Mannheim University, Steinbeis University in Berlin and the Katholische Universität Eichstätt-Ingolstad. I also worked closely with the Frankfurt-headquartered Institute for Corporate Culture Affairs (ICCA), which has played a central role in promoting CSR in Germany, not least through the publications it has sponsored, such as *The ICCA Handbook on Corporate Social Responsibility*, *The A to Z of Corporate Social Responsibility* and *Responsible Business*. Former Director of ICCA, Nick Tolhurst, and I co-edited *The World Guide to CSR*, and he and his ICCA colleague, Aron Embaye, also wrote an excellent chapter on CSR in Germany for that book.

Tolhurst and Embaye explain how the national psyche of Germany is strongly predisposed to sustainable business, with influences ranging from German philosophers such as Kant and Marx to political developments such as the social welfare state and the Green Party. There has been business leadership too. The entrepreneur Robert Bosch was one of the first entrepreneurs in Germany to introduce the eight-hour working day in 1906, while companies such as Faber Castell AG, ThyssenKrupp AG, Volkswagen AG and many others show a deeply rooted culture of social engagement. In fact, I remember from South Africa how Volkswagen's system of participatory decision-making – known as *mitbestimmungen* – was highly praised for ensuring that workers were fairly treated and had a direct say in how their company was run, even before apartheid had crumbled.

I also know from my work on *Landmarks for Sustainability* that Franz Hermann Schulze-Delitzsch established the first credit unions in the 1850s in Germany, thereby giving the 'unbanked' an opportunity to borrow from the savings pooled by themselves and their fellow members. Now, the World Council of Credit Unions boasts 172 million members, through 46,000 credit unions in 97 countries. Perhaps it is not surprising, therefore, that Germany also leads on SRI, having promulgated a law that obliges investment funds (predominantly pension funds) to disclose the extent to which social, environmental and ethical criteria are accounted for in their investment policies.

Another area of leadership is in ethical consumption. The world's second eco-labelling scheme, the Blue Angel Seal, was launched in Germany in 1978 (the first was the Organic label, established in the United Kingdom in 1967). Given this pioneering start, it is hardly surprising that ethical consumerism in Germany is among the strongest anywhere in the world. According to research from market research group GfK NOP, German consumers are willing pay a 5–10% price premium for many ethical products. In order to share best practices, the German government has also established a Round Table on Corporate Codes of Conduct, which aims to improve labour and social standards in developing countries through voluntary codes of conduct.

Achievements and challenges

Beyond these general areas of progress, there are some great case studies of sustainable business in German companies, such as the way in which business ethics is used as a management instrument at Henkel. CEO, Ulrich Lehner, writes in *The ICCA Handbook on Corporate Social Responsibility*, 'Henkel does not regard business ethics or related issues like corporate governance or corporate social responsibility, including corporate citizenship, as cost centres, but as value-creating (at least value-conserving) regulative instruments of modern enterprises.'

Another case, profiled in *Responsible Business*, looks at how sustainable business is used as a corporate strategy (rather than a marketing tactic) at the small generic drug firm, Betapharm, in the historical Bavarian town of Augsburg. Its view, as Nick Tolhurst discovered in his interview with the head of the Beta Institute, Horst Erhart, is that 'you cannot dissociate CSR and say, this is "my CSR bit." [Rather] I am CSR – it's me, in the way I interact with employees, the way I deal with resources, the way I deal with this or that.' Another celebrated case is BASF, voted Europe's most socially responsible firm in the 2007 Good Company Ranking and today making great strides on climate protection, energy efficiency, occupational health and safety, education and sustainable investment.

Of course, sustainable business in Germany is not without its challenges. One area of ongoing concern is gender equality. Germany has one of the highest gender pay gaps in Europe; the average gross hourly earnings of German women are 77% of men's in the public sector and 73% in the private sector. Furthermore, German women are only half as likely as men to hold a managerial position.

Another sustainable business issue that has been in the spotlight is in the area of data privacy. As *TIME* magazine reported on 27 May 2008, the corporate spying scandals in Germany began in 2005 and 2006 with Deutsche Telekom employing a private security firm to scrutinize the phone records of journalists and members of its supervisory board. Hans-Olaf Henkel, a retired IBM executive and former president of Germany's main business lobby, condemned the practice as 'reprehensible and disgusting', comparing it to the 'methods of the East German Stasi' secret police. 'This is not capitalism', he said. 'It's not my understanding of the market economy.'

Then, in 2008, there was the infamous case in which the German retailer, Lidl, was accused of spying on its employees, recording personal details in an operation that included surveillance records with comments on whether employees seemed capable, what kind of friends they had, and even how often they went to the toilet. Conversations were recorded in minute detail. Electronics giant Siemens has also been accused of spying on employees, and employees alleged that staff doctors at automaker Daimler reported on employees. Uwe Wesel, an emeritus law professor at Berlin's Free University, said that:

> although the language of the courts is very clear that this kind of behaviour is not allowed, there does appear to be a certain cultural shift taking place. Perhaps driven by the debate about the threat of terrorism, certain standards are weakening.

Sustainability is boring

My other connection with Germany is less to do with the country and more to do with an individual, the German Michael Braungart, co-founder and co-author with Bill McDonough of the 'cradle to cradle' (C2C) concept. I interviewed Braungart in 2008 for *The Top 50 Sustainability Books* and was inspired (and entertained) by much of what he had to say.[12] Braungart told me his story as follows:

> In 1987, I was looking at complex household products and I identified in the TV set 4,360 different chemicals, and I thought it doesn't help just to take any toxic stuff out of it. I asked the simple question, do you really want to own 4,360 different chemicals? Or do you want to watch Larry King Live on TV? And I was claimed to be an eco-communist for that.

12 My interview with Michael Braungart is available on the Cambridge University website www.cpsl.cam.ac.uk.

In fact, it was probably Braungart's leading role in Greenpeace's protests against the Swiss chemical industry that earned him that dubious title. But the net effect was still positive. The chairman of Ciba Geigy, Alex Krauer, approached Braungart and challenged him to work in partnership on solutions for 'green' or sustainable chemistry, with a budget of about $2 million.

Braungart accepted the offer, and immediately set about challenging his benefactor.

> I told him that sustainability is boring. I said to Alex Krauer, 'What would you say if I would ask you about your relation- ship with your wife? How would you characterise it? As sustain- able?' If this is the bigger goal, sustainability, then I feel really sorry because it doesn't celebrate human creativity and human nature.

Braungart is similarly scathing about the concept of green chemistry.

> I'm just talking about good chemistry. Chemistry is not good when the chemicals accumulate in the biosphere; that's just stu- pid. Young scientists immediately understand that a chemical is not good when it accumulates in mothers' milk. Chemistry is not good when it changes irreversibly biological systems like EDTA; it's just primitive chemistry. So we can now make far bet- ter chemistry, far better material science, far better physics, and we don't need to put this into 'green' or 'sustainable' niches.

Braungart went on to found the Environmental Protection Encourage- ment Agency (EPEA), which developed a system of 'lifecycle develop- ment' in the 1990s. Then he met the American architect, Bill McDonough, and they began to work together, writing the book *Cradle to Cradle* and founding MBCD, which offers C2C certification. He reflected that:

> Bill helped me a lot to phrase it in a way that people really could understand, [as being] about the management of the biosphere and of the techno-sphere, as technical nutrients and biological nutrients. So there is no waste, it's just materials going back into the techno-sphere and the biosphere, and then they can be beneficial.

One of the things I love about Braungart is not only his feisty spirit, but also his inherently positive approach. In his usual grasshopper-minded way, he began by telling me, 'Another thing which I learned was that the biomass of ants is so much higher than of human beings, and they are not an environmental problem, because they do different nutrient management than we do.' Then came his quasi-philosophical message:

> So we don't need to apologise for being on this planet. We don't need to minimise our footprint. We can have a big footprint, but make it a wetland. I understand when you have a real lack of something – not enough light, not enough energy – then you need to minimise, to reduce or avoid that. But when you have more than enough input [such as solar energy], then you can make things which celebrate abundance.

Here, Braungart makes a very important technical point.

> The thing is the differentiation between efficiency and effectiveness. Nature is completely inefficient, but amazingly effective, whereas the traditional eco-efficiency only optimises the existing stuff and makes it less bad. At the end, it's perfectly bad. Using this logic, East Germany has been protecting the environment far more than West Germany, just by inefficiency. So when you do something wrong, don't make it perfect. What happened in the last 20 years, we basically lost 20 years by optimising the wrong stuff.

This gets to the heart of Braungart and McDonough's cradle-to-cradle message of making things 'good' by design, not just 'less bad'.

Similarly, he says, it is not about respecting diversity:

> it's about supporting diversity. It's about celebrating diversity. And the social dimension is at least as important as the environmental one. We think that we can make things which are good for economy, good for society, and good for the environment at the same time. So the human footprint can be beneficial – and you can see this even in the city of Berlin; species diversity in Berlin is four times higher than in the surrounding agricultural area. So we can be beneficial. We don't need to apologise that we are here.

Limits to growth

Another link I have to the region is also based on an interview I did for the *Top 50 Sustainability Books,* in this case with Dennis Meadows, co-author of the 1972 *Limits to Growth.*[13] Meadows is not German, but I interviewed him in Vienna, where he was teaching. The *Limits to Growth* study was the world's first comprehensive computer model of the world's economic, social and environmental systems, and all the scenarios it ran predicted an 'overshoot and collapse' outcome for society. Unfortunately, his conclusions haven't altered and his vision of the future is far less sunny than that of Braungart. Even so, I think it is a message we need to hear.

When I asked Meadows what his hopes for the future were, he answered rather bleakly, saying:

> I don't have hope that we will sustain our current Western industrial society. In 1972 it would still have been possible, I think, and that was our analysis – that there was still time to slow down and to sustain something more or less indefinitely. But since 1972 there's been phenomenal growth, and now we're far above the limits. And there is, as far as I can tell, absolutely no possibility whatsoever of sustaining industrial activity, material consumption, energy use and air pollution flows at current levels. They need to come down drastically. Every moment they're above the limits, we're damaging and deteriorating the basic productive capacities of the planet. So I don't hope for that.

I pressed him on how he felt the future might unfold. 'I see some drivers', he said.

> I see that oil depletion and climate change are quite far advanced. Water is going to be a really serious problem soon. But there's lots of 'stuff'; it's just that we're running out of some things. I think those shortages will drive the system. Which way, I don't know. Take energy, for example. Generically there are two ways you could imagine the global community responding to the perception that oil is now declining. One is to set up international research institutes, which begin to look for ways of generating power from renewables, and sharing that technology widely.

---

13 My interview with Dennis Meadows is available on the Cambridge University website www.cpsl.cam.ac.uk.

The other way is that the big energy users basically try to grab whatever they can and hold it for themselves – and that's what we're doing. So you see, the future has two generically different paths. I don't think humans will disappear off the planet. I think our current industrialised society will profoundly change. I think our political systems will change. I don't think democracy is going to survive the downturn. There's a drift already in important countries towards a more centralised, less democratic form of government. So there will be big changes.

Meadows did conclude with one small, positive concession, which is about attitude. We were talking about his ex-wife and co-author of *Limits to Growth*, Donella Meadows, and he told me, 'I always remember on her office door was a little motto which said, "Even if I knew the world would end tomorrow, I'd plant a tree today".' And that seems a good note to end the chapter on. Next, we make our way to Hungary.

Breakdown and breakthrough
Navigating the chaos
(Hungary: 2003, 2011)

Capitalism in crisis

I first visited Budapest in August 2003, when I presented a paper on 'Corporate social responsibility and personal meaning in life' at the European Business Ethics Network (EBEN) Conference. This captured some of the early findings from my PhD research (more about this in Chapter 22). I stayed, together with my academic colleagues from Nottingham University's International Centre for CSR, at the fabulous Danubius Hotel Gellert, in the central district of Buda, with the River Danube on one side and a green hill on the other. The hotel (and my visit) is most memorable for its thermal pools, built in 1918.

I had another opportunity to visit in November 2011, as a keynote speaker at CSR Hungary's annual conference. One intriguing question I remember from the conference was: Is the employment of disabled people a neglected issue in sustainable business? I think it is, but that may be because it gets swept up in the HR (human resources) function, under the topic of diversity management. For those interested in this question, my Malaysian friend Sanjukta Choudhury Kaul is researching this topic for her PhD at Monash University. Another memory from the conference (far more profane than profound) was a surprising and delightfully delicious Hungarian dish that we had for lunch – rice and sour cherries.

These visits aside, what I really want to share in this chapter are some of the things I have learned from two Hungarians, even though I have not met one of them (George Soros), and the other (Ervin Laszlo) I interviewed by telephone. Both were profiled in *The Top 50 Sustainability Books*, for their books *The Crisis of Global Capitalism* and *The Chaos Point*, respectively. They are two very different characters: Soros, a Hungarian-born billionaire investor, philanthropist and author; and Laszlo, a Hungarian scientist and leading writer on systems philosophy and general evolution theory. And, yet, they both bring us warnings of how our global society is at risk due to poor systemic design. Let's begin with Soros.

Soros is one of the super-rich 'winners' of Western capitalism. In 1992, he earned himself international notoriety and the nickname of 'the man who broke the Bank of England' after speculating on the pound sterling, believing it was overvalued, and earning himself $1.1 billion in the process. Beyond this single speculative jackpot, however, his Quantum Fund is one of the most successful managed investment funds ever, increasing more than 30% annually over a 30-year period. Such an impressive track record makes it all the more interesting that he is highly critical of Western capitalism in general and global financial markets in particular.

In *The Crisis of Global Capitalism*, Soros warns that global stability is threatened by the emergence of market fundamentalism – the belief that our 'common interest' is best served by individual decision-making and that any attempt to maintain the common interest through government intervention distorts the market mechanism. 'It is market fundamentalism', Soros insists,

> that has rendered the global capitalist system unsound and unsustainable. The ideology of market fundamentalism is profoundly and irredeemably flawed. Market forces, if they are given complete authority, even in the purely economic and financial arenas, produce chaos and could ultimately lead to the downfall of the global capitalist system.

Soros believes that the development of a global economy has not been matched by the development of a global society. International law and international institutions, insofar as they exist, are not strong enough to prevent war or the large-scale abuse of human rights in individual countries. Ecological threats are not adequately dealt with, and global financial markets, which are inherently unstable and do not care about social and environmental needs, are largely beyond the control of national or international authorities. He says,

> We live in a global economy, but the political organization of our global society is woefully inadequate. We are bereft of the capacity to preserve peace and to counteract the excesses of the financial markets. Without these controls, the global economy is liable to break down.

Towards open societies

Soros criticises the global capitalist system on two counts. First, market fundamentalists erroneously believe that markets tend towards equilibrium. However, financial markets are characterized by booms and busts as a result of self-reinforcing loops in the economic and trading system. Hence, the potential for disequilibrium is inherent in the financial system; it is not just the result of external shocks. As he told Congress,

> Financial markets are supposed to swing like a pendulum. Instead, financial markets behave more like a wrecking ball, swinging from country to country and knocking over the weaker ones. It is difficult to escape the conclusion that the international financial system itself constituted the main ingredient in the meltdown process.

Soros's second critique is the failure of politics and the erosion of moral values on both the national and international level. Soros distinguishes between 'making rules' (which is a collective decision) and 'playing by the rules' (which is an individual decision). He notes that this distinction is rarely observed, particularly with politicians who too often put personal interests above public interests. This is exacerbated by the 'promotion of self-interest to a moral principle'. The result is that markets are enjoying free rein in areas where they should not have influence, ranging from moral values and family relationships to aesthetic and intellectual achievements, with 'destructive and demoralizing effects'. He believes that:

the choice confronting us is whether we will regulate global financial markets internationally or leave it to each individual state to protect its interests as best it can. The latter course will surely lead to the breakdown of the gigantic circulatory system, which goes under the name of global capitalism.

Soros believes capitalism needs democracy as a counterweight, because the capitalist system by itself shows no tendency towards equilibrium. While communism has been worse than the disease it tried to cure, market fundamentalism is not the cure either.

Communism abolished the market mechanism and imposed collective control over all economic activities. Market fundamentalism seeks to abolish collective decision-making and to impose the supremacy of market values over all political and social values. Both extremes are wrong. What we need is a correct balance between politics and markets, between rule making and playing by the rules.

The solution Soros proposes is the promotion of an 'open society', a term coined by Karl Popper and meaning a society that is, in contrast to totalitarian societies, founded on democracy and the rule of law – both elements that Soros believes market fundamentalism erodes. Within an open society, there is an acknowledgement that institutions are flawed and that errors are made. But rather than this being a reason to abandon the institutional arrangements, it simply calls for error-correcting mechanisms to protect both markets and democracy. Soros makes it clear that he does not want to abolish capitalism. 'In spite of its shortcomings, it is better than the alternatives. Instead, I want to prevent the global capitalist system from destroying itself.'

Chaos looming

Laszlo comes at the problem from a different angle. He serves as president of the Club of Budapest, a futures-oriented think-tank, and as head of the General Evolution Research Group, which he founded. As the author of a staggering 70 books, Laszlo has tirelessly sought to understand how society and the environment function as a complex, evolutionary system, and how we can (and must) intervene to prevent our own self-destruction.[14] He told me:

> I have been working with systems theory, especially with the way complex systems evolve over time and I've been recognising that this evolution is strongly non-linear. That means it goes through periodic quantum leaps. And if you apply this to human society, then you get to the insight that when you reach a critical threshold in the development of society, then a sudden non-linear change is likely to occur. That particular conviction has led me to think about whether we are approaching such a threshold, and if we are, how to call attention to it, because such change is normally unforeseen, often unpredictable and it's extremely abrupt. It needs to be anticipated as much as possible and prepared for, because even though it's unpredictable, it's not un-guidable, which is a big difference.

I was especially intrigued that Laszlo spoke about this 'chaos point' we are entering as essentially having only two outcomes – breakdown or breakthrough. When I asked him about this, he said,

> That is the particular meaning of a tipping point; it is not just a phase-change. A tipping point has an uncertainty element – it can go this way or that. I usually say that a tipping point is known by the fact that only two things are impossible at the tipping point. One is the status quo and the other one is returning to a past level of stability, which you can no longer re-establish exactly the way it was. So you either find a way to move forward – to re-establish stability on a new level in a new form – or you risk the collapse of the system.

Laszlo talks about two paths of growth that society can pursue. The first is based on conquest, colonisation and consumption, and the other is based on connection, communication and consciousness. I asked him to elaborate on these.

> We can also talk about external growth or internal growth. Typically external growth is conquest. If you want to annex, conquer, or colonise more and more, you're becoming richer, becoming more powerful and extending your dominion over things. This

14 My interview with Ervin Laszlo is available on the Cambridge University website www.cpsl.cam.ac.uk.

was possible while we still had areas like the Wild West, uncon-quered areas. You could colonise people, you could move over to fresh areas and obtain new resources. Now we have reached the point of saturation in this respect. There is nothing else left to colonise. In fact, the formerly colonised people are rising up and saying that they want to have their own identity, their own autonomy. So you can't just simply proceed like this.

This may be true politically, but surely we are seeing a new pattern of conquest in the economic sphere, as the West shifts its investments to emerging markets, and emerging markets seek out resources to fuel their growth, such as China in Africa? Laszlo agrees, saying,

This is an attempt to extend the power and the sphere of influ-ence of business companies, so people will buy their products and they will be able to become richer and more powerful through a larger and larger territory that they can cover. So that is also an extensive form of growth, but it's not the only kind.

Connection and consciousness

I knew from reading Laszlo's book that the other kind was more about connection and communication, but I wondered if that was purely driven by the IT revolution, or something different? Lazslo answered that it is driven by a consciousness revolution, of which the IT revolution is only one element. 'It is a recognition', he explained,

that development is not only a horizontal extensive develop-ment. Development means very largely an intensive develop-ment – increasing the quality of life, as opposed to the quantity of the material standard of life. A certain level of material stand-ards is necessary for a quality of life, but beyond that it becomes self-defeating. So the ambition in the longer term is to go for quality. That means the kind of relations that people have to each other and to their environment, which has to be a multi-faceted closed connection; a connection of communication. In other words, a sort of communion rather than a relationship of conquest and subjugation.

I wanted to ground the conversation a bit, so I asked about how all this is relevant to business. Laszlo explained that:

> If you think of yourself as being separate from the world – if you think of the world as being material and mechanistic – then you try to manipulate it and to just pursue your own interests independently of the interests of the others; you try to simply impose your own thinking and your own interests on others. This kind of mind-set is creating the problem, and in business it is creating the shareholder philosophy – the idea that business only is responsible to its own shareholders, its owners, and its responsibility to anything else is secondary, if it exists at all. The shareholder philosophy is the concept that one business is separate from other businesses, separate from the communities in which it operates, separate from nature; it has only itself to account for because it is an entity purely in its own right. Now this has been changing towards a stakeholder philosophy.

That is certainly true, although the grip of shareholder-driven capitalism is still an iron fist with deadly force. Perhaps climate change is a global challenge that can shake off the short-termism of the markets and get us thinking systemically about our shared long-term future. I asked Laszlo what he thought. 'Climate change is a two-edged sword', he said.

> It could be a very positive thing and it could also be of course a dangerous thing depending on its consequences. If James Lovelock is right and we'll have only 600 million people being able to survive on this planet for the next 100,000 years, then it's a catastrophic process. If, however, we can still turn it around, not necessarily going back to the previous climate but to make the climate liveable for the entire human population, of course it could be a very positive thing. Because it is visible – it is experienced by people much more so than the intricacies of the world's financial system. Climate change is evident and therefore it triggers a mentality of change, so in that sense it's very good. The big $64 billion dollar question is whether this reaches a point where it becomes irreversible and catastrophic, or whether this threat that is evident in the change of the climate can motivate positive behavioural change, operational change, in society in time.

Given the odds, and Laszlo's deep knowledge about how social and environmental systems adapt and change, is he optimistic or pessimistic about the future? 'I wouldn't consider myself an optimist', he told me.

> Because I think an optimist is a dangerous person, in the sense that an optimist might believe that this is the best of all possible worlds, or at least a very good world. If you do that then you're not particularly motivated to change it. A pessimist is just as dangerous because he thinks you can't change this world. You have to be in between – you have to recognise that the world is changeable and that it's in need of change. My kind of systemic optimism comes through in the fact that I find that the world is in need of change and at the same time it's beginning to change, quite rapidly in fact. People are waking up to the fact that you can't go on as you have and you'd better start changing. This was not even the case in the 1970s when the Club of Rome report first came out. It has started becoming the case in the 90s and now in the last five years, it's been moving forward very rapidly.

I think Laszlo's right. And even if he isn't, I believe the only way to be effective in the world is to be an activist for making things better.

9
Partnerships and poverty
New governance for a new world
(Switzerland: 2008)

Responsible competitiveness

I first visited Switzerland in 2002, while I was still Director of Sustainability Services for KPMG in South Africa, in order to establish contact with the World Business Council for Sustainable Development (WBCSD), headquartered in Geneva. I have since returned several times, for various meetings on sustainability and CSR hosted by the European Academy for Business in Society (EABIS), Net Impact and others. However, for this chapter, much like the last, I want to focus on two fascinating individuals I happened to interview in Switzerland, even though neither is Swiss. The first interview was in the lakeside city of Geneva with Simon Zadek, then still CEO of AccountAbility, and the second was in the skiing town of Gstaad with Muhammad Yunus, founder and then still CEO of Grameen Bank.

I first met Zadek in 1996 while I was completing my MSc in Human Ecology and he was at the New Economics Foundation (more about this in Chapter 21). Since then, I have followed his career and thinking over the years and our paths have crossed several more times. On this occasion, in August 2008, I had travelled to Geneva to interview Zadek about his book *The Civil Corporation*.[15]

Reflecting back on the book, which was published in 2001, and on what has changed since, Zadek pointed to the geopolitical shift towards Asia and Russia, the increasing influence of investment markets, the re-emergence of a strong state role and greater emphasis on partnerships and collaboration. I wondered what had prompted his more recent focus on accountability and responsible competitiveness. The former came out of his work for the New Economics Foundation to work on 'a theory of organisation at scale' and the latter, Zadek explained, emerged largely as a response to the views of David Henderson, expressed in his book *Misguided Virtue: False Notions of Corporate Social Responsibility*.

Henderson argued that corporate responsibility increased poverty, because it reduced market flexibility and added costs, whereas markets were the route to prosperity. 'It was a rather caricatured view of everything', claimed Zadek. 'But the underlying point made came through to me, which was: what are the macroeconomic effects? We've all been concentrating on the micro side.' Zadek began to realise that:

> micro-level innovation would be halted if the national policy implications of advancing corporate responsibility at the micro-level would undermine national or regional competitiveness. So to understand the political economy of corporate responsibility or sustainability or citizenship required an understanding where national competitive strategies and the political dimensions of that 'hit the road' on this agenda.

To illustrate what he meant, Zadek noted that:

> the debate about a post-Kyoto deal is a debate about competitiveness. What's going to prevent it moving on is a zero sum view without a pay-off matrix; that is, about a loss of competitiveness at both the top of the economic pyramid and mid and low levels in the pyramid.

I pushed him to elaborate. 'Climate change is the perfect storm', he said.

---

15 My interview with Simon Zadek is available on the Cambridge University website www.cpsl.cam.ac.uk.

It is credible systemic risk accompanied by demonstrable failure of our two primary large-scale instruments of change, namely public policy and capital market allocation. Because public policy is not reshaping markets to be forward looking at anything like the pace that's needed, and capital markets are not recognising the value-added opportunities, or factoring them into their asset valuation methodologies. And so at that point the importance of collaboration, new models of partnerships, new ways of constructing market rules, becomes the game.

Collaborative governance

I asked what he means by new models of partnership, and Zadek explained that we need to:

move businesses into the rule-making business. We've spent a decade and a half experimenting in that with the ETIs and the FSCs and the MSCs and the EITIs. All very interesting, but the thin end of the wedge is the kind of social compact, or political compact, that is going to be needed to address the next round, if capital markets continue to fail and traditional multilateralism doesn't deliver the goods.

I wondered if we're looking also in the wrong place, by expecting incumbent large multinationals – which are benefiting from the status quo – to come up with a solution, be it collaborative or not. What about small entrepreneurial ventures that go to scale? What about the next Google or Facebook, but for sustainability? Zadek agreed that this might work, but only when it's a straight technology solution that the market appreciates. 'But not,' he cautioned, 'if the market is backward looking and doesn't incentivise the change. And not if the political economy of the changes is not acceptable to some influential parts of the world.' Zadek's conclusion is that new rules will be needed, not just more clean tech. 'For sure, the clean tech space is exciting and flourishing and emerging every day. But for the innovations to take hold at the scale and pace that we need, we have to change the rules of the game.'

So, how do we change the rules of the game? Clearly, we don't have the answers yet, but Zadek speculates about how it might unfold:

The question is whether, through a mixture of public and private actors, we can create rule systems that help businesses and countries navigate away from first-mover disadvantages in advancing sustainability, by creating micro-climates within markets that are trans-border and offer competitiveness upsides without having to have everybody play ball. If one can advance rule systems that can do that, either they themselves will move to a system level, or the transaction costs of maintaining them at ever larger scales will eventually trigger statutory regulatory moves at a trans-border level.

What are the implications of these imperatives, I asked Zadek, for companies interested in sustainable business? 'The companies that have been most interesting in the sustainability area', he observed, 'are ones that have tried to create space, not only for themselves, but for other companies to advance, whether it be responsible drinking, cheaper drugs, improved labour standards, or less corruption.' Many other companies, Zadek believes, have improved their own sustainability practices, but failed to innovate at what he calls the 'meso-system level' – in other words, the intra-sector and cross-sector collaborative space. That is also why, according to Zadek, many companies that have tried to make a stepwise shift in the approach to their business model have failed.

All this talk about changing the rules of the game made me wonder if Zadek still believes in 'the civil corporation', especially in light of the growing critique of the version (or brand) of capitalism the world has been practising. Is he suggesting that in order for companies to make the necessary changes, we need far more profound changes in capitalism? He answered in three parts.

First, the fiduciary model of business is almost done – the primacy of financial stakeholders is not sustainable as an effective basis for achieving success. Second, it doesn't seem to me that our liberal democratic model can survive the challenge of sustainability. It has embedded a short-termism that is in danger of driving a frenzied hedonism as we rush towards the precipice, rather than a reflective long-term view as to how to build societies in different ways. Third, we're creating a possible new set of institutional processes that can help us, but that re-converge political and economic power into a single system, without the safeguards to maintain them as separate powers that need to balance each other. Take a trivial example like forestry or marine or labour standards. We are actively bringing businesses back into the process of political decision-making and legitimising them in the spirit of sustainability. That is tactically the right thing to do, but the potential end game is profound.

These are clearly big issues with big implications. Is Zadek optimistic and hopeful? 'I feel quite optimistic about the experience of the last decade and a half', he admitted.

I think we've experimented in how to create norms in different ways – radically different ways in a global economy where national rules don't work in relation to global institutions, pushed by civil society pressure that didn't exist before. I think we've achieved some extraordinary innovations. There have been some impacts on the ground with real people and real rivers not being polluted. But also I think we've gone through our first phase of learning and that we need to be ready to take the next step. How do we create the next lot at a larger scale and in a more effective way, by implication, needing to include some of the new players on the global stage, which has never been done before in those spaces? This will probably mean NGOs being less important than they were in the first round; certainly, Western brands being less important; and governments being more important, albeit within a non-statutory space.

'My hope doesn't arise from a sense that amazing things are about to happen', said Zadek.

Or that human nature is about to change; that global consciousness is about to be formed; that a revolution is about to take place; that technology will solve a problem; or even in a sort of Margaret Mead way, that there's always some fantastic person down the road doing something amazing, which of course is true but to be frank is not enough. My hope comes from my own internal process of trying to understand what's going on and my very direct experience of trying to make change. I think it's through the habit every day of trying to make change that one maintains an ambition about the possibility. It's the habit of action, of taking risks, of challenging others, of finding voice. And as Ed Mayo, the executive director of the New Economics Foundation used to say to me, of always getting up in the morning slightly angry at the injustice in the world.

Worm's-eye view

After speaking to Zadek in Geneva, I took a train through the picturesque Swiss Alps to Gstaad, where Muhammad Yunus was speaking at a conference on microfinance, the movement he helped to seed through the example of the Grameen Bank. I was impressed by Yunus's quiet and humble demeanour, while his passion and determination shines through. I was speaking to him about his book *Banker to the Poor*, and more generally about his views on poverty, microcredit and the role of women.[16] The story of how he founded the Grameen Bank in 1976 after a famine stuck Bangladesh is well worn and I won't repeat it here. What I would rather share is some of his wisdom.

One of the first insights was his emphasis on what he calls the 'worm's-eye view' of the world. 'All this academic life that I had all these years gave me kind of bird's eye view', he explained.

> I can see the whole world; I can see the terrain, but I don't see the details. And, since I don't know the details, I make up those details in my imagination. Now, coming to the village, I see the details in very, very clear terms. I don't have the global perspective, but I know the person's daily routine, what she is eating today, what's her hope for tomorrow, what disasters befall her family. I said, 'Oh, my God, what I'm getting now is the worm's eye view.' Then something hit me and I said, 'This is an advantage. If you have the worm's eye view then you can find the solution right away.' So I think it's much more powerful than just being up in the sky and speculating about things.

Part of Yunus's 'worm's-eye view' perspective was a gradual realisation that microfinance works best when the loans are given to women. To start with, Grameen Bank was only aiming for parity between loans to men and women, which took them six years to achieve. 'Then we started noticing', said Yunus, 'that money going to the family through women brought so much more benefit to the family. So gradually we changed our policy, and today, with seven and a half million borrowers, 97% are women.' Explaining why this may be the case, Yunus said,

16 My interview with Muhammad Yunus is available on the Cambridge University website www.cpsl.cam.ac.uk.

A woman has certain features in her character, in her being, which is convenient for achieving the goals that microcredit wants to achieve. As soon as she makes money her first attention is the children. And a woman has a longer vision – she wants to get out of this miserable situation as fast as she can. She is the best manager of scarce resources. She is very careful with the money we give her. And it changes the society, bringing empowerment to a woman, because she is always neglected, always ignored. Now she has a bank account, she owns a bank, she has her savings and she is income-generating. So self-confidence and dignity come back to her.

Social business rising

Relating this to business, I was curious to know if the 'bottom of the pyramid' (BOP) strategies popularised by C.K. Prahalad and Stuart Hart were also taking us some way towards this 'worm's-eye view'. To the contrary, Yunus is quite critical of BOP strategies.

I see that now the businesses are trying to discover a new world of poor people and I feel uncomfortable with that kind of attitude, because it promotes the idea that you can make money. It's not getting them out of that situation; you want to make yourself rich out of the people who live there. The bottom of the pyramid is a challenge for humanity: how to raise them out of that level that they're in? The pyramid will always be there, but the bottom shouldn't be as miserable as it is today. So our primary responsibility is to lift them, rather than see it as an opportunity to make money.

Yunus was not only critical about the attitude implicit in BOP strategies, but also the rationale that selling things to the poor will bring them out of poverty. 'We should not look at them as consumers of our product', he suggests.

We should see them as potential producers; potential creative people who can take charge of their own life and transform it. And our role is to be presenting ourselves into a supportive role, and that's where I talk about the social businesses – business not for making money, business to change the world, change people's lives.

I asked him to elaborate on this idea of a social business. 'It a non-loss, non-dividend company with a social objective', he explained.

> Today, economic theory presents the human being as a single-dimensional being: all you enjoy is making money. That's a mis-interpretation of the human being. To represent the totality of the human being, we have to have at least two kinds of business – one, which is concentrated to me; another, which is totally dedicated to others. So a profit-maximising business is a means to make money, to expand, to grow. And then social business is the end; what do I do with the money? I want to change the world; I want to change people's lives. And that's where I put the signature on this planet – this is what I have done. Making tonnes of money doesn't give me the right to be remembered in this world.

Yunus's intergenerational perspective on sustainability was perhaps what I took away most from the interview. He said:

> We are not plunderers on this planet, we are residents. This is our house and we want to make it safe. We want to make it beautiful, for when we hand it over to our next generation. And the next generation's job will be to make it more beautiful and more safe when they hand it over to the next generation. We're doing the reverse – we're making it worse. That's not a way to go, so we have to reverse that process.

And reversing that process, in Yunus's view, includes nothing short than ending poverty. 'I'm totally convinced that we can create a world where there'll be no poor person at all', he said.

> People have unlimited potential to change their own life and contribute to this planet. But unfortunately, they aren't given a chance. All we are doing [through microcredit] is removing the barrier that society has created. Once the barrier is out of the way, they will come out of poverty. It's like coming out of prison – you just unlock it and they come out; you don't have to go and drag them out. So this is the situation and it's happening in many, many countries. Now we have to bring all our energy to get rid of this last bit of poor people that we have on this planet

and declare country by country that we are free from poverty from now on. And then create poverty museums, so anybody who wants to see poverty should go and visit the museum.

Cycles and cradles
Faster, further and higher
(The Netherlands: 1997, 2002, 2009, 2011)

Stakeholder politics

Despite my Dutch heritage – my father was born in Holland, I have a Dutch passport and I speak Afrikaans, which is a version of the Dutch language – I was 27 years old when I first visited the country. This was at the time that I was establishing KPMG's new Environmental Unit in South Africa and the Netherlands was (and still is, I believe) the largest and strongest of KPMG's national sustainability practices.

My first meeting was with George Molenkamp, then Chairman of KPMG Global Sustainability Services and Special Professor of Business Studies at the University of Amsterdam. He generously shared their intellectual resources with me, including an environmental self-assessment auditing tool that KPMG had developed on behalf of the Dutch government. I learned that KPMG had, in fact, conducted the first environmental audits in Europe, and was already a pioneer in the field.

The company was also emerging as a leader in non-financial reporting and report verification, working with Shell, Philips, Unilever and many others to help define an approach to triple-bottom-line reporting that the GRI would later formalise and refine. KPMG's first international sustainability reporting survey was conducted in 1993 and has been repeated every three years since. Today, this research database provides unbridled insights into historical trends in sustainability reporting, and corporate social and environmental performance.

Alongside Molenkamp, one of the people who has been intimately involved in these developments is Jennifer Iansen-Rogers, a long-serving senior manager in the Dutch sustainability practice. Iansen-Rogers has, perhaps more than any other person over the past 20 years, been at the heart of evolving sustainability accounting, auditing and reporting agendas, not only in the Netherlands, but globally. It was for this reason that I asked her to write multiple entries for *The A to Z of Corporate Social Responsibility* – on assurance, auditing, environmental auditing, the ISAE 3000 Standard for Assurance Engagements, non-financial reporting, report verification and social auditing – as well as the chapter on CSR in the Netherlands in *The World Guide to CSR*.

It was from Iansen-Rogers that I learned that Dutch socioeconomic development was based on the Rhineland model – a stakeholder-based approach for economic development, which promotes the principles of solidarity and cooperation between the owners of companies, government, employees and customers. It provides a balance between free market forces and social and environmental responsibility for longer-term societal stability. Intervention by the state in industry and the labour market is encouraged to ensure just working conditions for employees and to prevent social inequality.

This model has developed further into the 'Polder Model', which describes the current consensus-based decision-making model in Dutch politics and economics. Its use is thought to date from the 1982 Wassenaar Accord, an agreement between government, employers and companies to revitalise the economy by increasing employment through wage restraint and shorter working hours. This tripartite relationship also supports a strong tradition of volunteering. Among the unique partnerships this model has seeded is the Social and Economic Council of the Netherlands (SER), which brings together employers' representatives, union representatives and independent experts to help shape Dutch policy and legislation on social and economic affairs.

I have visited the Netherlands many times since 1997 – in 2000 for an ISO 14001 meeting; in 2002 for an environment, health and safety audit of a chemical plant; in 2010 at the invitation of the CSR Academy and to give training for Alliander; in 2011 to lecture at the Open University, hold workshops for MVO Nederland and give the keynote address at the Dutch National Sustainability Congress; and in 2012 to lecture at the Radboud University in Nijmegen. If I try to distil what I have learned from these visits, they probably fall into five main areas: mobility, climate change, finance, leadership and cradle to cradle practices. So let me try to unpack these insights one by one.

Cycle mania and climate defence

Anyone visiting the Netherlands for the first time is immediately struck by a strange phenomenon: bicycle mania. Not that bicycles are a novelty, but the Dutch have turned cycling into a national pastime and the bicycle into a cultural icon. Wherever you go in the country, there are swift-flowing rivers of cyclists that threaten to sweep you up in their tide if you're an unsuspecting pedestrian from abroad. Outside all of the stations are colourful reefs of bicycles, stacked layers deep and storeys high, on a scale unlike anything you have ever seen before.

The statistics back up the visceral experience. The population of the Netherlands is just 16 million – roughly twice that of New York or London – yet they make more cycle journeys than 300 million Americans, 65 million British and 20 million Australians put together, and they do so with greater safety than cyclists in any of those countries. Londoners only make around 2% of journeys by bike, and New Yorkers even less at only around 0.6% of commutes. Meanwhile, in the Netherlands on an average working day, 5 million people make an average of 14 million cycle journeys.

So why, in an age desperate for more sustainable transport solutions, has the Netherlands succeeded so spectacularly where others have tried and failed? I am no expert, but there seem to be a few obvious reasons. First, the country is relatively flat. Second, it is fairly small, so vehicle space is at a premium. Third, the government has invested heavily in supporting infrastructure (bike lanes, storage facilities, etc.). And, fourth, cycling is complemented by a well-developed public transport system of trains, buses and trams.

There is also the very important issue of safety – both perceived and actual. The accident statistics show that the Netherlands is the safest place in the world to cycle. There is obviously a 'safety in numbers' effect, and good infrastructure design is vital. But there are also legal sanctions. For example, there is an interesting law in the Netherlands called 'Strict Liability' or 'Article 185 WVW'. In essence, the law makes car drivers financially responsible in the event of a crash with bikers. Of course, there is a cultural effect as well. Since everyone cycles regularly, there is a prevailing empathy and safety awareness on the roads.

A second distinctive feature of the Netherlands is that most of the country is below sea level and much of it comprises land reclaimed from the sea, and so is especially vulnerable to climate change and the anticipated rise in sea levels, storm activity and flooding. However, this also makes the Netherlands one of the most prepared and technically advanced countries in terms of climate change mitigation and adaptation. Its complex system of dykes and pumping stations has been built up over centuries and was significantly reinforced over the last 60 years through the Zuiderzee Project (enclosing the IJsselmeer) and, after the flood disaster of 1953, the Delta Project in Zeeland. I fully expect that Dutch geo-engineers will be in high demand all over the world in the decades to come.

But it is not only in adaptation that the Dutch have something to teach us; they have been very progressive in climate mitigation as well. To meet its commitment to reduce greenhouse gas emissions by 30% from 1990 levels by 2020, the government has introduced a range of policy instruments called 'Clean and Efficient' in its work programme for both industry and citizens. This includes measures to reduce energy use (e.g. higher taxes on fuel and emission-related variable taxation for cars) and to stimulate renewable energy (mainly wind and biofuels) to achieve 20% of total energy use (up from 2% in 2007). It has also extended emission trading to sectors that fall outside the European ETS.

Ethical finance and leading 'big'

Third, on the issue of sustainable finance, the Dutch have led with social banks such as Triodos and ASN Bank, as well as more mainstream banks, including ABN AMRO and Rabobank. I first researched Triodos when I was doing my Master's thesis on sustainable finance in 1995, and found their model fascinating. All of its loans and investments are screened on ethical criteria. In addition, as a customer, I have the option to link my savings account to investment in causes I believe in (renewable energy, organic farming, social enterprise, etc.), or to take a lower interest rate and pass on the saving in the form of lower interest loans to sustainable businesses.

Another area of sustainable finance where the Netherlands leads is SRI. By the end of 2009, the SRI market in the Netherlands was around €396 billion, up 37% from 2007 and representing a remarkable 33% of total assets under management. While all major Dutch banks offer ethical investment products, Rabobank has been especially progressive, having developed sophisticated rating systems to assess and score the sustainability of the companies they are investing in. Rabobank also consistently scores top of its sector in the annual Transparency Benchmark survey, which assesses sustainability reporting in the Netherlands.

The fourth area I want to comment on is the values-based leadership approach that seems to be inspired by the Dutch culture. One supreme example is Paul Polman, CEO of Unilever. When he launched its Sustainability Living Plan in 2010, this confirmed something Unilever's Chief HR Officer Sandy Ogg said in research I did for Cambridge University:

> There's so much going on now in the world that if you don't have amplification and time compression, then it doesn't rumble. So I call that leading big. You can't let it drool or dribble out into an organisation like ours and expect to have any impact.

In this case, for Unilever, Polman's 'leading big' means seeking to double the size of the company, while halving the environmental footprint of its products. In addition, the company plans to source 100% of its agricultural ingredients sustainably by 2015 and help a billion people out poverty.

According to Ogg, Polman stands out as a sustainability leader because he understands the changing global context and expresses empathy in a multi-stakeholder environment. In Polman's own words, 'This world has tremendous challenges – the challenges of poverty, of water, of global warming, climate change – and businesses like ours have a role to play in that. And frankly, to me, that is very appealing.' Hence, 'the art of leadership is to look reality in the eye' and 'positively influence someone'. Most importantly, Polman believes his leadership of Unilever on sustainability issues must be through action. As he puts it, 'You cannot talk yourself out of things you've behaved yourself into.'

Philips is another Dutch company that has been showing leadership. As you might expect, with lighting comprising about 50% of its revenues, it has focused strongly on environmental issues. Its fourth EcoVision programme contains challenging targets including 25% improvement in the energy efficiency of its operations, €1 billion investment in green innovations and 30% of total revenues from green products by 2012. However, it has also started to innovate by supplying products to so-called BOP markets.

For instance, Philips has collaborated with C Quest Capital (CQC) to supply 2.6 million free compact fluorescent lamps (CFLs) to official residences of employees of the Indian Railways. The project is funded through the certified emission reductions (CERs), which accrue to CQC and help cover the product costs. Another example is Distance Healthcare Advancement (DISHA), carried out by Philips India with the support of a consortium of partners. The project aims to deliver high-quality, low-cost diagnostics to low-income rural communities that are not addressed by the existing healthcare system. To reach its goal, DISHA uses a custom-built 'tele-clinical' van equipped with appropriate diagnostic devices and medicines. In the partnership, Philips Medical Systems supplies appropriate diagnostic equipment such as x-rays, ultrasound and ECG devices to the tele-clinical van.

Another great BOP initiative I came across is the Dutch social enterprise called connectthepipe.org, which is simultaneously promoting local water saving practices and investing in water access projects in developing countries.

Cradle to cradle country

A final area in which the Netherlands seems to be making significant progress is on C2C production and consumption. The Dutch government has taken an especially proactive role in promoting C2C practices, and the local authority of Venlo aims to be the first C2C region. It is also using C2C principles in its plans for the 2012 Floriade (the World Horticultural Expo).

At the Dutch National Sustainability Congress where I keynoted in 2011, C2C companies and initiatives were in profusion. Examples ranged from an electric waste truck that uses energy from the waste it collects (Van Gansewinkel) to workspaces designed to be carbon neutral and to produce more energy than they consume (Ahrend). Other leaders are OCE (part of Canon), which manufactures C2C certified paper, and Desso, which makes C2C carpets and artificial grass.

One C2C product I was especially impressed by was Marmoleum®, Forbo's own brand of linoleum floor covering. Marmoleum® already complies with more environmental quality marks – such as The Nordic Swan, Blue Angel, and Nature Plus – than any other flooring product in the world. According to a life-cycle assessment by the University of Leiden, Marmoleum® is the most sustainable, resilient floor covering in the world. Behind its sustainability credentials is the fact that it is a biodegradable, natural product made from 97% natural raw materials, 70% of which are rapidly renewable. It also contains 40% recycled content. The main raw materials from which it is made are linseed oil (from the seed of the flax plant); wood flour from controlled forests; and jute, the natural backing material onto which the Marmoleum® is calendered.

It is no coincidence that Michael Braungart, one of the co-originators of the concept, has taken up a position as Cradle to Cradle Chair at the Dutch Research Institute for Transitions (DRIFT) at Erasmus University in Rotterdam. In the interview I did with Braungart, he reflected on why the Netherlands has been so proactive on C2C thinking, while other countries have lagged behind.[17] According to him, it's because:

> the Dutch never romanticised nature, so it's different to the United Kingdom or Germany. There's no 'mother nature', because with the next tide they would just swim away. It was always a culture of partnership with nature, learning from nature, and that's what we need. We can learn endlessly from nature, but it's not about romanticizing nature.

The second reason why C2C has been so successful, according to Braungart, is that the Netherlands has a culture of support, whereas the Americans, Germans, British and Swedish have a culture of control.

---

17 My interview with Michael Braungart is available on the Cambridge University website www.cpsl.cam.ac.uk.

> They assume human beings are bad anyway and we need to control them to be less bad. But the Dutch culture is a culture of support, because if you don't support your neighbour, you will drown (because then your neighbour couldn't take care of your dyke). Even if you don't like your neighbour, you need to support your neighbour. So cradle to cradle is a culture of support.

Braungart contrasts the American company Interface and the Dutch Desso to further illustrate how the Dutch 'get' C2C.

> Desso, the second biggest maker of carpets, is different to Interface which is using recycled PVC with toxic plasticisers. They first say: 'what is the right thing to do?' And then say, in the year 2016 all their carpets will be cradle to cradle. So it's no longer about buying less, like all these green labels, or if I don't buy it it's even better. No, it's about the more you buy the quicker we are changing for the better. So it's a positive agenda, instead of trying to be less bad. The goal is not zero emissions – even if I would shoot myself right now, I would have emissions, so the zero emission goal you can't achieve anyway. Instead of that, we want beneficial emissions.

For such a small nation, the Dutch always seem to punch above their weight, whether it is in football or sustainability. At the heart of this achievement, I believe, is their collaborative approach. To illustrate the point, the Netherlands' Sustainable Trade Initiative, which has a mission to transform and mainstream sustainable product markets, does this by promoting investment by coalitions of companies, which receive match funding from the Dutch government to improve the productivity and scalability of sustainable production and consumption. When people ask me which country is leading on sustainable business, I always point to the Netherlands and say 'watch this space'. Of course, the Dutch are horrified by this, as self-criticism is another national pastime they take very seriously. As far as I can see, it's a win–win. The Dutch will continue to push themselves 'faster, further, higher' in the sustainability Olympics, and the rest of the world will continue to benefit from the lessons they are learning.

Part 3
Asia Pacific

Kaizen and kyosei
Driving a better future
(Japan: 1990)

Discovering kaizen

As I mentioned in the opening chapter, in September 1990 I headed to Japan for AIESEC's World Theme Conference on Sustainable Development. This was an opportunity of a lifetime. A management student at that time, I was all too aware of the rise of the Asian tiger economies, especially Japan. The West was spellbound by the revolution of total quality management (TQM), which the American statistician Edward Deming had introduced in Japan in the 1970s. The Japanese had perfected TQM through their *kaizen* philosophy of continuous improvement or 'change for the better'. In fact, I wrote an undergraduate paper on Japanese management techniques for one of my courses, singing the praises of 'just in time' (JIT) production methods and the cultural concept of *wa*, or harmony. I had also read about the shadow side of Japan's economic miracle – of how the production line system exploited employees, who worked long hours performing meaningless tasks under poor factory conditions.

Understandably, therefore, I was breathless with excitement when I arrived in a steamy Tokyo – humidity was almost 100% – on 21 August 1990. At the conference itself, we had presentations from people such as J. Hugh Faulkner, who joined with Swiss industrialist Stephan Schmidheiny the same year to form the Business Council for Sustainable Development (BCSD), serving as Executive Director. The BCSD in turn was invited by Maurice Strong, chair of upcoming 1992 Rio UN Conference on Environment and Development (UNCED), to provide a business perspective on sustainable development. It was no coincidence, therefore, that one the key outcomes of our AIESEC conference was a publication called 'A Youth Action Guide on Sustainable Development', presented as our contribution to the Rio Earth Summit.

Beyond the conference itself, we also had 'study tour' visits, most notably to the Toyota headquarters in Nagoya, where we met with the senior management team. We were served a *sushi*-style lunch in square plastic trays, each morsel neatly and aesthetically arranged. Apart from glimpsing the highly automated production line, we had a chance to explore the company's R&D display area – where it had numerous eco-efficient and alternative fuel technologies already in the mature stages of development. This made the deepest and most lasting impression on me. There was even an engine that was powered by light!

Having seen all this in 1990, it was no surprise to me that Toyota led the motor industry with its sustainability reforms nearly 20 years later, launching the Toyota Prius hybrid technology and RAV4 EV all-electric vehicle in 1997. By September 2010, 2 million Prius cars had been sold and although the RAV4 EV – which was offered on a lease scheme – was discontinued in 2003, Toyota is reportedly working with Tesla Motors to relaunch a second generation in 2012. Ever since Toyota's breakthrough, automotive companies have been falling over themselves to catch up and introduce their own hybrid and electric models. This is one of those rare moments when we are seeing a 'race to the top' on environmental performance.

Having said that, there is still a danger of this being a niche market for so-called 'ethical consumers'. In its report entitled 'Mobility 2020', the UK government's Business Taskforce on Sustainable Consumption and Production noted that:

> transport is the only major sector of the economy which – because of growth – will not contribute to CO_2 reductions. While the energy sector is likely to achieve promising cuts in the period 2005–2015 and industry as a whole will make more modest reductions, transport is showing a steady rise.

This seems to be a case of lack of will, rather than lack of technology. A typical family car, the report says, emits around 200 g of CO_2 per km; a smaller car around 130 g/km. Using *existing technologies*, the industry could reduce these figures to 130 g/km and 80 g/km, respectively. Easy wins for the industry include more efficient tyres and wheels, low friction oils, fewer extras and smaller fuel tanks. More radical redesign might involve photovoltaic panels to power cooling systems, waste heat recovery, greater use of lightweight materials and a smart dashboard indicating CO_2 emissions in real time. The technology is already available. The report concludes that with a new approach, a 60% cut in car-related carbon emissions could be achieved by 2020. 'There is impressive innovation in the industry, but it is linked to individual products and brands, not a system-wide solution. What is needed is vision.'

Driving a sustainable vision

Vision, I learned on my trip, is something the Japanese do very well. Shortly after my visit and ahead of most companies in the world, in 1992 Toyota issued its Environmental Guiding Principles and adopted its own Earth Charter. What is interesting is not that it has these principles (after all, many companies have flowery statements on their boardroom walls now), but rather the way they are expressed, which I believes conveys a qualitative difference in aspirations.

For instance, in its Guiding Principles it commits to 'honour the language *and spirit* of the law' (emphasis mine); to 'enhancing the quality of life everywhere'; to 'foster a corporate culture that enhances individual creativity'; and to 'pursue growth in harmony with the global community'. And in its Earth Charter, it is already striving to 'pursue production activities that do not generate waste' and to 'participate in the creation of a recycling-based society'. Note that it does not say 'activities that *reduce* waste'; they say activities that 'do *not generate* waste'. Long before Ray Anderson at Interface conceived his much-celebrated 'Mission Zero' or McDonough and Braungart had popularised C2C practices, Toyota had understood and integrated the concept of a circular economy.

Of course, it is not just Toyota that has understood these principles. In August 2000, Fuji Xerox became the first company in Japan to achieve

Zero Landfill from collected used products. Extending its success to the region, by 2010, Fuji Xerox Eco-Manufacturing in Thailand was able to announce that it had effectively accomplished the Zero Landfill goal by recycling 99.8% of used products and consumables in 2009. This is not just a business phenomenon; the philosophy pervades the whole of Japanese society. For example, the town of Kamikatsu wants to eliminate all waste by 2020, and has already achieved an 80% recycling rate.

With this kind of national psyche, it is no surprise that Japan led the adoption of the ISO 14001 environmental management systems standard, which was launched in 1996. After all, it was based on the ISO 9000 quality standard, for which the Japanese were already the world's leading experts and practitioners. The number of ISO 14001 certifications in the Far East grew from 4,350 in 1999 (31% of global share) to 112,237 in 2009 (50% of global share). For many years, Japan led the ISO 14001 international league tables, but by 2009, it had slipped to second with 39,556 certifications, behind China with 55,316. Congruent with Japan's leadership on ISO 14001, a study by EIRIS in 2007 found that the percentage of high-impact companies with advanced environmental policies was 90% in Japan and Europe, as compared with 75% in Australia and New Zealand, 67% in the United States and 15% in Asia (excluding Japan).

Sustainability accounting pioneers

Japan has also led in the field of sustainability reporting in general, and environmental auditing and accounting in particular. As far back as 1993, the Japanese Institute of Certified Public Accountants (JICPA) set up an Environmental Auditing Subcommittee. This was followed by an Environmental Auditing Technical Committee in 1998, an Environmental Accounting Technical Committee in 1999, and a Greenhouse Gas Emissions Trading Technical Committee in 2002. Later, in 2005, the old Environmental Auditing Technical Committee was reorganised as two technical committees: the CSR Information Technical Committee and the CSR Assurance Technical Committee. As a result, there are now four technical committees.

The Japanese government has been a major factor in promoting environmental auditing, accounting and reporting. In May 2000, the Environmental

Agency (now the Ministry of Environment) published an Environmental Accounting Guideline. It also published Environmental Reporting Guidelines in 2001. In 2004, the Ministry of Environment established the 'Law Concerning the Promotion of Business Activities with Environmental Consideration by Specified Corporations, by Facilitating Access to Environmental Information, and Other Measures'. This obliges companies to publish an environmental report every year and to enhance the reliability of the report by having it verified.

Of course, sustainability reporting has now become commonplace, following the introduction of the GRI's Sustainability Reporting Guidelines in 1999 and their revision in 2002 and 2006 (the so-called G3). And indeed, Japan continues to be among the leading reporters in the world. Of the roughly 1,800 GRI reports published in 2010, 7% were by Japanese companies (on a par with Brazil, but behind Spain with 9% and the United States with 10%). One indication of Japan's leadership is that 65% of Japanese CSR reports address supply chain risks, according to KPMG's 2008 International Survey of Corporate Responsibility Reporting. However, it is on the phenomenon of environmental accounting that I believe we can learn the most from Japan.

As it happens, when I started KPMG's Environmental Unit in 1997, my second project was to develop an environmental accounting procedure for a national chemical company. At the time, the leading authority on the subject was the English accounting academic, Rob Gray, founder director of the Centre for Social and Environmental Accounting Research, and editor of the *Social and Environmental Accounting Journal* from 1991 to 2007. His books include *Accounting for the Environment* (first published in 1993) and most recently a four-volume set called *Social and Environmental Accounting* (2010, with co-editors Jan Bebbington and Sue Gray).

From his research, I learned that the pioneers in social and environmental accounting were companies such as Baxter International, BT and Ontario Hydro. I fully expected that this was the next big wave. And, yet, disappointingly, environmental and social accounting faded into the background, as sustainability reporting – led by the efforts of the GRI, AccountAbility and others – took centre stage. There is good reason for this. Quantifying physical social and environmental impacts is a natural prerequisite to translating them into financial impacts; and as I discovered in my KPMG project, estimating the financial costs and revenues associated with environmental (let alone social) externalities can be challenging.

As far as I am aware, Japan is the only country that has stuck consistently to the vital task of developing and promoting environmental accounting. In 2005, the Japanese government issued an updated version of its Environmental Accounting Guidelines, which includes detailed data table templates and advice on how to quantify environmental costs and benefits.

Kyosei at Canon

Another lesson that I believe Japan can teach the rest of the world is how to develop and nurture a philosophy of care, respect and honour. Fujio Mitarai, president and CEO of Canon, writes in the *ICCA Handbook of Corporate Social Responsibility* that:

> To be honest, I was somewhat puzzled when I first encountered the term 'CSR'. In Japan, whenever something is introduced as an acronym of a concept expressed in English, we tend to view it as an entirely new and novel idea. The moment we translate the term into Japanese, however, we soon realise that, more often than not, it is a concept that we have long been familiar with. This, too, is the case with the term 'corporate social responsibility'.

Canon's first president, Takeshi Mitarai, introduced three guiding principles during the 1940s, which are not a million miles away from today's concept of sustainable business. They were: 'health first', which stresses the importance of healthy and happy employees; 'familism', to nurture a spirit of harmony between workers based on trust and understanding; and 'meritocracy', to ensure that employees are evaluated fairly for the abilities and skills they bring to their jobs. Then, in 1988, Canon expanded these concepts beyond the boundaries of the company and expressed its philosophy as 'the achievement of corporate growth and development with the aim of contributing to global prosperity and the well-being of humankind'. This is the idea behind Canon's corporate philosophy of *kyosei*. More succinctly, at Canon they define *kyosei* as 'living and working together for the common good', which is as good a definition of sustainable business as you'll ever find.

As Luke Poliszcuk and Motoko Sakashita report in their chapter on Japan in *The World Guide to CSR*, this is the same sort of philosophy that resulted in the *tokugawa* sustainable forest management practice that started around 1700 in response to deforestation, and continued to evolve for the next 150 years. Another example is the *sanpo yoshi* business philosophy practised by merchants in the Edo period (1603–1868); this literally means 'three-way good': the notion that business should benefit the company, the customer and society.

Some of these Japanese concepts, such as 'glocality', even make their way into our English sustainable business lexicon. The term 'glocal' – a portmanteau of global and local – is said to come from the Japanese word *dochakuka*, which simply means global localisation. Originally referring to a way of adapting farming techniques to local conditions, *dochakuka* evolved into a marketing strategy when Japanese businessmen adopted it in the 1980s. It is said that the English word 'glocal' was first coined by Akio Morita, founder of Sony Corporation. In fact, in 2008, Sony Music Corporation even trademarked the phrase 'go glocal'.

Of course, all of this does not mean that Japan is devoid of irresponsible business practices. For example, there were pollution-induced illnesses in the 1950s caused by the release of methyl mercury by a chemical factory in the city of Minamata. There have also been the corporate governance banking scandals of the past two decades and the catastrophe at the Fukushima nuclear plant that resulted from the Japanese earthquake and tsunami of March 2011. However, I believe that culture, values and philosophy are more enduring drivers of long-term success than short-term greed and negligence, and that Japan will rise again as one of the leaders of our post-industrial, low-carbon economy.

Almost every week we see sustainable innovations coming out of Japan, and it is no coincidence. The Japanese government is strategically investing in clean technology in the same way that it invested in the motor industry in the 1970s and the micro-electronics industry in the 1980s. To give just one example, in February 2011, the Mitsubishi Chemical Corporation announced its launch of new product called ALPOLIC®/gioa®, a combination of thin-film solar cells and aluminium plastic composite panels. The new building material enables effective photovoltaic generation on vertical walls.

We can expect to see many more of these kinds of social and environmental innovations coming out of Japan in the next ten years, especially now that the country has such strong competition from South Korea and China. After my visit more than 20 years ago, it is clear that another trip to Japan is long overdue.

Yin and yang
Striving for harmony
(China: 2008, 2010)

Waking dragon of the East

Long before actually visiting China, I had, in common with so many before me, been fascinated by Chinese culture, history and religion. In fact, growing up, I was so inspired by Eastern philosophies that on my 21st birthday I added 'Tao' as a middle name. Later, in 2004 on a family road trip through California, I remember devouring a pocket edition of the *Tao Te Ching*, that beautiful and wise book of poetic philosophy ascribed to Lao Tzu, the reputed founder of Taoism who lived in China in the 6th century BC. Not only was I intrigued by China's ancient philosophies, but I was also seduced by the artistic beauty of its calligraphic writing and impressed by its impending economic rise to power as one of the 'waking dragons' of the East. I even registered for a correspondence course in Mandarin through the University of South Africa in 1994, but never completed the course.

In any event, I finally made it to China in 2008, after it had (I noted in my diary) 'so long drifted like a cloud across the sky of my dreams'. I arrived in June and gave a talk at the China Europe International Business School (CEIBS) conference on Responsible Competitiveness, in Shanghai. My co-author Dirk Matten and I also took the opportunity to launch our new book *The A to Z of Corporate Social Responsibility*. After the CEIBS event, I attended the Being Globally Responsible conference, and acted as a judge for the Innovate China International MBA competition. I also met with Professor Zhu from Tongji University, since that university was to be a partner – together with the University of Cambridge – in a Sustainability Leadership Institute that was being proposed for the planned eco-city at Dongtan.

As a result of these meetings, I formed the opinion that, in the medium to long term, China may very well set an example for other countries and companies in terms of sustainability and responsibility. A clue to my optimism came from something that William Valentino, CSR Director for Bayer in China, said to me: 'Above all else, China prizes stability. And stability, in turn, can only be maintained under conditions of social upliftment and environmental improvement.' Despite labour conditions remaining a concern, human rights abuses are starting to become the exception rather than the rule, and I believe China's sustained economic boom is doing far more social good than harm.

Reconciling its new-found addiction to growth with environmental constraints, however, may prove its most difficult challenge yet. Yet, even here, there are early signs that the government understands the problem and is acting decisively to address it. For example, when I was there, I read that Shanghai was spending 3% of its city GDP on environmental clean-up. Although it clearly has a long way to go (the smog is so bad, I didn't see blue sky once during the seven days I spent there), this level of environmental spend by far exceeds anything in the West.

The danger, on the other hand, is that China will get stuck in the 'CSR as philanthropy' mode. My visit in 2008 was shortly after the devastating Sichuan earthquake and one of the fascinating things was to see was how Chinese bloggers were publicly ranking (and rankling) companies based on their response to the disaster. For me, that represented good news and bad news – good news because it meant that civil society was becoming more active, and bad news because it was entrenching a philanthropic view of CSR. The other experience I had during that visit, which confirmed my fears, was my role on the judging panel for an MBA competition on CSR, where the project we selected (which involved setting up an e-waste recycling facility) was passed over for a philanthropic project (which involved giving money for setting up a school). However, if this can evolve into a more holistic understanding of sustainable business, built on the platform of the government's policy of 'harmonious society', I really believe China may surprise the West.

A dangerous opportunity

In 2008, apart from visiting China, I was working on the Cambridge *Top 50 Sustainability Books* project. This gave me the opportunity to visit and interview some of the world's greatest thinkers on sustainability, and in each interview I made a point of asking their views on China. A number of responses stood out: for example, Amory Lovins, founder of the Rocky Mountain Institute and author of *Winning the Oil Endgame*, shared these thoughts with me:

> I recently had occasion to do the concluding keynote at the China/ US climate summit, and addressed our Chinese guests in a way I don't think they had heard before. I said, 'Look, your society has five millennia more experience than mine. You've got five times as many brains in China as we do in America, quite possibly better ones. About 90% of the technologies underlying the Western industrial revolution were invented in China. You've got the only country that's cut its energy intensity over 5% a year for a quarter of a century. You came off the rails in 2002 for about five years bingeing on energy-intensive basic materials, but you're fixing that now. And you're the world leader in distributed renewable sources of power. You have seven times as much of that as you do of nuclear, and you're growing it seven times faster. You've got the only country that has energy efficiency as its top development priority, not because of a treaty but because your paramount leaders understand that you can't develop otherwise. To be sure, implementation is at an early stage. You face many difficult challenges – heaven is high and the emperor is far away. So a lot of things happen at a provincial and municipal level that are not as the planners in Beijing would wish. But you have better leaders than we do. You're more highly motivated and you work harder. So for all these reasons, I think we can rely on China to lead the world out of the climate mess.' Once they'd

got over their shock of not being patronised, I think they rather
liked this idea.[18]

Others, quite naturally, were not so optimistic. Elizabeth Economy,
author of *The River Runs Black*, has studied China's environmental challenges in depth and believes the crisis they face is deep and intractable.
The facts she cited in my interview with her were sobering, to say the
least.[19] She told me:

> China has 20 of the world's 30 most polluted cities in terms of its
> air quality. Seven hundred and fifty thousand people die prema-
> turely every year in China because of respiratory diseases related
> to air pollution. China has only 25% of the world's average per
> capita availability of water. Something like almost 30% of the
> water that runs through China's seven major river systems and
> tributaries is unfit even for agriculture or industry, much less
> any form of drinking or fishing. A lot of Chinese water experts
> will say that in the northern part of the country they antici-
> pate that between five and ten cities will completely run out
> of water by 2050. In fact, by 2050 China will face a water short-
> age equivalent to the amount of water that it consumes today.
> China is roughly one-quarter desert, and the desert is advancing
> somewhere between 1,300 and 1,900 square miles per year. In
> the United States we would say roughly the size of the state of
> Rhode Island is lost to desert every year in China. Furthermore,
> 10% of China's agricultural land is contaminated with heavy
> metals and other contaminants.

She concluded that 'we're just on the cusp of understanding all of the
ramifications of China's environmental degradation and pollution for the
health of the Chinese people'.

William McDonough, co-author of *Cradle to Cradle*, was a little more
upbeat.[20] He told me that while 'they're not going to become an eco-par-
adise overnight', nevertheless, 'at the senior level, they've recognised the
idea of closing cycles as being a critical part of any long-term plan'. The

---

18 My interview with Amory Lovins is available on the Cambridge University
   website www.cpsl.cam.ac.uk.
19 My interview with Elizabeth Economy is available on the Cambridge University website www.cpsl.cam.ac.uk.
20 My interview with William McDonough is available on the Cambridge University website www.cpsl.cam.ac.uk.

only difference is that they call it the 'circular economy', rather than C2C. McDonough believes this will be driven by necessity rather than virtue. Apparently, Premier Wen Jiabao has stated that, if China continues its urbanisation at the current rate, it will lose 20% of its farmland by 2020. 'This is a horrifying prospect,' says McDonough. 'But from a design perspective, that gets us all excited about the idea of cities with farms on roofs and things like that.'

McDonough's co-author, Michael Braungart, laughingly told me that the Chinese ambassador claims that after Karl Marx, *Cradle to Cradle* is the second most-printed book from Germany in China.[21] He agrees that 'the Chinese think in cycles' but sees the fastest adoption of C2C in Taiwan. He believes that mainland China may still need to go through the eco-efficiency phase, before it accepts the more radical steps needed to tackle the dilemmas of bio-accumulation of chemicals, of endocrine disrupting chemicals and of materials which basically interfere with biological systems.

Two years is a long time in China

I returned to China in June 2010, as part of my CSR quest world tour, staying first on the Peking University campus in Beijing, where I was delivering a seminar. The campus is breathtakingly beautiful, with an old tower and a large lake where I spent many hours working and sketching. After Beijing, I took the overnight train to Shanghai and began preparing for an evening talk at CEIBS. The next day, I met with Jacylyn Shi, founder of Women In Sustainability Action (WISA), where I gave another evening talk.[22] World Expo 2010 was taking place while I was there, so I stopped by for a visit. There were some fabulous buildings and exhibits, even though I only saw about one-quarter of the Expo site. It is probably no coincidence that the quietest pavilions were those showing eco-designs, while the oil and Cisco (technology) displays were among the most popular.

---

21 My interview with Michael Braungart is available on the Cambridge University website www.cpsl.cam.ac.uk.

22 My interview with Jacylyn Shi is available on the csrinternational channel on YouTube.

It was interesting to observe how things had changed in the two years since I had last visited. As my Chinese colleagues kept reminding me, in China two years is a long time. The first thing I noticed was that the country was awash with CSR conferences, workshops and training, so much so that generic meetings no longer pull the crowds. Companies know what CSR is and now they want to know how to implement it. Not surprising, then, that the CSR reporting trend has finally taken off in China as well. For now, this is seen by many companies as an end in itself – often to satisfy Western markets – rather than a first step on a much longer journey. However, along with the reporting trend, there is at least more talk of strategic CSR, even though the evidence suggests this is more the exception than the rule. A company such as State Grid is among this progressive minority, but most large companies are still stuck in a philanthropic, project-based mode of CSR.

The main drivers for sustainable business seem to have shifted as well. Whereas before, Western pressure mainly drove the process through the supply chain, now the two main advocates seem to be the Chinese government and the workers themselves. The government has latched onto the CSR concept and is bedding down many elements in legislation, ranging from labour rights to cleaner production. There are also increasing numbers of protests by workers who are dissatisfied with the status quo. Sam Lee, founder of InnoCSR, told me the story that was in the headlines at the time of an abnormal number of suicides at Foxconn, which has added impetus to this growing workers' movement.[23] As China rises as an economic superpower and begins to dominate many industries, there is also far more emphasis on the safety and quality of products.

Apart from CSR management, China is investing heavily in the market opportunities provided by sustainable business issues, especially clean technology. Already in 2006, the richest man in China was reported to be Shi Shengrong, CEO of the solar company Suntech, and the richest women, Zhang Yin, made her fortune from recycling. A 2010 report published by the Pew Environmental Center found that in 2009 China invested $34.6 billion in the clean energy economy, while the United States only invested $18.6 billion. This explosive growth was brought home to me when, at the WISA event where I was speaking, I got talking to a supplier of wind turbines to Europe. His chief complaint was that he couldn't keep

---

23 My interview with Sam Lee is available on the csrinternational channel on YouTube.

up with the demand. He was turning customers away because there was already 12 months of orders in the pipeline.

In a related trend, I heard far more about environmental issues on my 2010 trip. In fact, visiting sustainable business scholar at Peking University, Mark Wehling, told me that green issues are moving companies away from philanthropic CSR.[24] World Bank estimates put environmental and associated health costs in China at 3% of GDP, with water pollution accounting for half the losses. These costs have not escaped the attention of the Chinese government, which is now driving environmental legislation and incentives much more strongly. Many Chinese talk about the 2008 Olympics as some kind of watershed on environmental issues. At the time, the government shut down many factories around the city and restricted vehicle access. As result, Beijing enjoyed unprecedented blue skies during the Olympics. When it was over and the government prepared to go back to business-as-usual, the public objected – they wanted to keep their blue skies – and so at least some of the pollution control policies remained in force.

Phases of CSR evolution

So, yes, there have been changes over the past few years, and there has been some movement towards strategic CSR. However, my overall impression is that most companies still view sustainable business as a philanthropic and public relations exercise. As Jacylyn Shi reminded me, CSR award schemes are booming, which is a sure sign of progress, but also of the immaturity of the market. Perhaps she is right to place her hope in the women of China to be the new pioneers. After all, there has been no shortage of testosterone-fuelled growth in China (and the world), which remains at the heart of the problem. We could benefit from less male *yang*, and more female *yin*, in China and in the CSR movement.

Shortly after leaving China, my book *The World Guide to CSR* was published, which includes an excellent chapter on China by Sam Lee and Joshua Wickerman. They report on a number of interesting trends,

---

24 My interview with Mark Wehling is available on the csrinternational channel on YouTube.

observing that many contemporary scholars claim that China's first experience with CSR was during the Maoist era of collective agriculture and state-owned enterprises, the period of the so-called 'iron rice bowl'. During Mao's reign, companies were both organised and required to *ban shehui*, or 'administer socially', which meant taking care of everything including workers' food, housing and marriage arrangements. This resulted in the social phenomenon called *chi da guo fan,* or 'eating from the same big pot' (getting the same reward or pay as everyone else regardless of individual performance). The 1978 reforms left a vacuum of state and company services that set the stage for debates about CSR.

According to Lee and Wickerman, China's CSR has evolved rapidly with its fast-paced economic growth, and can roughly be broken down into four categories:

1. *Official scepticism and hesitant engagement (~1994–2004).* During this stage, government attitudes towards CSR ranged from sceptical to hostile. After the economy opened in 1978, Chinese government and business attitudes focused on spurring economic growth by developing an industrial, export-oriented economy competing on cost and quality. Hence, attitudes towards international CSR best practice, along with statutory and non-statutory standards, were seen as means of discriminating and blocking Chinese enterprises from 'going out, going global', or as a pretext for denying markets for exported Chinese products

2. *Multinational company-led CSR (2004–2007).* At this point multinational corporations had been publishing CSR reports and integrating social and environmental sustainability into business strategies for several years. The first sustainability report was issued in 1999 by Shell China, and in February 2006 the first national CSR Summit was held in the Great Hall of the People

3. *Government-led CSR (2008–2010).* On 1 January 2008, the Chinese state-owned Assets Supervision and Administration Commission of the State Council (SASAC) published its 'Notification on issuance of guidelines on fulfilling social responsibility by state-owned enterprises'. This was the first concrete guidance from the Chinese government on how it expected central state-owned enterprises to implement CSR, based on the 2006 company law that first mentioned CSR. CSR also became more linked

to competitiveness. In the 2009 *Fortune China* survey, 81% of respondents felt that 'social and environmental responsibility can improve business performance in the long run', up from 67% in 2007 and 76% in 2008. As more companies operating in China go abroad, they are adopting and promoting global standards and sustainable business practices acceptable to stakeholders outside of China

4. *Global hybrid CSR model (2010–).* As Chinese companies continue to use 'going out' strategies, they are starting to pay more attention to the role of international civil society, namely groups that promote voluntary social and environmental standards, campaign for or against companies, or certify products according to values determined by multi-stakeholder governance processes

Build your dreams

Speaking of hybrid models, one of the case studies from China that I have been most engaged by is the story of Wang Chuanfu, founder of BYD, which manufactures batteries and electric cars. By 2009, Wang, aged 43, topped the annual *Hurun* Rich List of the nation's wealthiest, with assets of $5.1 billion, jumping 102 places from the 2008 ranking. BYD is derived from the Chinese name of the company, but has come to stand for 'Build Your Dreams', which gives some sense of Wang's character and ambition.

Starting business in 1995, it took just five years for BYD to become the largest manufacturer of mobile phone batteries in the world. Not content to dominate just one product market, in 2003 Wang bought a failing Chinese car company and entered the automobile market. When BYD launched a plug-in electric car with a backup gasoline engine, it went ahead of GM, Nissan and Toyota. BYD's plug-in, called the F3DM, could travel further on a single charge than other electric vehicles and sold for $22,000, less than the competing plug-in Toyota Prius and the Chevy Volt.

Despite Wang's meteoric rise to success in China, most people in the West had never heard of BYD. But that all changed in 2008 when investment mogul Warren Buffett bought a 10% stake in the company for $230 million. Chiefly, this was on the advice of his business partner in Berkshire Hathaway, Charlie Munger, who told Buffet, 'This guy is a combination of Thomas Edison and Jack Welch – something like Edison in solving technical problems, and something like Welch in getting done what he needs to do. I have never seen anything like it.'

Wang told CNN, 'Urban pollution, reliance on petroleum and emission of carbon dioxide are three problems that entrepreneurs have to consider for basic social responsibility.' Interestingly, he characterises this as 'making our Earth bluer'. In a BYD video, we are told: 'Glaciers are melting. Sea levels are rising. Who can guarantee that the next victims won't be us? Where is Noah's ark to save human beings?' Wang, it seems, is attempting nothing less than building that very ark – in the shape of BYD – that could take us to a sustainable future.

As I sat on the plane from Shanghai to Athens, my 2010 visit over, I thought about what I was taking away. At a trivial level, I had bought some music at the airport with my left-over Yuan – some Chinese pop and traditional instrumental music, a documentary on Confucius and a little book about Lao Tzu. But at a more profound level, China had given me the gift of hope. It seems to me that the country epitomises the Chinese word for 'crisis', which contains the two characters meaning 'dangerous' and 'opportunity'. There's a palpable sense here that the only way is up; that the future is all to play for and that a combination of vision, national pride and hard work make all dreams possible. It all seems rather familiar – the same sort of ideals that built the American Dream. I have no doubt that the 21st century will be the century of the Chinese Dream.

I remember reading in *China Daily* that the character for learning (*xi*) is partly derived from the non-simplified character meaning 'feather' or 'wing'. Hence, the concept is inspired by a bird learning to fly. Nothing could be a more apt metaphor for China, which is like a young chick that has flown the nest and will soon be at home in the sky, so long as its two wings – social and environmental integrity – do not become damaged by the economic sun in its rapid upward flight.

My visits to China have been all too few and too brief. And, yet, much like China on its path to embracing corporate sustainability and responsibility, I have taken the first steps towards understanding the country. And as the *Tao Te Ching* reminds us, 'the journey of a thousand miles begins with the first step'.

13
Too much sun
A slow starter
(Australia, 2010, 2011)

Launching ISO 26000

At the invitation of Leeora Black, Director of the Australian Centre for CSR (ACCSR), I travelled to Melbourne in early 2010 to give a keynote address on 'Leadership for social responsibility' at the ACCSR annual conference. The conference theme was 'ISO 26000 in a post-financial crisis world' and I was sharing the platform Jonathan Hanks, a South African friend and colleague, who also happened to be Convenor of the ISO 26000 Integrated Drafting Task Force and Managing Director of Incite, a South African sustainability consultancy.

In my talk, and no doubt much to Jonathan's chagrin, I suggested that ISO 26000 is similar to a teddy bear – something cute and fluffy, which may help companies sleep better at night – but having nothing in common with the grizzly bear that we really need to shake business out of its CSR complacency. Of course, it was unfair of me to make so light of a five-year international process of negotiation involving over 90 countries, which managed to reach some measure of agreement on such tricky issues as human rights and fair operating practices. But I really do believe that, as a non-certifiable guidance standard that promotes a strategic approach to CSR (rather than a transformative CSR 2.0 agenda), ISO 26000 may prove to be more of a damp squib than a big bang.

Having said that, I must give ISO 26000 its due – as a foundation document that encapsulates the international consensus on social responsibility, it is to be applauded and recommended. Its greatest achievement – and what I expect may prove to be its most enduring legacy – is the way in which it broadens the scope of CSR, first beyond big corporates to any organisation, and second beyond an exclusive focus on philanthropic community development to incorporate six other core subjects, namely organisational governance, human rights, labour rights, the environment, fair operating practices and consumer issues.

Besides this, countries such as Denmark are ignoring ISO's strong declaration against the ISO 26000 guidance document being used as a certifiable standard and have begun developing their own certifiable national standard, DS 26000. I expect consultants will also increasingly offer ISO 26000 compliance auditing services, irrespective of whether these are sanctioned by ISO. The fact is that business, governments and civil society alike want standards on social responsibility that have 'teeth'. A decade of weak standards without sanction, such as the UN Global Compact and AA 1000, as compared with tougher certification schemes such as SA 8000 and the FSC, have taught us where real value lies.

At the ACCSR conference, I was impressed by a number of people and organisations, and took the opportunity to interview, among others, Vince Hawsworth, then CEO of Hydro Tasmania; Vanessa Zimmerman, a legal advisor to the UN Special Representative on Business and Human Rights; Nathan Fabian, CEO of the Investor Group on Climate Change Australia/ New Zealand; Bruce Harvey, Global Practice Leader on Communities for Rio Tinto; and Neil Birtchnell, General Manager of Business Community Investment for Transfield Services, a global provider of operations, maintenance, and asset and project management services.[25]

---

25 My interviews with Vince Hawsworth, Vanessa Zimmerman, Nathan Fabian, Bruce Harvey and Neil Birtchnell are available on the csrinternational channel on YouTube.

Too much sun

Besides the conference, I was invited by Suzanne Young, Associate Professor at La Trobe Graduate School of Management, to teach a module on its Master's in Business in Society course.[26] I also ran one-day workshops for ACCSR in Melbourne and the University of New South Wales in Sydney, and gave talks for the consultancy Banarra, CSR Sydney and Victoria University. My overwhelming sense from all of these interactions in 2010 was a huge frustration among people working in sustainable business in Australia. The biggest reasons cited were an unsupportive (some even say backward) government policy on environment, and the negative lobby power of Australia's two biggest industries – extractives (mainly mining) and agriculture.

I was really surprised that, after about ten years of severe drought, fatalities from runaway bushfires in Victoria in 2009, and unprecedented flood and storm damage from Tropical Cyclone Yasi in 2011, most Australians still seemed to be in a state of climate change denial. But perhaps that is testimony to the power of vested interests supporting the status quo. Also, at the time, the opposition party was scoring cheap political points by saying that everything to do with climate change was a tax, and hence to be avoided at all costs. It failed to mention, of course, that according to the Stern Review it may cost around 1% of GDP now, but it could cost as much as 20% of GDP later if immediate action is not taken. That is politics – tax the future 20 times as heavily, in order to get easy votes today.

I did hear one other explanation for why the take-up of sustainable business in general, and climate action in particular, is so lacklustre in Australia. 'There's too much sun', said my friend and sustainability consultant, Samantha Graham. She was making a point that Australians are too laid-back about life. They are eternal optimists who believe that things will get better sooner or later. There may be a grain of truth in this, but I also saw some really progressive work going on in stakeholder engagement and social impact management among the mining companies (such as by Alcoa) and biodiversity management (such as by Rio Tinto). Also, I noticed that, having had a banking scare about a decade earlier, Australia's tight corporate governance practices sheltered it from the worst

26 My interview with Suzanne Young is available on the csrinternational channel on YouTube.

effects of the global financial crisis. Of course, it also helped that China's demand for Australia's natural resources continued unabated.

An experiment in generosity

One of the highlights of my 2010 trip was spending some time with Shanaka Fernando, founder of the Melbourne-based restaurant chain, Lentil As Anything, who was introduced to me by New Zealand sustainable business academic, Colin Higgins.[27] Fernando is one of those rare pioneers who are prepared to live by their convictions, flaunt social convention and challenge the status quo.

After a failed stint as a Buddhist monk in his home country of Sri Lanka (he fell in love with a nun, had a torrid affair and got kicked out), he came to Australia and dabbled in law studies. It wasn't fulfilling, so he gave it up to travel on a shoestring around the developing world for six years, learning about culture and community along the way. When he returned to Australia, Fernando started a business importing saris made from recycled fabrics, which made him enough money to start his current social experiment – Lentil As Anything.

I call it a social experiment, because the business goes beyond simply being a social enterprise. In common with other social businesses, Lentil As Anything embraces the entrepreneurial spirit while it 'seeks to have a significant, positive influence on the development of the community'. But there is something unique, more challenging, more sublime and more subversive – it gets to the heart of human nature and the essence of Western capitalism. I am talking about generosity and money.

Through Lentil As Anything, Fernando is trying to foster a culture of generosity. What would happen, he wondered, if there were no prices? What if people only paid what they could afford, or what they thought the food was worth, or what they were inspired to pay? Is there enough generosity left in Western society to run a viable business on the principle of giving and sharing, rather than profit maximisation? Would the 'free rider' problem kick in, with people taking advantage of the 'free' food?

27 My interviews with Colin Higgins and Shanaka Fernando are available on the csrinternational channel on YouTube.

According to Fernando, all kinds of interesting things happen when people are faced with 'the magic box' – the mini treasure chest that people can place their donations in as they leave. A few (very, very few) take advantage. Some, who genuinely can't afford to pay, offer to chop vegetables or do dishes. Others make their own assessment of what is a fair price to pay. Some are quietly generous, while others make a theatrical gesture of placing their donation in the magic box.

But it goes beyond the money. Other unexpected things happen too. As you look around, you notice that this is not a 'people like me' experience, where those from your own socioeconomic or ethnocultural strata surround you. Lentil has succeeded in mixed it up, cutting across traditional divides. And because of the philosophy of the place, you may find a wealthy businessman striking up a conversation with a subsistence artist.

When you create these kinds of creative connections, it is a potent recipe for innovation, for rediscovering what it means to be human. Fernando insists that Lentil is first and foremost about good food (interestingly, vegetarian food, because that is the most inclusive, making concerns about halal or kosher or meat-based preparation irrelevant). But it is clearly more than that. It is an invitation to restore our faith in the essential goodness of humanity and the wholesome nature of community.

What, you may ask, has all this to do with sustainable business? Well, I believe it is entrepreneurs such as Fernando who are at the forefront of the CSR 2.0 wave. If we subject Lentil to the five tests of CSR 2.0 (more about these in Chapter 25), it scores well: is Lentil creative? (yes); is it scalable? (not sure); is it responsive? (extremely); is it glocal? (yes, it thinks globally but acts locally); and is it circular? (mostly, yes, local production and recycling are part of the philosophy and practice).

Even on scalability, Lentil gave me pause to think about what I mean by that. If we accept the 'long tail' approach to scalability (popularised by Chris Anderson), Lentil does not have to go from four to 40,000 restaurants to be scalable. It could be that 10,000 independent restaurants – inspired by the Lentil philosophy – pop up all around the world and turn the generosity experiment into a global movement.

As the world recovers from the age of greed that culminated in the global financial crisis, it is refreshing to be reminded of the rightful place of money in society. Money is always a means to an end; never the end in itself. Melbourne – and indeed the world – would be a poorer place if brave experiments such as Lentil As Anything were allowed to fail. Let us make sure that, in the battle of generosity versus money, generosity wins hands down.

The state of CSR

In 2011, I was back in Melbourne to teach at La Trobe again and to help launch ACCSR's State of CSR Annual Review 2010–2011. The findings, based on the survey responses of almost 500 mid-to-senior level managers across a broad spectrum of organisations and industries, are as follows:

- 80% agreed that CSR had contributed to strengthened reputation (as compared with less than 40% in 2008), while just over 60% said CSR contributed to reduced costs in their organisations (versus less than 20% in 2008)

- Reducing environmental impact and building understanding of CSR within their organisations were rated the most important issues for CSR managers in 2011

- CSR staff and budgets cut in the first years of the global financial crisis were rebounding, with a strong increase in hiring and spending forecast for 2011.

Reflecting on the findings, Leeora Black told me she was struck by the ambiguous signals that Australian businesses are giving about the role of sustainable business in their organisations.[28] On the one hand, it's clear – and very heartening – to see that more organisations are seeing value from sustainable business that goes beyond reputation and risk management. But on the other hand, most of the respondents said that getting organisational buy-in is the biggest single obstacle to their success with sustainable business.

According to Black,

> the issue lies with the nature of the CSR function itself: probably the most cross-functional, cross-silo business discipline to

28 My interview with Leeora Black is available on the csrinternational channel on YouTube.

emerge so far in the history of management. It requires a profound level of cross-business functionality and integration to be effective. This is a real challenge to most companies, which are founded on vertical accountabilities.

One of the survey findings I considered most interesting and encouraging was that there was a significant decline in organisations reporting the need to understand climate change, but an increase in organisations using sustainable business as part of their regulatory response. Might this suggest that Australian organisations were beginning to move towards a more integrated approach to managing climate change? Was this a sign of a shift from its position of climate change denial – if not on the public streets, then at least in the plush boardrooms of Australia?

A new era in climate policy

As it turned out – in a move that shocked, surprised, delighted and infuriated many across the country and the world – it was from Australia's parliamentary halls rather than its corporate suites that the most significant reforms on climate change emerged. In November 2011, Prime Minister Julia Gillard successfully guided 18 Clean Energy bills through the Senate, which included the provision for a $23 per tonne carbon tax to be paid by 500 big polluters from July 2012.

The carbon tax, which begins as a fixed price before converting to an emissions trading scheme in 2015, is forecast to raise $24.5 billion in the first three years. To compensate households for the impact of the tax, the government will distribute $15.4 billion through pension and benefit increases, tax cuts and other assistance for higher power bills and related cost increases. The government will also spend $10.3 billion compensating business, particularly trade-exposed polluters in sectors such as steel manufacturing.

In launching the radical policy, Gillard said (and not without justification):

> We have made history – after all of these years of debate and division, our nation has got the job done, and from 1 July we will see a price on carbon pollution. This comes after a quarter

of a century of scientific warnings, 37 parliamentary inquiries and years of bitter debate and divisions.

According to *National Affairs*, the Clean Energy Future package relies on a significant expansion of cleaner gas-fired power generation to help replace coal-fired power and meet the targets of cutting Australia's carbon emissions by 20% by 2020, and 80% by 2050. Renewable energy, such as wind and solar power, will expand even faster, helped by the new $10 billion Clean Energy Fund, a condition of the Green Party's support for the legislation.

These are encouraging signs indeed. I still think that Australia faces an uphill battle against the vested interests and economic power of its mining and agro-industrial sectors, not only in the climate change space but also in adopting transformative CSR. But perhaps if its labour government remains strong and its more forward-looking and image-conscious financial and tourism sectors can take up the CSR 2.0 challenge, we might just see Australia leapfrogging from being CSR laggards to sustainable business leaders.

After my 2010 visit, I concluded a blog on sustainable business in Australia entitled 'Too much sunshine?' with the cheeky words: 'Why worry about disaster scenarios for 2050 when the sun is shining, the skies are blue, there's a cracking footie (or rugby or cricket) game on? CSR – what? Surf's up!' I will be more than happy to have my words be proved unfair and inaccurate.

14

Merlions and orang-utans
A new breed of entrepreneurs
(Singapore, Malaysia, Thailand: 2010, 2011)

An unnecessary extra?

I arrived in Singapore in March 2010 as part of my CSR quest world tour. Apart from the balmy weather, there is a lot to like about Singapore. It is organised without feeling over-policed (despite the joke that it is a fine city – for everything, there is a fine). The city is efficient and the people are friendly. Because of the mix of cultures and the cornucopia of shopping malls, there is a very cosmopolitan feel about the place. And, yet, it is not all neon lights and concrete; there are plenty of green spaces and cultural sites to visit.

Singapore literally means 'lion city' and has five colossus merlion statues in the city. I like the story of how the merlion – Singapore's national icon – represents Singapore's past as a fishing village (hence the mermaid's tail) and the future (a lion representing power and progress). One particular memory I have is walking along Orchard Road, a busy boulevard, just when the sun was setting, and the trees were roaring with the deafening sound of birds roosting for the night.

During my visit, I gave a talk on 'The future of CSR' hosted by the ever-amiable Thomas Thomas and his Singapore Compact for CSR, as well as giving the closing address at the EU conference on CSR.[29] I returned to Singapore twice in 2011, in September to deliver the keynote speech on sustainability at the International Singapore Compact CSR Summit 2011, and in October to give a keynote speech to the Fairprice retail conference on CSR 2.0 in the fast-moving consumer goods (FMCG) sector.

As far as sustainable business in Singapore goes, I have mixed impressions. Evidence of 'explicit' CSR (reports, policies, managers, etc.) is extremely limited and certainly lags other developed nations and some developing countries, including those in Asia. However, I did find myself asking the question: If a government is extremely effective – as arguably it is in Singapore – does that limit the need for and scope of sustainable business?

Over the past 50 years or so, the Singapore government has succeeded in growing the economy, creating job opportunities, ensuring good working conditions for nationals and raising the standard of living, all in a tiny city-state with few natural resources. It has even cleaned up the rivers, lowered air pollution, greened the city and virtually eliminated its dependence on Malaysia for water. Could it be that sustainable business is an unnecessary extra, practised only to placate Western markets and investors?

On reflection, I think this would be a premature and misplaced conclusion. First, there seem to be some issues where, although progress has been made, there are still serious concerns. For example, the rights and conditions of migrant contract workers on which the economy is dependent are still sub-standard. Transparency and integration of sustainable business issues into corporate governance and financial markets is also weak, and reducing the carbon intensity of the economy – which includes the biggest container port and biggest gas refinery in the world, and a prolific construction industry – remains a vast challenge.

---

29 My interview with Thomas Thomas is available on the csrinternational channel on YouTube.

Sustainable competitiveness

In addition to these areas for improvement, I must confess to being surprised that, despite widespread perceptions (including my own) of the government being 'strong', there seems to be a reluctance to take a lead on many social and environmental issues. For example, after meeting with the CEO of the National Environment Agency, I had the impression that the government is extremely hesitant to introduce any bold regulations or controls that might be seen as a cost or risk to the competitiveness or security of Singapore's trade and industry.

The water issue is illustrative. It was only after a political crisis with Malaysia that Singapore instituted the range of measures, including leading-edge filtration and desalination technologies, that now make it not only virtually water self-sufficient, but also a leading exporter of water technologies. I did hear talk of Singapore becoming a green IT or clean-tech hub for Asia, but I think the government's softly-softly approach will leave it far in the wake of countries such as Korea, Japan and China.

Even so, there is a lesson to be learned from Singapore. As a geographically small city-state, with a relatively high population density, the government quickly faced up to the fact that there is no 'away'. It had to deal with its own externalities, rather than export them. Innovation was born of necessity. Poverty and pollution could not be tucked away in remote rural regions or ignored as the inevitable lot of a fringe slum society. Either the whole city prospered, or it didn't. There was nowhere to hide poor governance.

As the Asian tigers jockeyed for position in the region and the world in the 1980s and 1990s, Singapore made strategic investments in two areas – its people (creating a highly skilled labour force) and its infrastructure (making it one of the most friendly trade and investment hubs in the world). Singapore knew that if it didn't get these two things right, it would have no competitive advantage. Most crucially, it would lose its upwardly mobile workforce to Japan, Korea or the West, and global economic activity would divert to other parts of Asia.

We can all learn from this 'spaceship earth' (city-state) thinking of Singapore. But, for me, the jury is still out on sustainable business. Unless the government and companies can shake off the 'competitiveness at all costs' mentality, it may always be a sustainable business laggard, moving with the late majority; certainly not the worst, but far from the best.

Somehow, Singapore needs to answer for itself the 'why' question. Why is sustainable business relevant, or important in Singapore? I am betting this will inevitably lead straight to another question: how can sustainable business make Singapore more competitive?

Jack-out-the-box

There is a positive side-effect of Singapore's obsession with competitiveness. It breeds entrepreneurs, and occasionally, they turn out to be social entrepreneurs. Jack Sim is one such person, whom I was lucky enough to meet when I was visiting in September 2011. As Sim recounts in his inspiring autobiographical book *Simple Jack*, he grew up in extreme poverty in Singapore in the 1960s. This was a time when Singapore was poorer than Cambodia. His father was a provision shop assistant and his mother was a rural entrepreneur.

Jack started his own business when he was just 25, and by 40, he was financially independent and decided to quit the rat race. 'Capitalism is futile game after we've satisfied our basic needs,' he concluded, and proceeded to hand over his business to his staff. He decided to devote the second half of his life to something more meaningful, namely improving sanitation around the world. In 1998, he established the Restroom Association of Singapore (RAS) with a mission to raise the standards of public toilets in Singapore. He soon realised that there were existing toilet associations operating in other countries, but no channels available to bring these organisations together to share information and resources. There was a lack of synergy.

As a result, in 2001, Sim founded the World Toilet Organization. He joked with me that he had hoped the World Trade Organization (WTO), which hosted its inaugural summit in Singapore in 1996, would sue him for copying its WTO brand and that the ensuing media fuss would raise awareness about the 2.6 billion toilet-less people around the world. Sim forged ahead and declared 19 November as World Toilet Day, which is now celebrated in over 19 countries with over 51 events hosted by various water and sanitation advocates. He also introduced an annual World Toilet Summit and a World Toilet College.

He credits fellow Ashoka Fellow, David Green – who was dedicated to making eye operations affordable in developing countries – with inspiring him to replicate the social business model for sanitation. Green advised him not to depend on donors, but rather to drive down the product cost to a level that the poor were willing to pay, thereby making the operation financially viable. This meant achieving production economies of scale and using local distribution, while simultaneously driving demand by marketing toilets as a being a status symbol.

Sim went on to establish a sales agent model, first tested in Cambodia, whereby the World Toilet Organization supplies toilets to the local poor, who earn a commission for every toilet sold. He also engaged partners in the developed world. For example, he persuaded Index Award (the world's biggest design award body) to begin designing a SaniShop franchise to brand and design flat-pack sanitation products for scaling-up distribution in the developing world. Many other prominent research universities and institutions also joined in to share their experiences in the product design, while the US Agency for International Development (USAID), Lien Aid and Credit Lyonnais Securities Asia (CLSA) helped with funding.

Part of Sim's success can be ascribed to the World Toilet Organization's powerful aspirational model, which triggers the poor emotionally to buy toilets as a priority purchase. Sim makes the case that:

> Each toilet door opens to a bright future of healthy children, daughters graduating, respect from the community, wives appreciating their new privacy, elders giving the thumbs-up and people earning more money because no one is sick any more.

Despite the World Toilet Organization's success – with more than 235 member organisations from 58 countries – Sim is already working on its next big thing, which is to establish a BOP Hub in Singapore, referring to the 4 billion poor living at the bottom of the world's economic pyramid. The Hub will act as a trade centre for the poor in developing countries to formulate, cooperate and merge business solutions to transform emerging markets into vibrant marketplaces. It will develop market-based solutions in sectors such as water, food, housing, energy, transportation and telecommunication. It's another big dream, but knowing Sim, I wouldn't bet against it becoming a reality.

KitKat catastrophe

From Singapore, my 2010 CSR quest trip took me on to Malaysia, where Navin Muruga of FORS had arranged for me to deliver a training session. My first emotion, on stepping out into the baking heat of Kuala Lumpur, was relief. I was back in a developing country (albeit a fairly prosperous one). For me, it is like the difference between classical music (symbolising Europe, or Singapore), pop (the United States) and jazz (the developing world). I like all three styles, but jazz countries are where I feel most relaxed, most soulful. Typifying this anything-goes style, I stayed at a low-cost Tune hotel and was highly amused by the rooms. As I tweeted at the time: 'Woke up to Maggie in the bathroom – not a woman, but a billboard for noodles inside my hotel room. McDonald's looks over me as I sleep - scary!'

It was an interesting time to be in Kuala Lumpur, with the Greenpeace KitKat campaign against Nestlé having just gone viral. In a nutshell, Greenpeace accused Nestlé of endangering orang-utans through deforestation caused by its irresponsible palm oil supply chain in Indonesia. The campaign was specifically targeted at a Nestlé supplier in Indonesia, but Malaysia is also a major world source of palm oil and it clearly got the attention of plantation companies such as Sime Darby, a Malaysian company which supplies nearly 10% of the world market.

Fortunately for them, according to Chief Sustainability Officer, Puvan Selvanathan, they were ahead of the curve, with some plantations already certified by the Round Table on Sustainable Palm Oil (RSPO) and the rest scheduled for certification in 2011/2012 (whereas Unilever and Nestlé are only committing to have fully converted supplies by 2015).[30] Leaving aside the specific companies involved, the Greenpeace–Nestlé palm oil debacle highlights the increasingly important role of sector-based codes and social media as new mechanisms for corporate governance and stakeholder accountability.

The RSPO is part of the new generation of multi-stakeholder sustainable business codes, which have far more credibility than their industry-led predecessors (such as Responsible Care). It still has its problems, especially the ability for plantations to offset carbon rather than actually

---

30 My interview with Puvan Selvanathan is available on the csrinternational channel on YouTube.

to convert to sustainable practices, and the certification bottleneck that seems to be slowing things down. Nevertheless, it is part of the new web of sustainable business governance mechanisms that is needed to take responsible behaviour to scale. It will only work, however, when companies such as Nestlé, Carrefour and Unilever 'choice edit', so that unsustainable palm oil is phased out completely.

As far as social media goes, I believe the Greenpeace–Nestlé campaign will become a classic sustainable business case study. One estimate calculates that within four days the Greenpeace report and shock-video may have reached half a million people through social media such as Twitter and Facebook. This viral effect was seemingly boosted by Nestlé's attempt on its Facebook page to censor comments made by its critics. The fact that Nestlé took swift action by dropping the accused Indonesian supplier, and that its hands are effectively tied by a lack of available sustainable palm oil, did little to quell the angry reactions of online activists. In the end, it took six months of negotiation and promises by Nestlé before Greenpeace dropped the campaign.

For peat's sake

A related but different issue that I became aware of during my time in Kuala Lumpur, through a chance meeting with eco-activist Matthias Gerber, is that most of the world's peat forests are in Indonesia and Malaysia.[31] These underground forests are a colossal carbon-sink asset for the world and their loss poses a significant climate change threat. They are in urgent need of protection, but instead, intensive farming and deforestation is lowering the water table, drying out these organic soils (comprised mainly of undecayed leaves) and resulting in peat forest fires, which release massive amounts of CO_2 into the atmosphere and are hard to put out once they begin.

This is exactly the sort of issue CSR should be tackling in Malaysia, where, according to research by CSR Asia, Malaysia is marginally ahead of Singapore and the Philippines, but behind Hong Kong. My observation

---

31 My interview with Matthias Gerber is available on the csrinternational channel on YouTube.

– which was confirmed by Tan Lin Lah, Executive Director of the UN Global Compact for Malaysia – was that strategic, embedded sustainable business is still limited to very few large companies, such as those involved in the local UN Global Compact network.[32] The progressive role of the government on sustainable business, however, may yet pay dividends. This includes, for example, presidential awards for CSR, the creation of a Green Technology ministry and the implementation of a Green Buildings Index.

There is even talk of impending reforms to company law, to redefine corporate purpose in terms of meeting stakeholder needs, rather than continuing to follow the global model of shareholder fiduciary duty. If it was any other country, I would take this with a pinch of salt, but this is Malaysia, which dared to defy the International Monetary Fund (IMF) hegemony after the Asian financial crisis. If there is any government bold enough to challenge shareholder-driven capitalism, it is Malaysia.

I, for one, hope it has the courage to do so, because until we reduce the stranglehold that shareholders and financial speculators have over our companies and markets, it will always be like trying to sail against a gale, using only a handkerchief – namely CSR – as a sail. The trade winds of the market will always blow, but rather than tinkering with the sails, we need a new kind of vessel – a new model of responsible business – that can not only navigate through the tempest, but also sail for calmer waters, where long-term thinking is possible and preferable.

Street democracy

After seeing Malaysia on the CSR quest world tour, I headed to Thailand, a country I first visited in November 2008, where I was attending the CSR Asia Summit in Bangkok and taking advantage of the opportunity to launch *The A to Z of Corporate Social Responsibility*. I also gave a keynote address on 'CSR and the financial crisis' at the NGO-biz NETWORK conference and arranged a meeting of the local members of CSR International.

---

32 My interview with Tan Lin Lah is available on the csrinternational channel on YouTube.

When I was back in Bangkok in April 2010, I took in the usual tourist sites – a visit to the Grand Palace, a canal boat ride, a tour of the floating markets and a trip to the city's electronics mega-shopping malls. As part of the CSR quest world tour, I then talked to a packed house at an event hosted by the Thailand Stock Exchange, with sponsorship and support from Thai Health Promotion Fund and NGO Business Partnership.

As it happened, the hotel where I was staying was located right in the heart of the 'red-shirts' anti-government protests, which were going on at the time. That made for a very noisy 36 hours, with constant sloganeering and speechifying over loudspeakers, day and night. I didn't really mind. The protests were all peaceful at that stage, although unfortunately they turned violent a few days later. I felt somehow privileged to have such an intimate window on Thailand's rising social movement for democracy.

Cabbages & Condoms

The most interesting sustainable business-related discovery in Thailand was undoubtedly Cabbages & Condoms, which I first visited in 2008, thanks to a recommendation by one of Thailand's sustainable business stalwarts, Alex Mavro. Behind this story is an organisation, the Population and Community Development Association (PDA), and its Founder and Chairman, Mechai Viravaidya. Today, PDA is one of Thailand's largest and most successful private, non-profit development organisations. Among the many programmes and projects it runs is the quirkily-named Cabbages & Condoms restaurant in Bangkok, a social enterprise dedicated to raising awareness on family planning and HIV/AIDS.

Through PDA and his other activities, including serving as a Senator in the Thai government and Chairman of some of Thailand's biggest companies, Viravaidya has played a pivotal role in Thailand's immensely successful family planning programme, which saw one of the most rapid national declines in fertility in the modern era. The rate of annual population growth in Thailand dropped from over 3% in 1974 to 0.6% in 2005, and the average number of children per family plummeted from seven to under two.

Viravaidya was also chief architect in building Thailand's comprehensive national HIV/AIDS prevention policy and programme. This initiative is widely regarded as one of the most outstanding national efforts by any country in combating HIV/AIDS. By 2004, Thailand had experienced a 90% reduction in new HIV infections. In 2005, the World Bank reported that these preventative efforts helped save 7.7 million lives throughout the country and saved the government over $18 billion in treatment costs alone. As a result of his outstanding work, in 1999 Viravaidya was appointed the Joint United Nations Programme on HIV/AIDS (UNAIDS) Ambassador.

I conducted an interview with Viravaidya and was most intrigued by his views. I started by asking him what demonstrable impact social enterprises can make on society's problems, using Cabbages & Condoms as an example. He told me:

> We originally referred to the Cabbages & Condoms Restaurant as a 'Business for Social Progress', which is commonly known as a social enterprise in the West. The profits from our restaurant directly benefit our NGO, the PDA. The impact has included promotion of family planning in Thailand, HIV/AIDS prevention through condom usage, poverty alleviation and education in north-eastern Thailand. The restaurant has been a successful social enterprise, and we always encourage civil society leaders in Asia to set one up to help maintain financial sustainability.

So what then are the barriers to scaling up social enterprises such as Cabbages & Condoms? 'The biggest hurdles to social enterprise', said Viravaidya, 'are good ideas and funds for large-scale endeavours. It is best for new organisations looking at establishing a social enterprise to seek advice from the business community and start small.'

Conscious of his extensive involvement in politics, I was curious about his view of government's role in enabling social enterprises to succeed. He said this varies from country to country. Whereas in the United Kingdom the government is quite active in its support, the Thai government currently plays no role in incentivising social enterprise. What's more, Viravaidya would like to keep it like that: 'The best thing they can do is to kindly stay out of the way.'

So why use business as the vehicle for responding to the needs of society? Why not just have a charity? 'We needed to ensure that our poverty eradication and education initiatives performed under our NGO had long-term sustainability,' explained Viravaidya.

And we're not entirely dependent on outside donations. The social enterprises we have established have earned approximately $150 million over 25 years and fund approximately 70% of our development endeavours. We would not have been able to accomplish half as much as we have without our social enterprises.

This seems a good lesson for the entire region and the rest of the world to heed. While governments need to be more actively involved in supporting sustainable business, companies and societies should not wait to be handed social solutions on a platter. Social entrepreneurs make things happen.

15

Access and justice
Purpose out of chaos
(India: 2010)

Colours in the dust

After Thailand, where I also spent a lovely week in Koi Summui attending my sister's wedding, and Cambodia, where I took a short tour of Angkor Wat with my parents, I headed for India in April 2010. My friend, fellow CSR Nottingham alumnus and author of the chapter on India for *The World Guide to CSR*, Bimal Arora, had arranged a packed itinerary for me.

My first few days in India were all work and no play, but rewarding nevertheless. The evening that I arrived in Mumbai, I interviewed the founder Vinay Somani and researcher Tanya Mahajan of Karmayog, a CSR-promotion organisation.[33] The following day, I travelled to Raipur to deliver a talk on 'The future of CSR', hosted by the Confederation of Indian Industry (CII). The flight back to Mumbai was via Bhopal, which felt somehow poignant given the number of times I have used the 1984 Bhopal disaster as a case study in my talks and writing. We should never forget that, in what is still described as the world's worst industrial disaster, an

---

33 My interviews with Vinay Somani and Tanya Mahajan are available on the csrinternational channel on YouTube.

explosion at Union Carbide's pesticide plant in Bhopal released a cloud of methyl isocyanate, killing at least 2,000 and injuring 50,000 people.

Travelling on to Delhi, I did a workshop on 'CSR around the world', hosted by the national power supplier (NTPC). Several power cuts during my stay at its guesthouse seemed ironic, but just highlight the scale of the challenges India faces. Next was a workshop on 'CSR, marketing and PR', hosted by the National Association of Software and Service Companies (NASSCOM), as well as talks for ArcelorMittal, the University of Delhi, the Indian Institute of Foreign Trade and the Business & Community Foundation. In Chennai, I did a session for the Institute for Financial Management & Research on 'New directions in CSR' and ended the itinerary with a trip to Pune, where I delivered a workshop on 'CSR in developing countries' at Genteel School of Business & Economics.

It was my first visit to India and I didn't get the 'assault on the senses' that I had expected, other than the heat – it was 43°C during the day and 30°C at night, the highest April temperatures in 52 years. Poverty was everywhere in evidence, but nowhere near as overwhelming or pervasive as I had expected. Perhaps I am just accustomed to slums and scenes of hand-to-mouth existence, having grown up in South Africa and travelled extensively in developing countries.

What was more notable was the traffic. Not only are the roads swarming with cows, bicycles, bull carts, rickshaws, auto-rickshaws, taxis, cars, buses and trucks, but there appear to be no rules of the road, other than 'take the gap'. Traffic lanes, stop signs and traffic lights have no meaning. Hooting is compulsory. Many cars and trucks even have signs saying 'Horn ok please' painted on their bumpers. Somehow, the absence of rules makes drivers more alert and aware, so in a chaotic way, it works – sort of.

Shining through the dust and the smog (in Delhi) are iridescent colours – of women's saris, brightly painted trucks and temples, shrines, gods and goddesses. I find this fascinating – that the hottest, driest and often poorest places in the world are also the most colourful. Perhaps it is compensation for a harsh and bland environment, or perhaps it is simply the richness of indigenous cultures.

There is also a real sense of diversity and dynamism among the people of India – constantly busy and bustling, wheeling and dealing, in animated discussion, struggling to make themselves seen and heard amid the crowd, manoeuvring, manipulating, engaged in the cut and thrust of survival. What is also remarkable is that people and animals mix and move freely together, on the streets and pavements, through waste dumps and in markets. It is a mobile morass of life that is unmanageable and incredible.

I formed a number of impressions on sustainable business, based on my short trip. First, as expected, CSR is still largely philanthropic, building on long and proud traditions from family empires such as the Tatas, and concepts such as Gandhi's trusteeship. Yet we do see government playing a very active role. On the one hand, it guarantees 100 days of work each year for each of India's 60 million rural households, which is amazing; but then it also requires all public companies to set aside 2% of net profits for CSR programmes, which is, in my view, misguided.

Now there is a proposal to extend this 'mandatory CSR' to private companies. This is essentially just an added tax and should not be called sustainable business. In my view, governments should focus on effective regulation of the issues that sustainable business is trying to address (biodiversity loss, labour conditions, climate change, transparency, etc.) rather than regulating sustainable business activities per se. Regulating sustainable business directly simply creates bureaucracy, stifles innovation and invites corruption.

A little world

A more positive trend is seen in the social entrepreneurs who are popping up all around India. Among the most inspiring is Anurag Gupta, the founder of A Little World (ALW), which provides hi-tech innovations for the rural poor in India, including micro-banking, lighting, media and sanitation. I had the chance to interview Gupta and he explains how biometrics and LED technology is being used to serve the poor.[34] I wrote up the story more fully in *The Age of Responsibility*, and Bimal Arora has also published it as a case study, but I will share the highlights here.

Essentially, Gupta has designed a system of rural banking that allows a mini-branch – comprising one woman working from her home – to use a

34 An interview with Anurag Gupta is available on the csrinternational channel on YouTube.

mobile phone and biometric scanner to take a customer's voice imprint, photograph and fingerprints, thus enabling them to open a basic bank account within two days. The phone holds up to 50,000 customer records and the mini-branch acts on behalf of the big national banks. This is no mean feat in a country where, according to Duvvuri Subbarao, Governor of the Reserve Bank of India, only 40% of the population have a bank account, 10% have life insurance coverage and less than 1% have non-life insurance. Furthermore, a mere 5.2% of Indian villages have a bank branch.

When I interviewed Gupta in 2010, four years after the launch of ALW, it was on the tipping point of serious scalability, with 11,000 micro-bank branches operating in all states of India and serving 5.5 million customers. Part of the reason for its success has been Gupta's relentless pursuit of efficiency and low-cost options, so that today each micro-bank branch costs less than $85 a month to run, and customers are only charged around 5 Rupees (10 cents) a month to use the bank's services. Gupta expected ALW to become the largest micro-banking system in the world within six months and – pending capital injection of around $60 million – to have set up in 150,000 locations in India over the next 2–3 years.

Believe it or not, Gupta is just getting started. He sees the branch network as an enabler to deliver all kinds of other essential services to India's rural poor. Already, he has innovated rechargeable LED light boxes to replace polluting and hazardous kerosene lamps, as well as enhancements to wood or cow-dung burning stoves, using a fan that halves cooking time and fuel requirements, and almost eliminates the poisonous smoke. Future innovations include water filters, bicycles, televisions, spectacles, radios, medicines and textbooks.

To make all these products affordable, Gupta plans to use a lease–purchase model, whereby costs are divided into weekly instalments for 6, 12, 18 or 24 months, depending on the product. So, for example, a rural villager pays just a few Rupees for one week's use of a rechargeable LED lamp. At the end of the week, he returns it and pays the next week's instalment for a fully charged LED light-box replacement. Using a similar approach, villages will also be able to buy communal toilets, with monthly instalments of just 20 Rupees (40 cents) for a period of 5 or 10 years.

ALW's vision remains ambitious: to touch a billion people through innovative technologies and alliances at the BOP for delivering multiple financial and other services at the lowest cost, through mainstream financial and other institutions. Having spent a little time with Gupta, I would not bet against his inspiring vision becoming a reality. ALW is a testimony to Gupta's creativity and to the power of using innovation – not only in technology, but also in partnerships and business models – to tackle some of society's most intractable social challenges.

Aligned to social enterprises such as these is the power of social activism. I came across a great example in the form of the aforementioned Karmayog.org, which has created an online platform that allows citizens to publicly report (and presumably embarrass) agents of corruption, such as officials asking them for bribes. It is also used to pool NGO resources during times of crisis, such as flooding, and to share CSR ratings that they have conducted on Indian companies.

The other positive sign from India is the trend of 'inclusive business', where bigger companies such as Tata are designing products and services to cater for poor customers at the BOP (which in India is just called 'the market'). The Tata Nano – a small eco-efficient car for $2,500 – is a case in point. What is even more encouraging is that these products are not being accepted without question. In one of my workshops, we had a raging debate about whether it is a good thing to have every Indian driving a car, Nano or not.

Greener is not always better

In 2011, my attention returned to India during a research project I did for Cambridge University in preparation for its *State of Sustainability Leadership* publication. One of the interviews I conducted was with Dr Emma Mawdsley, a Senior Lecturer in the Geography department who is particularly interested in how India's growing middle classes experience environmental change. She want to know what impacts these changes have on the poor and marginalised sections of society, and thus the implications for environmental politics in India. I asked her what evidence there is in India of rising public interest or concern with sustainability.

'In terms of public interest,' Mawdsley said,

poorer people in India have always been acutely aware of sustainability issues – not necessarily framed in an 'environmental'
way, but from the basis of trying to defend biomass-depend-
ent livelihoods (fishing, agro-forestry, small-scale agriculture,
etc.) In terms of more urban, educated populations, there has
long been a rather elite concern with wildlife and conservation, but often at the expense of poorer, rural people's access to
resources. Similarly, forest management has traditionally been
tilted towards managing for 'national' need and industry, rather
than local and subsistence needs. The 'ordinary middle classes'
have traditionally displayed little or no direct concern with sustainability. However this is changing to some extent, partly as
a result of education and the media, and partly due to growing environmental problems like air pollution. Such concern,
though, doesn't necessarily translate into socially just or progressive 'environmentalism'. While there are progressive organisations and individuals, in general middle-class environmental
attitudes tend to be rather anti-poor and authoritarian, blaming
unsustainability on a growing population and poverty rather
than also thinking about wealth and consumption.

This critical perspective is in evidence throughout Mawdsley's research.
For example, she questions the so-called environmental Kuznets Curve, a
model which argues that greater economic growth is positively correlated
with reduced pollution. She sums up the Kuznets hypothesis as follows:

> For many politicians, policy-makers and citizens in lower-in-
> come countries, the message is clear: developed countries went
> through their phase of dirty industrialisation, became wealthy
> and only then could afford to clean up. Developing countries
> such as India therefore argue that they have the right to industri-
> alise. They acknowledge that this may result in environmental
> degradation in the short term, but hold that these problems will
> eventually be addressed when the country has become wealthy.
> Moreover, according to technological optimists, 'leapfrogging'
> would help 'tunnel through' the worst phase of environmental
> degradation as industrialisation gets under way.

Mawdsley is sceptical about whether the environmental Kuznets Curve
constitutes a universally achievable – or indeed, desirable – model. She
points out that not all pollutants follow this pattern (e.g. CO_2 has continued to rise with economic growth) and that one reason the West has

followed the curve in some respects is simply the shift towards the service sector, which changes the geographical distribution of environmental degradation (i.e. polluting production moves 'offshore' to emerging markets). Furthermore, even if the environmental degradation associated with rising economic growth will eventually decline, it may be too late to reverse it completely.

Delhi's uneven development

Mawdsley recognises many of these tensions and debates in India's capital city, Delhi.

> There has been a huge drive towards the idea of making Delhi a 'world class city'. One element of this is the campaign for a so-called 'clean, green Delhi'. Initiatives include the massive project to retune all public transport to run on Compressed Natural Gas (CNG) and relocate polluting industries away from the centre. Some elements of air pollution have significantly improved. Other aspects of this drive include slum demolitions, and investment in new transport infrastructure (largely aimed at car drivers, and individuals who can afford to travel on the new Metro system). Branding events like the Commonwealth Games are meant to highlight Delhi's global status as a desirable city.

Mawdsley believes that, while pride in the city and support for its agenda are widespread, and some environmental benefits have certainly been achieved, we should not lose sight of the deeply regressive nature of much of the process.

> Slums and informal settlements have been demolished even when they have been legal, while malls and elite housing apartments have been allowed to be constructed illegally. Poorer people have lost their livelihoods as hawkers and street vendors, and small-scale manufacturing has been driven out of the city. The Delhi Government and the Supreme Court have actively sought to marginalise and exclude these populations from their vision of a new Delhi.

This pattern of social injustice is reflected in the way Delhi is tackling its air pollution problems. The policies have been critiqued for impacting badly on the poor (small polluting industries were relocated, for example, with little or no compensation for owners or workers); for only displacing pollution rather than reducing it (older non-CNG vehicles were sold to other city transport fleets, while the industries were relocated rather than reformed); and for representing a middle-class priority, rather than the most pressing need of the poor – clean, available water.

Looking at the issue of water, Mawdsley is similarly critical. Building on work by one of her PhD students, Yaffa Truelove, she draws attention to the fact that the poor are often criminalised for water theft (estimates indicate that as much as 50% of Delhi's water is unaccounted for in official meter readings and thus 'wasted'), while the authorities turn a blind eye to middle- and upper-class illegality. This often consists of the falsification of meter readings and technologies that can enhance water amounts extracted from already legal connections or from illegal/unregistered ground water sources (through tub and bore wells). Even the much-lauded Bhagidari system of citizen participation in governance suffers from a structural bias towards wealthier groups, since the scheme is limited to 'authorized colonies', and not the unauthorised colonies and slum areas in which the majority of Delhi's poorer inhabitants reside.

Mawdsley concludes that the main sustainability leadership lesson we can learn from India is not to lose sight of social justice in the pursuit of environmental improvement.

> The pursuit of profitable environmental policies, technologies and change is desirable if we are to move towards greater sustainability, but the political and social nature of their impacts must be recognised. 'Green' does not automatically mean 'good'. There will always be winners and losers, but there is a real danger in India at least that the drive towards greater sustainability will have some regressive social outcomes.

In light of my own experiences and research, I believe India is certainly a space to watch on sustainable business, and its progress is far from being a foregone conclusion. Whereas there is a sense of order and control in China's great transition, India is far more chaotic and unmanaged (or unmanageable?). It is almost as if there is a grand experiment in sustainable business – democratic, messy, ad-hoc Indian style, versus controlled, managed, sanctioned Chinese style. Which will prevail is a question for future historians. I think it's too soon to place bets on either. If we're lucky, both will succeed in their own way.

Part 4
Americas

16

Mythology and pathology
Unmasking the corporation
(Canada: 1992, 2008)

Meditations on business

My encounters with the Americas (North and South) began right at the beginning of my career, in fact when I was still a student. As I mentioned earlier, AIESEC's International Traineeship Exchange Programme arranged for me to work in the spring and summer of 1992 for the Royal Bank of Canada as a management trainee in the picturesque university town of Kingston, at the mouth of the St Lawrence River in Ontario. I spent a lot my spare time squirrelled away in the Kingston University library, which had search-access to university library databases across the whole of North America. The terms I was searching were not 'sustainable development' or 'social responsibility', but rather 'new age business' and 'holistic business'.

There were two breakthroughs in my search. The first was discovering a remarkable book called *Meditations on Business: Why Business as Usual Won't Work Anymore*. The author, John Dalla Costa, had been a seminarian who studied for the Roman Catholic priesthood for seven years, and then opted for a business career, becoming President and CEO of one of Canada's most successful advertising agencies. In the book, he argued for a 'new business paradigm' based on reciprocity – giving back to nature, to our people, and to our society, as much as we in business extract from them. 'Since these values are expansive', said Dalla Costa, 'extending beyond self-interest to embrace the broader needs of nature and humanity, I've called them spiritual.'

This kind of thinking really struck a chord with me, as did the themes explored more widely in the book, such as business and the quest for meaning; the dehumanizing vocabulary of business; the crumbling mythology of business; searching for new heroes; the feminine and masculine disequilibrium; the ennobling potential of business; expanding profit and human potential through art; and working towards a true balance sheet – all manna from heaven, as far as I was concerned. Happily, I had the opportunity to meet with Dalla Costa in Toronto at the end of July 1992. Among the sage advice that he gave me, and which I recorded in my diary, was: 'follow your heart', and 'try to infiltrate rather than confront the business community; hence, be cautious in the use of "new age" concepts and terminology'.

The second breakthrough in my research was finding a series of booklets under the title *New Age Business: Community Corporations That Work*, by Canadian academic Greg Macleod. These were case studies of what Macleod called 'community development companies', such as New Dawn Enterprises in Cape Breton, Canada (which Macleod founded) and Mondragón, a worker-led cooperative in Spain. I was especially fascinated by the Mondragón story. In a small town in the mountainous region of north-eastern Spain, and based on the teachings and initiatives of a Roman Catholic priest who taught the application of the gospel to business and the economy, one electric stove manufacturer with five employees established in 1955 grew into an 84,000 employee-strong worker-owned cooperative, which actively pursues a philosophy of local community development. I recommend reading the more recent reflections by Jeffrey Hollender, co-founder and former CEO of Seventh Generation and co-author of *The Responsibility Revolution*, who visited Mondragón in July 2011 and blogged on his observations.

What is a corporation?

I returned to Canada in 2008 as part of the *Top 50 Sustainability Books* research that I was conducting for Cambridge University. In Vancouver, I interviewed the legal academic and writer, Joel Bakan, famed for his 2004 book and documentary film, *The Corporation: The Pathological Pursuit of Profit and Power*, which has won 25 international awards and been translated into numerous languages.[35] For the rest of the chapter, I want to focus on insights from this interview, because I believe it gets to the heart of sustainable business – namely, changing the nature of the corporation itself. For an excellent overview of CSR in Canada in more conventional terms, I recommend Dermot Hikisch's chapter in *The World Guide to CSR*.

I began by asking Bakan about the evolution of the corporation as a legal structure. He explained that the original notion of the corporation was that the sovereign power would grant the status of 'corporation' to a group of business people in order to acquit themselves of some responsibility to create something that was in the public good. For example, an early corporation in London in the 17th century was created to transport water.

> So the idea was that you had a public interest that needed to be met and you would create a business entity that could meet it, but under very strict guidelines. The notion that this was simply about creating wealth for the owners of the company was alien. It was really about serving some public interest.

According to Bakan, the emergence of the corporation as a legal and financial tool – as opposed to a vehicle for the common good – is linked to industrialisation. With the creation of the railroads in Britain and the United States, which needed massive amounts of capital, the corporation starts to become a unit that is legally separate from the people who manage it; in other words, the owners are separate from the managers and the entity itself is separate from the owners. As a result, you can have an infinite number of owners. Their role is limited to providing capital and their gain is limited to making money, or having wealth created for them. But

---

35 My interview with Joel Bakan is available on the Cambridge University website www.cpsl.cam.ac.uk.

they are silent, they are invisible, they have nothing to do with running the company.

The challenge then became how you can ensure that the money is used for the investors' benefit, rather being than siphoned off by managers and used irresponsibly. As a result, the law developed the notion of the 'best interest' principle, which imposed a responsibility on managers always to act in the best interest of the shareholders. Bakan explained that:

> the law tended to see – and continues to see – the best interests of the shareholders as only one, and that is getting a financial return on the investors' investment. So what the 'best interest' principle has done is essentially impose upon managers, and the corporation as a whole, an obligation to put the creation of wealth above every other interest, including the interest of the environment, the interest of society.

Pathological pursuit of profits

This brings us to the central thesis of Bakan's book – the idea that a corporation is pathological. His argument depends on another aspect of corporate law, which is that it grants legal personhood to the corporation. Hence, the law creates a 'person' in the form of a corporation and then it requires the person always to act within its own self-interest. This is where Bakan's analogy becomes clear.

> If we have a person who is only able to act in his or her own self-interest, in a human being, we generally call that person a psychopath. That is, in a way, the diagnostic definition of what a psychopath is: a person who is unable to understand – or be empathetic towards or be concerned about – other people's interests.

I wondered how Bakan's view squared with the fact that companies, by the very nature of what they do, provide goods and services to meet people's needs. Not only that, but we don't see major corporations practising wholesale abuse of their employees and other stakeholders any more, at least not without being named and shamed if they do. Bakan was not persuaded.

> A company has to be sensitive to the context in which it oper-
> ates, just as a psychopath does. In your own self-interest you
> have to serve the interests of those around you to some degree,
> otherwise they'll either lock you up, or turn away from you
> and have nothing to do with you. We often hear, for example,
> about the charm of the psychopath. Sometimes the most charm-
> ing people in our society are also psychopathic; they use their
> charm in order to attain their own self-interests.
>
> The concern about other people's interests must be strategic.
> Legally it has to be strategic in terms of serving the self-interest
> of the company.

Hence, in the case where serving consumers' best interests is not in the
best interests of the company – Bakan uses the example of Coca-Cola marketing unhealthy products – the company nevertheless has an incentive:

> to propagate the view that it is serving other people's interests
> when it may not be doing so; to create and market products that
> may actually be very harmful to people, but convey a sense that
> they're not harmful, and that in fact people should like them.

Social responsibility is an oxymoron

So what does this say about sustainable business? Bakan is a CSR
sceptic.

> The so-called social responsibility that we hear about is a bit of
> an oxymoron, because legally a corporation can't really have a
> responsibility to society, unless it can justify the presence of such
> a responsibility as somehow ultimately serving its own interests
> in creating wealth. My scepticism about social responsibility is
> really driven by my sense that there's a better alternative than
> social responsibility and that alternative is democratic govern-
> ment. I believe we have a better option in the form of not try-
> ing to persuade companies – pleading with them to be socially
> responsible – but just demanding that they be so through laws,
> through regulation.
>
> My concern is that increasingly we're living in a rhetorical
> and ideological world where people are putting their energies
> into social responsibility in a way that suggests they've given

up on democratic regulation. The fundamental difficulty with
social responsibility remains the fact that we haven't changed
the nature of the corporation. It is – and continues to be – patho-
logically constituted, in the sense that it still must put its own
interests above all others. And that makes it a very unstable kind
of institution for achieving public goals, and for self-regulating.

You can create many environmental conditions around a psychopathic human being that are going to make him or her less
psychopathic. You can monitor their activity. You can create
incentives for them to be responsible and to be kind and to not
engage in mass murder, or whatever other things psychopaths
might do. You can do all of that, but isn't it a better alternative
to create laws that say 'Actually, you're not allowed to murder,
you're not allowed to steal, you're not allowed to exploit, and if
you do we're going to punish you.' That seems to me to be more
effective than looking at the psychopath and saying 'Oh, but we
should respect that psychopath's autonomy, and just try to educate them and prod them and push them a little bit, and hope
that we can make them see that it's in their best interests not to
engage in those type of behaviours'.

Bakan is not alone in his argument. He quotes Noam Chomsky as saying, 'Yes, sure, you can create various incentives to make a tyrant more
benevolent, but isn't it better to do away with tyranny?' Pressing home
the point, Bakan observes that there were some slave owners who treated
their slaves better than other slave owners,

> but wouldn't it be better to do away with the institution of slav-
> ery, than to rely on slave owners to be nice? It's better, I think,
> to change the nature of the institution and do away with it alto-
> gether, rather than simply tweaking around the edges.

I agree, but I wanted to know if Bakan was suggesting doing away with
sustainable business practices altogether. After all, isn't there an argument that suggests that sustainable business through the ages has been
a lead-indicator for legislation? In other words, companies have tended
to go ahead of the law (as a result of stakeholder pressure or some other
reason) and then governments catch up and turn the new norms into legislation. Bakan responded:

> My argument is not that we should get rid of social responsibil-
> ity. We should continue trying to persuade corporations, whether

through investor markets or consumer boycotts or through generating information, and through having NGOs monitor what corporations do. We should continue all of that, because with human behaviour and corporate behaviour, legal restrictions are not enough. You have to create a culture where people, whether as individuals or as corporate actors, actually want to comply with various social norms. So I don't see a difficulty with continuing to push the social responsibility concept. Where I have difficulty is seeing that push and that pressure as being an alternative to government regulation. I see social responsibility and government regulation as a hand-in-hand proposition.

Legal nature of the corporation

Many critics of Bakan's book would say that he's really overstating the point. Are companies really comparable to tyrants or psychopaths? We have companies operating all around the world that people support; at the very least, we buy their products. Surely, we see them as benevolent institutions? I asked Bakan whether the negative examples aren't the exceptions rather than the rule. In reply, he said:

> The case I'm making is not a case against this or that company. The case I'm making is a case against an institution that is legally set up in a particular way. And I don't think anybody has criticised me for overstating the legal structural nature of the corporation. I think everybody would agree with how I describe it; not necessarily as a psychopath, but in terms of the primacy of wealth creation. My point is that, given that structural nature, what you've created is a potentially (not always, manifest, but a potentially) very dangerous institution. And I've provided examples in my book of places and times and instances where those dangers became manifest. At other times those dangers may be less manifest, and some companies may be run differently than other companies.

One of the points Bakan stressed to me was that the human factor is important.

I don't believe that the people who run corporations are necessarily worse than the people who run many other kinds of institutions, whether it's churches or unions, or whatever. I think you have some nasty people and you have some good people. And I do believe that corporations will have different cultures, and will act differently in part dependent upon the types of men and women who are running those corporations. Nevertheless, it remains the case that even the best companies – and that's why I use British Petroleum as an example in my book, because their primary imperative is to create wealth for their shareholders – they will do some bad things.

I think Bakan's conclusion sums up his message quite nicely. He says:

My book is really a caution. It's not saying every company in the world is wreaking havoc. It's not saying that companies aren't providing important and useful services. It's not saying any of that. What it's saying is that in certain conditions, given the nature of this institution, it can act in pretty dangerous ways, and many of those conditions are currently in place, and many of those dangerous behaviours are currently manifest. We don't often hear about them, because the media isn't that good necessarily at revealing how dangerous they are.

Despite's Bakan's central thesis about the pathological nature of corporations, he remains optimistic.

I suppose what gives me the most hope is that we're moving in the right direction; my sense that there is a palpable desire among people on the ground. It is created in part by a sense of need and a sense that their lives are degrading – as the income and wealth gap widens and as the rich get richer, and the poor get poorer; as people see environmental effects actually happening; as the media turns onto this. I think that there is a sense among people that there are problems that need to be dealt with; that we can't simply proceed with business as usual. There's a broadening public consciousness around these issues. So that palpable sense that things need to be different is probably is what causes me the greatest optimism.

17

Plantations and houses
The lessons of shared responsibility
(Guatemala, Mexico: 2007, 2008, 2009, 2010)

A new CSR pyramid

Travelling to a new country, and soaking up the sights and sounds of a different culture, gives me a real high. It has something to do with discovering the unexpected, observing the world with senses on high alert and mentally registering similarities and differences.

This is how I felt when I visited Guatemala in 2007. I am always inspired by the stories I hear, such as those of my Antigua guide, who escaped into exile in the United States at the age of 12. The aesthetics of a place make a big impression, such as the luminous craft markets and the earthquake-crumbled ruins of convents and cathedrals in Antigua.

In Guatemala, I felt strangely at home. I put that down to the 'developing worldliness' of the place – its colourful, jumbled, hustling, diesel-smoke belching, smiling friendliness. Of course, the uniqueness of the country is also invigorating, especially the traditional dress of the women, and the rich Mayan history, which happily still shines through in the people, art and architecture.

In some senses, my CSR quest tour started back in December 2007, on this trip to Guatemala. The main purpose of the visit was for Dirk Matten and me to launch *The A to Z of Corporate Social Responsibility* at the Inter-American Development Bank (IADB) annual conference on CSR. That was when the seed of the idea was planted – while talking to Dirk over a glass of celebratory champagne in the hotel bar late one night.

One of the greatest insights for me had come after visiting a local sugar plantation. The company had prepared a presentation on its approach to CSR, and imagine my delight when I saw that it also had a CSR pyramid! The interesting thing, however, was that it was not Carroll's CSR pyramid or a Prahalad and Hart's BOP pyramid. Economic responsibility was still at the base of the pyramid, but the next most important responsibility was to the families of its employees. The third tier was community responsibility and, rather intriguingly, the apex of the pyramid was 'engagement in responsible national policy development'.

Was that company right and others wrong? Of course, they were both right. That is the beauty of 'glocality'. It is not an 'either–or' mentality, but a 'both–and' approach. The other interesting observation is that they had formed a cooperative of farms in order to tackle CSR. Individually, they were too small to justify a sustainable business programme, but collectively, it made sense. This is one of the ways that SMEs can address sustainable business, through pooling their resources and collaborating.

I gained more insights into sustainable business and SMEs when I visited Mexico in 2008, at the invitation of Jorge Reyes, Director of the IDEARSE Centre at Anahuac University, which is doing some excellent work on the subject.[36] In 2009, I was invited back to deliver the keynote address at its 7th International CSR Conference, and again in 2010 to run a workshop, so I got to know a little bit about its research programme, which I will try to summarise briefly here.

In response to a government-sponsored programme aimed at SME growth acceleration, IDEARSE put together an approach for supporting growth of the businesses through the implementation of a sustainable business administration model that would develop competitive advantages for the companies. Built into its business training programme, therefore, were six elements for SME development: self-regulation, stakeholders, human rights, environment, labour and social/community impact. Working with the supply chains of big brands such as Sony, Coca-Cola and CEMEX, IDEARSE have taken more than 70 SMEs through the programme, with

---

36 An interview with Jorge Reyes is available on the csrinternational channel on YouTube.

impressive results. On average across the six sustainable business dimensions, the SMEs improved from a score of 23% to 43%, while simultaneously showing average annual sales growth of 30%.

Heiligendamm Dialogue Process

In 2008, I returned to Mexico City at the invitation of the Heiligendamm Dialogue Process, which was meeting to discuss the major challenges in the world economy – including CSR – that had been identified at the Heiligendamm Summit in 2007. If you're wondering what the Heiligendamm Dialogue Process is, you're not alone. I had never heard of it until I got the invitation. In fact, it is probably the closest thing we have to a statement by the world's regional superpowers on how sustainable business fits into the bigger picture of global development. Here's how it is described:

> The leaders of the G8 and the G5 countries (Brazil, China, India, Mexico and South Africa) discussed the major challenges that have arisen in the world economy at the Heiligendamm Summit in 2007. They recognised the interdependence of their economies and the importance of an active exchange on the framework conditions of a globalised and competitive world economy. They decided to embark on a high-level, structured dialogue on specific challenges which was subsequently referred to as the Heiligendamm Dialogue Process (HDP).

And what does that have to do with sustainable business? Well, one of the four main topics for the Dialogue Process, which is hosted by the OECD, is 'promoting cross-border investment to our mutual benefit including the encouragement of responsible business conduct'.

A lengthier document on 'Growth and Responsibility In The World Economy', issued as a G8 Summit Heiligendamm Declaration on 7 June 2007, makes fascinating reading. Not least because, according to the G8, the world outlook at the time was all sunshine and roses. 'We note,' they said, 'that the world economy is in good condition.' How quickly the world can change! Beyond this piece of trivia, there is some very revealing content on sustainable business and broader socioeconomic and environmental trends. I find it interesting because this north–south group is at the fulcrum on which the future is being shaped. Below, I have summarised some of the main points from the Declaration:

1. *G8 agenda for global growth and stability.* This opening section makes it clear that the developed world's obsession with economic growth as the solution to social and environmental challenges continues. What is interesting (and different), however, is that there is now more acknowledgement about the importance of stability in financial markets and the distribution of the benefits of globalisation

2. *Systemic stability and transparency.* Reading this section produces a sense of déjà vu and shows that our current financial crisis did not arise from a vacuum or without the knowledge of the superpowers. In relation to global financial markets, especially hedge funds, they refer to 'potential systemic and operational risks' and 'the need to be vigilant'. I guess no one (or at least no one that mattered) was really listening

3. *Freedom of investment.* This is the familiar 'free capital flow' mantra, acknowledging that 'supporting protectionism would result in a loss of prosperity'. I cannot help wondering how this can be reconciled with the continued protectionism of EU agriculture and US fossil fuels

4. *The social dimension of globalisation.* The fact that this is even being acknowledged could be construed as progress. The emphasis is on 'promoting and developing social standards', such as the International Labour Organization (ILO) Tripartite Declaration, OECD Guidelines for Multinationals and the UN Global Compact

5. *Strengthening the principles of CSR.* In addition to emphasising and supporting the above-mentioned social standards, there is reference to 'the voluntary approach of CSR', encouraging 'the transparency of private companies' performance with respect to CSR' and 'clarification of the numerous standards and principles issued in this area'. Given that this is the main section on CSR, it is quite weak and disappointing, with a fairly limited conception of CSR

6. *Promoting and protecting innovation.* This section hints at technology transfer, but is far more about protecting intellectual

property (patents), claiming that 'trade in pirated and counterfeit goods threatens health, safety and security of consumers worldwide, particularly in poorer countries'. No guessing which country wrote this section

7. *Climate and energy.* This forms the bulk of the paper, focusing on energy security, energy efficiency and climate change. Although there are no revelations, it is quite a good summary of the position of the world on these issues, and how it has responded to date. For example, it talks about the global energy security principles, the post-Kyoto deal, deforestation, biodiversity, sustainable buildings, transportation, industry, power generation and energy diversification

8. *Responsibility for raw materials.* This focuses on transparency and 'sustainable growth' in the mining sector, mentioning programmes such as the Extractive Industries Transparency Initiative (EITI), the OECD Risk Awareness Tool for MNEs (multinational enterprises) in Weak Governance Zones, and the Diamond Development Initiative

9. *Corruption.* This final section is simply a restatement of commitment, referring to existing initiatives such as the UN Convention against Corruption and the OECD Anti-Bribery Convention

If this Declaration is anything to go by, at least the growth and globalisation debate seems to be getting more sophisticated, implicitly acknowledging that there is such a thing as 'uneconomic' growth and globalisation which does not share its benefits fairly; also that issues like poverty and climate change are critical to long-term economic prosperity.

My overall impression from the Heiligendamm Dialogue Process so far is that the battle to have sustainable business acknowledged as part of the social and environmental suite of solutions has been won, but the war to see CSR as a more holistic, embedded and strategic concept is in danger of being lost.

Sharing resources in times of stress

Beyond the SME agenda and the Heiligendamm Dialogue Process, Mexico has many other CSR insights to offer, which are expertly reported by Leonardo J. Cárdenas, Chair of the Graduate Program on CSR at Universidad Regiomontana in *The World Guide to CSR*. He observes that Mexico has a very long tradition of social responsibility, which can be tracked back to before America was 'discovered' when the indigenous cultures still dominated the region. For example, the Raramori, who still live in the mountains of northern Mexico in the state of Chihuahua, use the expression *korima*, which means 'to share'. Importantly, *korima* is not philanthropic in the sense of sharing surplus wealth, but is the practice of sharing resources in times of stress.

Cárdenas points out that in the middle of the 20th century, before social security was part of labour law in Mexico, one of Mexico's largest and oldest breweries, Cervecería Cuauhtémoc Moctezuma (CCM), located in Monterrey, voluntarily started providing health services to its employees and their families, including access to medicine, dentists, optometrists and various medical services (X-ray, surgery, etc.). Furthermore, CCM provided its employees and families with sporting, cultural and educational facilities such as libraries and theatres.

In the 1980s and 1990s, CSR in Mexico was often in response to crises, as several natural disasters hit the country. For example, in 1985, a large earthquake hit Mexico City. More than 10,000 people were killed and more than 30,000 injured. In response, hundreds of construction companies provided equipment and labour to help remove debris and rescue trapped people. Privately owned also hospitals opened their doors to anyone in need.

Similarly, in 1990, when a flood hit the state of Chihuahua and hundreds of families lost all their material possessions, industry owners agreed to be charged with a special tax for one year to help repair damaged areas and provide new shelter for those families. This scheme was so successful that industry leaders asked for the tax to become permanent and managed by an independent trust fund. This gave birth to FECHAC (Federation of the Chihuahuan Industry), an NGO supported by more than 38,000 industries that make voluntarily annual contributions.

One thing I learned from my visits was that in terms of biodiversity Mexico is one of the ten richest countries in the world. According to Achim Steiner, Executive Director of UNEP:

> Mexico is at the crossroads of the 'green economy' politically, physically and practically. Firstly it still has many challenges, from high air pollution in cities and dependence on fossil fuels to land degradation and the need to fight poverty. But Mexico is also emerging as one among a group of developing economies who are bringing much-needed leadership to the need for a new, comprehensive and decisive climate treaty.

How CEMEX empowers the poor

Another inspiration from Mexico is the case study of CEMEX, which has been expertly summarized by the consultancy Article 13. They note that the Mexican-based construction materials company has grown substantially since it began operations in 1906. CEMEX now operates in more than 50 countries and has trade relationships with over 100. Even though CEMEX's geographic reach provides it with a sizeable potential customer base, the company has remained committed to growing its home market through development of the Patrimonio Hoy (PH) housing project.

Concerned over high levels of homelessness in Mexico, which affects up to 20 million people, CEMEX set out to help Mexican families obtain this basic human right. By doing so it has been able to align its values and commercial objectives with the needs of communities. In 1998 CEMEX sent a team into the low-income community of Mela Colorado, home to some 90,000 people. The team spent the next 18 months there, getting an appreciation of the barriers preventing families from obtaining their own home.

Typically, low-income families build their own homes, working on them in the little spare time they have. This is made more difficult as they often have little experience in construction, leading to lower quality, inefficient dwellings and placing the families at the mercy of retailers who exploit their lack of knowledge. The PH project uses a simple but innovative financing system to help provide access to building materials and advice. Families group together to self-finance the projects and commit to save for ten weeks. To encourage high repayment rates all members must make their weekly contribution, otherwise all parties lose access to the programme.

Materials are provided during the second phase, once the group has demonstrated a commitment to their savings activities. In addition to the materials, CEMEX also provides warehousing facilities, access to its network of certified distributors and technical advice, including architectural advice tailored to their needs.

The social capital of the community is considered collateral enough and a 99% repayment rate would indicate that this is indeed the case. The programme has provided homes at 70% of the former cost and at less than one-third of the usual time. It develops competencies and promotes a sense of independence and family unity. In an unexpected outcome it has also contributed to economic development by fostering small business – more than 15% of families who have built a spare room use it to run a small business.

Article 13 concludes that, so far, the programme has helped more than 165,000 low-income families and is expected to expand to two million families throughout Mexico. In addition, the programme has already spread to Colombia, Venezuela, Nicaragua and Costa Rica, showing that it is possible to grow a business and encourage community development at the same time.

Emergence and convergence
Birth of a new capitalism
(United States: 2002, 2004, 2008, 2010)

Stakeholders are the enemy

The first time I visited the United States was in 1994 while I was a strategy analyst for Capgemini. I have returned numerous times, mostly on work-related trips – in 2002 to conduct a KPMG sustainability audit; in 2004 to attend the Global Mind Change Forum of the World Business Academy; in 2008 as part of my Cambridge University research for the *Top 50 Sustainability Books*; and in 2010 as part of my 2010 CSR quest world tour, where I was generously hosted by Josetta McLaughlin of Roosevelt University in Chicago, and also lectured to MBAs at Presidio Graduate School in San Francisco.

As you can imagine, there is a lot to say, so I have split my American insights into two chapters. To begin with, I touch on some of my own experiences and reflections and highlight some findings from the excellent chapter by Audra Jones in *The World Guide to CSR*. Then, I talk about my encounters with great sustainability luminaries like Amory Lovins, Herman Daly, Jeffrey Sachs, Joseph Stiglitz and Stuart Hart.

Let me start with some anecdotes. In 2002, I visited the United States as part of a safety, health and environmental governance audit on a chemical company. I was still Director of Sustainability Services at KPMG at the time and we visited facilities in five countries – South Africa, Germany, Netherlands, Italy and the United States. One of the things we always asked was for the company's records of legal non-compliances, including fines and penalties. This was a relatively straightforward matter in all the countries but one – the United States.

First, it had not just a few but thousands of non-compliances, which probably said more about the country's onerous legal requirements than the company's negligence. For instance, when we asked to see its air pollution permit documentation, we were directed to an entire bookshelf of lever-arch files. Second, staff did not know what liability these non-compliances represented, because they were in constant negotiation with the government over their exact settlement amount. This was, apparently, allowed under the Federal Sentencing Guidelines, which gives some flexibility to companies on legal sanctions if they can demonstrate due diligence; for example, by having an environmental management system in place, or conducting safety risk assessments.

We were not happy, but conceded the point and tried a different tack, asking to see the board meeting minutes for the past 12 months. We wanted to check the extent to which sustainability issues were being discussed at a top management level. Imagine our surprise when we were told that the company did not keep board minutes, for fear that these might be leaked to the public and so expose the company to the risk of being sued.

At this point, I am sure our heads were in our hands. So we tried again, enquiring whether the company mitigated against that sort of public risk through stakeholder engagement. The word *stakeholder* seemed to cause a little confusion. 'You know, interested and affected parties, the community, NGOs', I explained helpfully. Ah yes, the Managing Director understood perfectly now, and did not hesitate with his reply, spoken between gritted teeth, saying: 'NGOs are not stakeholders, they are the enemy!' It would be funny if it was not true.

Of course, I am in no way implying that this company is indicative of the state of sustainable business practice throughout the United States, where many of the finest sustainable business institutions and best case studies are found. One group that particularly inspired me in the early part of my career was the World Business Academy, founded by the futures researcher, Willis Harman, with the aim of achieving a 'global mind shift' by raising the consciousness of business. In fact, I ended up establishing a South African chapter for the organisation back in 1994, along with a chapter for the equally pioneering Institute for Ecological Economics.

Regulation-enabled CSR

The result of the tireless work of these and many other organisations is that there is a strong tradition of CSR and sustainable business in the United States today, albeit within a tough market environment. Audra Jones, Americas Director for the International Business Leaders Forum (IBLF) explores this in her chapter in *The World Guide to CSR*. She argues that, although CSR evolved in the first part of the 20th century, led by a few visionary business leaders such as Rockefeller, Carnegie, Ford, and Hewlett and Packard, the growth of CSR in the United States as a business imperative is due to regulation.

Beginning in the late 1960s and early 1970s, the US government established regulatory agencies that shaped much of the CSR benchmarks guiding business operations. For example, the OSHA (Occupational Safety and Health Administration), EEOC (Equal Employment Opportunity Commission), CPSC (Consumer Product Safety Commission) and EPA (Environmental Protection Agency) created standards and legislation for responsible corporate business practices, which have become thresholds for good commercial behaviour. Recent examples of industry-specific and sector-wide regulation include the Community Reinvestment Act in the banking sector, the Clean Air Act and, after Enron's collapse, the Public Company Accounting Reform and Investor Protection Act.

Corporate philanthropy also accelerated due to regulation. The formalized efforts of philanthropy in the early part of the 20th century by the Rockefellers and Carnegies fostered the first regulatory response to CSR in the form of tax-breaks to corporations making charitable contributions to non-profit organisations. Without that incentive, many corporations would not have engaged in philanthropy. This remains true in parts of the developing world where no such tax incentive exists.

Jones believes that, in the last 20 years, there has been a shift in CSR from regulatory compliance towards harnessing the potential for sustainable business to contribute to reputation, public policy and core business practices. This evolution has been encouraged by pressures on business from new stakeholders, such as institutional investors creating SRI funds.

The Dow Jones Sustainability Indexes were launched in 1999 as the first global indexes tracking the financial performance of the leading sustainability-driven companies worldwide. In the 1990s, many US corporations also began participating in voluntary principles such as the GRI. More recently consumers have expectations of business and – as American business integrates CSR into core business – there has been increased pressure on defining the value of corporate investment in sustainable business.

I have written extensively in my other books about many of these US-based initiatives, as well as the sustainable business case studies that have instructed and inspired us over the years – from the pioneering voices of Rockefeller, Carnegie, Rachel Carson and Ralph Nader to the seminal academic work of Archie Carroll, Ed Freeman, Stuart Hart and C.K. Prahalad. I have profiled the corporate fiascos of Exxon, Enron, McDonald's and Nike, and business visionaries such as Ben & Jerry's, Patagonia, Interface and Seventh Generation. Rather than repeat these here, for readers who are interested in this historical perspective, I recommend two of my books in particular – *Landmarks for Sustainability* and *The Age of Responsibility*.

Capitalism at the crossroads

For this rest of chapter, I want to share some insights from the American interviews I conducted for *The Top 50 Sustainability Books*, beginning with Stuart Hart, who perfectly captures the US entrepreneurial spirit in his thinking on sustainable business. Reflecting on his 30-year journey, he recalls that his 'Beyond greening' article in the *Harvard Business Review* in 1997 was really the turning point. By the time his 'Fortune at the bottom of the pyramid' piece with C.K. Prahalad came out in *Strategy and Business* in 2002, he had concluded in his typically understated way that 'there's a potential for some impact'.

Hart's thinking is synthesised in his book *Capitalism at the Crossroads*, and I was curious to know why he states his case in terms of capitalism, rather than at the level of sustainable business. He explained:

If you look at how capitalism evolved in the 19th century, it evolved in a very different direction than imagined by the progenitors of the concept – the classical economists in the 18th century. Karl Polanyi in The Great Transformation has referred to it as the dis-embedding of the economy. It produced a whole new organisational form called the large corporation, which solved a lot of problems and a lot of good came from that, but we haven't resolved the dark side of 19th century industrial capitalism.

I'm absolutely convinced that we're in the midst of the next transformation, just like capitalism transformed in a fundamental way between 1850 and 1890 – only it's from the 19th-century form of industrial capitalism to a sustainable form of capitalism that actually has the potential to solve social and environmental problems; to create wealth for everyone in the world and to take us more quickly to the next generation of potentially clean and sustainable technology.

Interestingly, unlike many other authors who have written on capitalism, such as Naomi Klein, Hart focuses on the positive role that business can play. I asked him if that is justified. 'I'm a pragmatist,' he replied,

In the sense that I look around and I try to assess where are the leverage points for change to occur most rapidly. We're headed rapidly for the cliff, so to speak. But there is also great potential to change quickly. What makes the world of commerce interesting in my mind is its ability to creatively destroy itself, to fall back on Joseph Schumpeter's term. We have a mechanism through which this change could unfold at the rate that it needs to in order to move us towards a sustainable world before it's too late.

That all sounds good, but aren't big corporations locked into incremental change? 'Schumpeter wasn't terribly optimistic about incumbent corporations' ability to engage in creative destruction', conceded Hart.

But what he bet on was the capitalist system – small entrants; new firms that would come in and creatively destroy the positions of incumbents. We probably shouldn't care very much whether large companies are able to do it to themselves or whether another large company from another industry does it, or whether it's a small start-up or an entrepreneur. The impor-

tant thing is the rate of acceleration of this whole process – that's
what we need to ramp up in whatever form it takes.

I spoke to Hart about the BOP model for doing business with the poor.
In response to criticisms of the model – that it simply turns the developing world's population into environmentally destructive consumers,
rather than lifting them out of poverty or introducing sustainable solutions – Hart talked excitedly about the evolving BOP 2.0 concept. 'That's
why the confluence of this idea of disruptive clean technology or green
technology innovation at the base of the pyramid is so important. I refer
to it as the great convergence', he said.

> It's almost like there are these two worlds. There is the clean-
> tech world – with people who have been very tech focused, very
> North American or Western European, very environmental, but
> haven't really looked at developing country issues, or poverty,
> or imaginative commercialisation strategies. But then there are
> the BOP people, who are much more business model-oriented,
> distribution oriented, with a focus on poverty alleviation, but
> they haven't thought much about the environment. And so the
> real challenge becomes: how do we begin to converge those two
> agendas in a fundamental way?

Hart, together with Ted London, has now pulled together this BOP 2.0
thinking in a book called *Next Generation Strategies for the Base of the
Pyramid*. He told me that the key to this new way of doing business is
co-creation.

> You have to change your mind-set and think: we could be
> partners and colleagues; we could work together to develop a
> business that combine the best of both; we could bring incred-
> ible next generation, clean technology, but there's a lot of local
> knowledge and if we combine those together, imagine what sort
> of interesting business we could create that could make a better
> way to live.

Our common wealth

Another person I interviewed, and who shares a similarly upbeat view of our potential to solve the problems we face, is Jeffrey Sachs, author of *The End of Poverty* and *Common Wealth*. He began by declaring that, contrary to popular opinion, 'If you take the big picture of development, it's been a resounding success against any backdrop of longer human history.' Elaborating, he said:

> For the vast proportion of human history, societies were economically stagnant and the overwhelming majority was living at the edge of survival. And during the last 50 years, almost all the world has gotten off of the edge of survival – and some quite far from the edge, into at least middle-income, if not high-income status. That counts in my view, because that's longevity; that's children not dying in infancy, or in childhood; it's healthier lives; it's greater opportunities – so it's worth accomplishing. Now the irony is that about a sixth of the world's population is still stuck in extreme poverty, but with the tools to end that extreme poverty at hand. We have the makings of the completion of what has been a very broad success of economic development, bringing it to those remaining parts of the world that have not yet experienced the sustained economic take-off. It can be accomplished.

Sachs is less optimistic than Hart about the role of business in solving the poverty dilemma.

> I love markets wherever they work, but I spend a tremendous amount of time also emphasising that markets don't work for everything. For cell phones, yes, you may be able to reach 40% penetration in Africa, and it's phenomenal; it's world-changing. But 40% penetration for immunisations won't do it. You might say that's a great success on a market basis, but if you leave 60% of the population unimmunised you've got epidemics and mass death. The same thing applies with bed nets. Of course we could sell bed nets to 25% of the population, but you will not control malaria that way. So we've got to get the model right. Business has scalability, information and management systems and it holds the technology. But if there's no market at the end for the public good that we need, then at a minimum we need a public–private partnership, where business does what it does,

but government makes the market, or provides the financing to get the job done.

In a futile attempt to dampen Sachs's optimism, I pointed out the unsustainability of Western lifestyles, which this rapidly emerging developing world is clamouring to replicate. Sachs conceded that, 'If we're not sustainable now, how would we be if the world economy were not seventy trillion, but two hundred and eighty trillion, because everyone's caught up? The answer is impossible.' He sees two contrasting views on the dilemma: one, that development has to stop – the rich have to become poorer so that the poorer can catch up – and two, that we have to make a global transition to sustainable technologies. Sachs told me:

> That's where I put my cards and my bet. That there are technologies that can do this. But I've argued in *Common Wealth that you* can't leave technological transformation to market forces alone. Of course, markets play a role, but technology is also a public good. With the environmental challenges we have two market failures: one is the mismanagement of the commons, like the greenhouse gases (what Nick Stern has called the greatest market failure in world history); and the second is the management of technological change, which I would argue, because of the public goods nature of knowledge, is itself intrinsically a public–private policy challenge. It can't be left to the markets alone. So I think we have those two transitions – manage the commons and manage knowledge and technology transformation.

Clearly (and happily), I had failed to dampen Sach's indomitable spirit, and he concluded by declaring:

> Every time I turn around – whether it's in India, whether it's in China and Malaysia, Tanzania – there's no shortage of reasons for optimism. What is the hardest part of all is managing change and having the understanding of how crucial and how fruitful cooperation can be right now. The problem isn't our lack of tools; the problem is our ability to manage all these wonderfully powerful tools that we have to a human effect. We have a challenge of management and understanding, of learning and cooperation. We're going to solve these problems. Extreme poverty will end by the year 2025. That's what I said in *The End of Poverty* and I think that's what's going to happen.

19
Globalisation and innovation
Redefining growth and progress
(United States, 2008)

How to tame globalisation

In this chapter, I continue my journey through the intellectual heartland of America's sustainability thought leaders. Let me begin with Nobel Prize winner in Economic Sciences and former World Bank Senior Vice-President and Chief Economist, Joseph Stiglitz. I wanted to know his views on globalisation, which is a theme running through many of his books. It is clear that Stiglitz is sympathetic to the critics of globalisation. As he puts it, 'We have learned how to temper capitalism – how to make the market economy work in the advancing industrial countries for most citizens, or at least we have until recently – but we haven't learned how to temper globalisation.'

The problem with globalisation, according to Stiglitz, is not with the concept or the trend itself, but with:

> the way globalisation was managed, which was disadvantageous to developing countries; even disadvantageous to many people in developed countries. One of the paradoxes was that, while in principle everybody was supposed to be better off as a result of globalisation, and therefore everybody ought to be supporting globalisation, in practice the opposition to globalisation rose

from both the north and the south. It had unified so much of the world against it because of the way it was managed. There were some winners but there were a lot more losers.

Stiglitz acknowledges that 'one of the concerns is that some special interests – corporate interests – have been able to do within the international agenda what they could not do within the domestic agenda'. For instance, America now has good environmental regulations for air and water.

> Many people in the corporate sector resisted the introduction of these but we now realise that they've made a tremendous difference to our standard of living – we can breathe the air, we can drink the water; it's made a big difference, and there's almost universal support. But what was put into international agreements like NAFTA[37] undermined some of these environmental safeguards. They were almost designed to make it more difficult to have good environmental regulations. And so in a sense they were undermining the democratic process.

I wondered if he felt the American position on climate change was part of this distortion of international standards by special interests. 'Climate change is a global issue and will only be solved globally,' Stiglitz replied.

> And so more than any other issue, it's brought to the fore that we share one planet and we have to work together. It can't be that the United States or Europe push their view of what has to be done on the rest on the countries. They won't accept it. The position under the Kyoto Protocol was that those who polluted more got to pollute more in the future. That doesn't make any sense. So I think it's going to take a very big change in mind-set to go from where we are to where we will have to be, namely an agreement to reduce emissions by some 80% in advanced industrial countries. The minimal acceptable framework is equal emissions per capita and I don't think the United States and the European Union are yet ready to accept that principle. But that's the only one that I think the developing countries will accept; it's a basic principle of sharing the burden of saving the planet.

37 North American Free Trade Agreement.

I asked Stiglitz whether he was optimistic about the future. He answered that:

> the most exciting developments are the result of the efforts of civil society to bring to the attention of everybody what has been going on. Before the Seattle riots, no one really understood what was going on. There was an enthusiasm that was not tempered by reality. As people started looking at what happened at the IMF and World Bank – failures of regulation of the global financial markets – there was a widespread recognition that something has not worked well. So understanding there is a problem is necessary before you're going to change.
>
> On the other hand there are some people who benefit from the system as it works today and they are going to make it difficult to make the changes that we have to make. For example, I don't think America or the developing countries benefit from our cotton subsidies. Our taxpayers pay and the developing countries are worse off. The same is true with our corn-based ethanol subsidies and our tariffs on imported sugar-based ethanol from Brazil. About 25,000 cotton farmers in the United States and a couple of companies are doing well from corn-based ethanol. But the number of losers is so much greater than the number of those who gain.
>
> So, overall there are some big opportunities for gains to both the developed and developing countries, but these special interests play an important role. That's why in some sense the problems have to do with deficiencies in democracies in the advanced industrial countries – corruption in the advanced industrial countries; corruption through campaign contributions. There's a growing awareness in the United States about the nature of that corruption. The question is, will we be able to do something about it?

Beyond uneconomic growth

Another former World Bank economist whom I interviewed was Herman Daly, the legendary author of books like *Steady-State Economics*, *For the Common Good* and *Beyond Growth*. For most of his career, Daly has been challenging the limits of his own profession. For instance, he began by telling me that:

what's really wrong with economics is that, in the very first pages of any textbook, you'll find a basic picture of the economy – a diagram of circular flow; of firms and households. It's an isolated system – so there's no environment; there's no physical context – and, having abstracted from all those relations, gets us in trouble when we try to apply the conclusions and the abstract models to reality. You have to go back and start over again.

This abstraction starts with what Daly calls *Homo economicus*, who is conceived as:

a kind of animistic individual who is related externally to other individuals and to the environment and other things. The relationships are external to the definition of a person. We want to substitute the concept of 'person-in-community' as our definition of the new Homo economicus, by which we mean that people are really not defined independently of their relationships to others; that relationships are really internal to the identity of a person.

Some of his ideas get quite esoteric and philosophical, but one of Daly's breakthrough concepts couldn't be simpler or more grounded – the notion of 'uneconomic growth'. I asked Daly to elaborate. 'It's quite possible', he said.

Given the fact that we live in a finite world – and all of our activities require some depletion and some pollution; some negative effect on the system of which we're a part – that the larger our economy gets, the heavier the burden on the rest of the system. There comes a point where the benefits (which are real) of expansion of the economy may be outweighed by the costs inflicted on the rest of the system of the expanded economy.

I asked Daly for some examples.

The biggest one right now is climate change. The costs resulting from economic expansion and consuming more fossil fuels. And likewise for things like acid rain, ozone layer depletion, the mobility of labour, uprooting communities, moving people around – these are costs. You might say, 'Isn't it better to be rich than poor?' Yes, absolutely. Most of our problems are easier to solve if we're rich rather than poor. But how do we get richer? And people say, 'Well, obviously by growth.' Well no, that's not so; that's not obvious any more. It may be that there's a point at which growth can become uneconomic and make us poorer rather than richer, and at that point we have to back off from growth.

Beyond simply being a theory, Daly and co-author John Cobb designed the Index for Sustainable Economic Welfare (ISEW), which subtracted these 'externalities' from gross national product (GNP) and revealed that the United States, the United Kingdom and other developed economies have seen a plateau in their net welfare since the 1970s, despite continued economic growth. Daly believes that the Index 'has not really been taken up very seriously by standard economists. They just still go right along with GDP and don't take on board the critique that we and other people have levelled against it.' That may be true, but Daly and Cobb's work has been adapted and expanded through other measures such as the Genuine Progress Indicator, the Human Development Index and the Ecological Footprint.

In common with Stiglitz, Daly is rather critical of the way the globalisation agenda is being advanced. He believes that:

> real community – historically where it exists and where we have institutions for mutual caring and taking responsibility – are pretty much at the national or sub-national level. What is happening is that instead of following the original charter of Bretton Woods and strengthening interdependence among separate national communities, we are abolishing or erasing the boundaries of these national communities through this concept of economic integration, free trade, free capital mobility and increasingly easy migration, so that nations really no longer have much clout vis-à-vis serving transnational corporations. And we're doing this in the interest of a very poorly defined, and historically baseless, notion of global community.
>
> That's why I praise the Bretton Woods institution. The way it was set up, it was going for what I might call friendship and mutual respect and good relationships among nations. So it was saying, 'Let's all be friends and work together.' But the new thing, it doesn't say 'let's all be friends', it says 'let's all get married and become one'. And I don't think we're anywhere near ready for that. It's a bit of a subterfuge or a ruse that covers a whole multitude of attacks on community where it really exists, in the name of some 'world without boundaries', which is a nice song lyric, but not much in the way of a policy prescription.

The art of barrier busting

Having exhausted my itinerary of former World Bank economists, I made my way across the country to Boulder, Colorado, to speak to the maverick engineer (or perhaps more accurately, 'imagineer'), Amory Lovins, Founder and CEO of the Rocky Mountain Institute. While Stiglitz and Daly focus largely on economics and policy reform, Lovins is more interested in business and technological solutions, or what he calls 'barrier-busting – turning into business opportunities each of the 60 or 80 well-known market failures to buying energy and resource efficiency'.

Lovins made his name as a co-author of *Factor Four*, published in 1997, which was about doubling wealth while halving resource use. 'The main thing that's happened since', he explained to me, 'is that our design methods and technologies have improved so much that we much more often achieve Factor 10 than Factor 4, and sometimes Factor 100 or more.' He was quick to point out that 'we're talking not so much of technologies, as of design methods, or design mentality'.

To illustrate what he means, he gave an example of how to save 92% of the energy in a pumping loop in industry in a way that works better and costs less to build.

> That's not because of any change in the pumps, or controls, or process, but because we're using fat, short, straight pipes instead of thin, long, crooked pipes. It's nothing new at all; it's good Victorian engineering rediscovered. It's optimising a whole system for multiple benefits, not isolated components for single benefits, and therefore getting multiple benefits from single expenditures.

From this sort of thinking, Lovins has created an entire philosophy.

> That sort of design is much more fun and it's the way nature designs. Nature doesn't do just one thing. And of course, the better the technologies you use the more you can achieve, but the design mentality is much more important than any technological novelty.

Talking to Lovins, you start to wonder why we haven't already solved all the world's problems. After all, he makes it sound so simple and economically lucrative. And yet many of these common-sense solutions have yet to achieve scale. I wanted to know why.

> We are seeing now some quite dramatic developments though. Many of the new buildings we're designing use no, or negative, amounts of energy – they create more than they use; they have very good economics. It's now perfectly normal to talk about tripled-efficiency cars, heavy lorries and airplanes.

Could Lovins name any pioneering companies?

> Walmart – of all people – have now demanded doubled efficiency heavy lorries at their suppliers, and they'll make billions off it, so they're highly motivated. We're using their demand-pull to drag those lorries into the market, so everybody can buy them. Walmart is quite straightforward that it likes that idea, and it's going to do the same with white goods for the household – making them very efficient at low cost and high volume. The lighting revolution is perhaps the best known, where we went from incandescent to compact fluorescent to LED. And Factor 10 is not at all unusual in that transition any more.

You can't fault Lovins's 'gift of the gab'. Once he got going, the examples just kept on flowing.

> United Technology has recently cut its energy intensity 45% in about five years. And DuPont has cut its greenhouse gas emissions to 80% below the 1990 level, and made three billion dollars' profit on the deal. Efficiency is cheaper than fuel. Dow made three billion. BP made two billion and so on, just substituting efficiency for fuel. So word is getting around that efficiency matters; efficiency is cheaper than fuel, therefore planet protection is not costly, but profitable. I think that once that is quite widely understood in the political realm, the main resistance will melt faster than the glaciers.

Natural capitalism and biomimicry

Another highly influential book that Lovins co-authored is *Natural Capitalism*. I asked him how that differed from *Factor Four*. He explained that not only was it for a business (rather than a policy) audience, but it was much more complex, because advanced resource productivity was only the first of the four interlocking principles of natural capitalism. Principle two is to produce things the way nature does, with closed loops, no waste and no toxicity. Principle three is leasing services or benefits, rather than selling products. And the fourth principle is to 'take the profits from the previous three activities and invest some of it back into the capital you're shortest of, namely nature, and therefore maximise biodiversity and the fecundity of nature'.

One of the concepts embedded in natural capitalism is Janine Benyus's notion of 'biomimicry'. Since Lovins is a bit of a 'techie', I wonder how he saw this approach, as compared with biotechnology. 'They're exactly the opposite', he declared emphatically.

> If I were doing biotech and I wanted to know how I make something like spider silk that's tougher than Kevlar® and stronger than steel, I would look for a gene that the spider uses and I'd stick it in a goat, and try to extract silk out of goat's milk and hope the gene doesn't go somewhere else. But if I'm doing biomimicry, I'd figure out how the spider makes the silk and then I'd imitate that process.

I concluded the interview by asking what gives Lovins hope.

> Three things stand out. One is the rapid rise of awareness and leadership in the private sector and the corresponding awakening of civil society, empowered by the emerging global central nervous system. Secondly, I'm encouraged by the fact that brains are evenly distributed – one per person – and as far as we know, there's nothing in the universe so powerful as six billion minds wrapping around a problem. And third, I'm very encouraged by the quality of the young people I see. They realise there is less time and they need to get on with it, and there's less frivolity and more focus on doing what's necessary. So I think the future is in pretty good hands.

Then, with his trademark quirky humour, Lovins ended by saying:

> It's really too early to tell whether this zany evolutionary experiment of combining a large forebrain with opposable thumbs will turn out to be a good idea. But the search for intelligent life on earth is starting to turn up some promising specimens.

20

Economics and evolution
Barefoot journeys towards abundance
(Chile, Argentina, Brazil, Costa Rica, Ecuador: 2010)

The barefoot economist

As part of my CSR quest world tour in 2010, I travelled from Chile to Argentina and Brazil, then up through Panama to Costa Rica and Mexico, before finishing back down in Ecuador. This chapter can only present a few highlights and insights from what was a fascinating and colourful journey of discovery, during which I mostly stayed in hostels and survived with virtually no Spanish, thanks to the generosity and patience of friends and strangers.

In Chile, I had the incredible good fortune to spend a few days in the beautiful Valdivia home of one of my intellectual heroes, 'barefoot economist' Manfred Max-Neef. When I was completing my Master's in Human Ecology in Edinburgh in 1996, I became familiar with his profound little book *Human-Scale Development*, and in 2008 I had the chance to interview him for the Cambridge *Top 50 Sustainability Books* project. His life's journey gives a sense of what a fascinating person Max-Neef is. Here is how he tells the story:

> I was the first economist in Chile who started speaking about the sociology of development. I was always concerned with

the non-material components of what was called development. The turning point was when I was in Ecuador, because I always wanted to be in the field where the poverty was; not like the typical expert that goes, spends five days and writes a huge report about poverty. I lived about ten years of my life in poverty-stricken areas, and that was the origin of the Barefoot Economics[38] book.

One of the things he learned was that:

the first characteristic of poverty is an enormous creativity. You must be tremendously creative to stay alive. And that means that you have tremendous potential. If you are to overcome poverty, construct on the creativity that people already have.

When I had been away from Chile for 20 years and while in Ecuador, there came a coup d'état, because we had mobilised about 300,000 peasants to do their own development process, and that is something militaries don't like. I was declared persona non grata and I had to leave the country, so I returned to Chile, and that was the beginning of 1973. A few months later came the coup in Chile and I had to leave again. I ended up after one year in the United States, then went back to Argentina and there started working on the concept of human needs. Next I had to leave Argentina again because there came the coup in Argentina, and then I ended up in a little village in Brazil. There I was 'discovered' by the Dag Hammarskjöld Foundation and they took me to Sweden and that's when I wrote Barefoot Economics. After that, when I'd finished my stay in Sweden, I received the Right Livelihood Award (the 'Alternative Nobel Prize') and with that I returned to Chile and with the money of the prize I set up the Development Alternatives Centre.

Out of his Development Alternatives Centre came Max-Neef's model of nine fundamental human needs. Unlike Maslow, Max-Neef believes that, beyond physical survival needs, there is no hierarchy. We all can satisfy our needs in any order or simultaneously. His great insight was that we often confuse needs with satisfiers. Hence, singing in a community choir and owning a sports car can both be satisfiers for the same basic need for recognition. Of course, the advertisers try to convince us that the best way

---

38 M. Max-Neef, *From the Outside Looking In: Experiences in 'Barefoot Economics'* (London, UK: Zed Books, 1992).

to satisfy our needs is to consume their products, whereas consumption often only produces pseudo-satisfiers. Building healthy relationships, for example, is likely to achieve more intimacy than drowning yourself in the latest 'cool' deodorant.

Max-Neef also had the insight that the divergence between GDP and Daly's Index for Sustainable Economic Welfare did not apply equally to developed and developing countries. This became known as Max-Neef's 'threshold hypothesis', which he explained to me as follows:

> If you have a country that has not reached this threshold and you have poverty, more economic growth is required to overcome that poverty. But if you are beyond that point, more growth will not do the trick, because every additional unit of growth has a greater component that goes into solving problems generated by growth instead of generating real development. You pass from a quantitative economy and after this threshold it becomes a qualitative economy and qualitative elements are much more important than the quantitative. That means a new economic theory.

This emphasis on the qualitative is reflected in Max-Neef's own life. 'I'm a musician, a pianist and composer', he told me. 'And music has been absolutely fundamental. I sometimes even say as a joke that I have put music into economics.' As it turned out, I was lucky enough to hear Max-Neef play one of his classical compositions, as I took in the idyllic landscape views from his glass-walled study. This was also where I had a chance to review the draft manuscript of his book *Economics Unmasked*. To honour Max-Neef, I wrote a poem called 'The Barefoot Don', which begins:

> He walks the mountains, plains and fields
> At home with forests, wolves and birds
> He's naked in the power he wields:
> The sword of truth; the axe of words

CSR tango

Travelling on to Buenos Aires, I delivered various workshops and presentations, hosted by Florencia Segura of AgendaRSE and Maria Irigoyen of ReporteSocial. I did interviews for the Argentine magazine *Calidad Empresaria* and Radio Cultura de Buenos Aires, as well as conducting my own interviews with Florencia, Maria and Cecilia Rena from confectionary company Arcor, and Ana Muro from BCSD Argentina.[39] I found out, for instance, that Arcor was linking sustainability performance to executive compensation, and BCSD (which was the first chapter of WBCSD set up outside Switzerland) has a great database of case studies. Its analysis of these cases suggests that most companies in Argentina still follow an eco-efficiency approach, with few adopting CSR, BOP or transformative models.

Maria Irigoyen explains in her chapter in *The World Guide to CSR* that the concept in Argentina has gradually evolved throughout the years, influenced by the country's cultural, historical and religious traditions. Its origins date back to the period of the Spanish viceroyalty, when the Catholic Church helped the poor through charity. When Argentina became an independent state in 1816, the governing class took over this role, mostly through philanthropic activities. During the mid-20th century, Peron's welfare state was marked by the concept of social justice, and in the 1980s civil society organisations played a stronger role in addressing society's needs through solidarity. In the 1990s, the concept of CSR was introduced in the media and some corporate circles.

According to research cited by Irigoyen, 94% of people interviewed in 2008 already thought it was essential for companies to communicate their CSR actions, compared to 87% in 2007 and 74% in 2006; and 87% of companies had implemented a CSR-related action during 2008, with a large focus on education and environment. Despite this progress, 41% of company directors interpret CSR as making contributions to society, and 33% of the public agree. The public agrees almost unanimously that beneficiaries should be included in decision-making processes, while 36% of the companies said that during 2008 this did not occur. Only 28% of businesses agree with the state evaluating the impact of CSR on society, compared with 50% of the public who think this is a good idea.

---

39 My interviews with Florencia Segura, Maria Irigoyen, Cecilia Rena and Ana Muro are available on the csrinternational channel on YouTube.

Lungs of the world

Travelling on to Brazil, I was hosted by Alda Marina Campos of the consultancy PARES in the beautiful city of Rio de Janeiro. I also had a chance to interview Alvaro Esteves, Director of Ekobe, in which he talked about his experiences in working with companies in sustainability and social innovation working in the favelas.[40] It was wonderful to have finally made it to Rio, after having narrowly missed out on attending the original Earth Summit back in 1992.

According to Camila Yamahaki and Tarcila Reis Ursini, authors of the Brazil chapter in *The World Guide to CSR*, despite a strategic approach to CSR being encouraged in Brazil since the early 1990s, in particular by business associations, CSR activities in the country mainly remain focused on philanthropy and community investment towards domestic issues.

This is despite the best efforts of the Ethos Institute, an NGO founded by a group of companies in 1998 with the aim of promoting sustainable business in Brazil. The Ethos Institute was responsible for developing the Ethos Indicators in 2002, considered instrumental in disseminating the CSR concept in the business sector. Another sustainable business framework that is influential in the management of many Brazilian companies, especially publicly listed companies, is the Sustainability Index. This was created in 2005 to select and encourage listed companies with good environmental, social and governance (ESG) performance. It has served as the basis for the creation of Brazilian SRI funds, hence encouraging companies to comply with its criteria.

One of the most progressive companies on sustainability in Brazil is Natura. Since its foundation 40 years ago, this Brazilian cosmetics company has led the way on analysis of the product life-cycle and control of the impacts of post-consumption waste. They are against animal testing, have a carbon neutral programme and prioritise responsible use of Brazil's biodiversity assets. This includes contributing to the income of traditional communities in the Amazon Forest through training on how to extract natural resources in a responsible manner. Another pioneer is Banco Real, the former Brazilian branch of ABN AMRO Bank and later

---

40 My interviews with Alda Marina Campos and Alvaro Esteves are available on the csrinternational channel on YouTube.

acquired by Santander Group. The bank has received many national and international awards, such as the *Financial Times* Sustainable Banking Award in two categories: the top Sustainable Emerging Markets Bank and the overall Sustainable Bank of the Year.

Inequality and deforestation remain among the biggest sustainable business issues in Brazil, along with corruption, child labour and racial discrimination. The poorest 20% of the Brazilian population are responsible for only 2.8% of the GNP, while the richest 20% account for 61.1%. Brazil has some of the richest biodiversity in the world, with the largest reserves of water and one-third of the world's remaining tropical forest. Hence, deforestation is a significant concern in terms of the loss of carbon storage capacity that it represents, exacerbated by the expansion of national and international markets for beef, soybeans and cocoa. If emissions from deforestation (i.e. lost carbon storage) were considered, the country would rank as the world's fifth biggest polluter. Ninety-three per cent of the Atlantic Forest, the most biologically diverse forest in the world, has already been devastated, while 12% of the Amazon Forest, the biggest tropical forest in the world, has also been lost.

Biodiversity havens

By contrast, travelling through Panama and on to Costa Rica, I discovered that Costa Rica is one of the few countries where biodiversity is increasing every year. I had a chance to interview Wilfrid Aiello, Director General of Horizontes, Cecilia Mora, Director of RSE Consultores, and Maria Morales, Corporate Citizenship Director for ITS InfoCom in San José. I also talked to Jessica Webb, Manager of Development & Tourism Communications for the Rainforest Alliance in Costa Rica, and she spoke about trends in sustainability certification in forestry, agriculture and tourism.[41]

The Rainforest Alliance is a great success story that demonstrates the power of combining values with collaboration. The result is that 157 million acres of forest and 1.24 million acres of farmland sustainably yield wood, nuts, coffee, tea, cocoa, fruit, ferns and flowers. On these certified

---

41 My interviews with Wilfrid Aiello, Cecilia Mora, Maria Morales and Jessica Webb are available on the csrinternational channel on YouTube.

lands, workers and their families enjoy clean drinking water, decent housing, healthcare and education, while wildlife habitat is protected, soils and waterways are healthy, and the gases that lead to climate change are absorbed. The hotel owners who work with Rainforest Alliance provide these same vital benefits to their employees, their neighbours and the earth. As a result of these efforts, consumers are now spending $12 billion a year on Rainforest Alliance certified or verified products and services.

In Ecuador, there are similar, positive stories of progress being made in the protection of ecosystems and cultural diversity. I have been hosted several times in Quito by my friend and colleague, Roberto Salazar, who has taken me to see, among other inspiring sites, San Pablo Lake at the foot of the Imbabura Volcano, the Otavalo traditional market amid the beautiful Andes, and Septimo Paraiso (Seventh Heaven) eco-lodge in the cloud forest of Mindo, run by Ana Lucia Goetschel.[42]

On one trip to Quito, in 2010 and on the last leg of my world tour, there was an attempted coup in which the president was more or less abducted and a firefight between the military and the police broke out, resulting in several fatalities. As soon as we became aware of escalating conflict, Roberto shut the office and I was kindly 'evacuated' to the safety of his home. These kinds of challenges do nothing to dampen the spirits of Roberto and his team; if anything, they only serve to underscore how necessary their dialogue services are if the country is to fulfil its great potential.

Roberto's company, Hexagon, does amazing work in bringing together diverse sets of stakeholders in structured dialogue sessions, using a range of online evaluation tools including the CSR 2.0 self-assessment diagnostic tool, which we developed together. Apart from running workshops hosted by Hexagon in Quito, I gave several presentations and workshops in 2010 and 2011 in Guayaquil, hosted by the British Chamber of Commerce, UNIAPAC Latin American Congress and the Business Council of Latin America. One of the interesting observations I made is that Catholic values are being translated actively into very detailed business guidelines and assessment tools.

In 2011, on one of my trips to Ecuador, I had the amazingly good fortune to be able to visit the Galapagos Islands, where I spent a few blissful days walking among the giant tortoises and marine iguanas, exploring a 300

---

42 My interviews with Roberto Salazar and Ana Lucia Goetschel are available on the csrinternational channel on YouTube.

m lava cave tunnel, climbing an extinct volcano, watching blue-footed boobies and white-tipped sharks, and generally soaking up the incredible and exotic biodiversity of these unique islands. Galapagos is not only a masterclass in evolution, but also a cautionary tale of the devastating effects of introducing foreign species (such as cats, rats and goats) into fragile ecosystems. It is also a heroic story of conservation success.

I was inspired to write two poems about these incredible islands, called Serenity and Galapagos. The latter begins:

> Genesis islands, straddling Hades and Eden
> Ancient follies forged in the fiery mists of time
> Land of contortion between struggle and freedom
> An ode to creation and its ebb-flowing rhyme

I hope you will also be inspired to visit not only Galapagos, but also Ecuador and Latin America. I believe we have so much to learn about sustainability and responsibility from this dynamic region, and my fleeting visits have only skimmed the surface.

Part 5
United Kingdom

21

Humans and ecology
From New Age to 'new' economics
(United Kingdom: 1992, 1995–1996)

Experiments in community business

This final section traces my physical and intellectual journey in and out and around the United Kingdom, where I have now spent ten years of my academic and professional life. It takes me back to where I started my career – to 1992 when I had just graduated and completed my management traineeship in Kingston, Ontario. After leaving Canada, I went to the United Kingdom as part of a three-week tour of Britain, which included visiting the northern Scottish community experiment in Findhorn. By then, I had read Paul Hawken's controversial book *The Magic of Findhorn*, so I was well aware of its reputation as a hippie-style community that, among other things, claimed to communicate and collaborate with nature spirits. I was more interested in how they were applying spiritual principles to commerce.

This began with the establishment of New Findhorn Directions (NFD) in 1979, a legal entity designed to serve as a framework within which private enterprise initiatives could emerge without violating the charitable status of the Findhorn Foundation itself. Subsequently, many promising business ventures were initiated, though not all have succeeded; nor have they all chosen to function under the umbrella of NFD. Those in operation when I visited included the Wood Studio, Bay Area Graphics, Findhorn Bay Apothecary, Weatherwise Solar and Alternative Data. They also had a pioneering eco-housing project (which included houses made from whisky barrels), under the leadership of John Talbott. The unique characteristics of these companies were that they were all trying to demonstrate their broader community philosophy of 'spiritual management' and 'work as love in action'.

Can we learn anything about business responsibility from these somewhat 'fringe' ventures? The common objective in places such as Findhorn in Scotland and Mondragón in Spain is community and environmental improvement, including through business activities. They are not hungry for short-term profits; rather, they are pursuing long-term sustainable development strategies. The desire is to be autonomous and self-sustaining and, most of all, to promote local self-development rooted in history and tradition. These two examples serve to illustrate that success stories in alternative ways of doing business do exist. The details of exactly how they are different, however, still need more thorough exploration.

First, a different set of values underscores community businesses. For instance, money is made to serve human development and not vice versa. The business is a means of human and community development and not an end in itself. Work is seen as an opportunity for creativity and personal development, as well as a contribution to serving the needs of society. Democratic action and consultation are encouraged, while integrity and competence in the management and conduct of business, as well as effective leadership, are considered necessary disciplines to be learned. There is also sensitivity to and solidarity with the local community as a prerequisite for a business operating in any particular area.

In order for these values to be translated into action, however, a community business needs to employ different structures to those traditionally used in private enterprise. For instance, there is a difference in ownership. Whereas conventional companies are owned by shareholders who may live anywhere, the shareholders of community businesses are people who live in the area where the company operates. The distribution of profits is also different. A traditional company tries to make a profit to return to the shareholders wherever they may live, but the community company aims to use its profits to start new local businesses and to improve life in the local community.

The benefits of the community business approach are readily apparent. Since its focus is local, a community business is more sensitive to local needs and opportunities in a way that traditional companies may not be. With the emphasis on people rather than on moneymaking, a community business will naturally be more responsive to human development in its staff and in its community than has been customary in the past. It would be a mistake to assume that these ideas are conclusive or easy to implement. On the contrary, growing 'spiritual businesses' is an open-ended and challenging experimental process, according to Francois Duquesne, past 'focaliser' of the Findhorn Foundation and present partner in the Alternative Data software company.

'I thought meditations on Monday mornings and being nice to customers would do it,' Duquesne says.

> Instead, I had to deal with intense personality conflicts in a system where power is equated with money. Yet there is great excitement. All the problems have had to do with perceptions of power. Power to stifle and manipulate, or to create, enliven and challenge. There is no other way of dealing with power issues except by bringing them out and working them through until there is some result.

Integrating business into an emerging community vision seems a natural path of societal evolution.

Eco-villages and sustainable communities

A few years later, I was back in the United Kingdom to begin my studies in human ecology, and back in Findhorn to attend a conference on 'Eco-villages and sustainable communities – models for 21st century living'. It was at this conference that the Global Eco-village Network (GEN) was launched with 12 members, to serve as an umbrella organization for eco-villages, transition town initiatives, intentional communities and ecologically minded individuals worldwide. Today, GEN links over 15,000 eco-villages on six continents, claiming to 'offer inspiring examples of how people and communities can live healthy, cooperative, genuinely happy and meaningful lifestyles – beacons of hope that help in the transition to a more sustainable future on Earth'.

GEN members include large networks such as Sarvodaya (2,000 active sustainable villages in Sri Lanka); the Federation of Damanhur in Italy and Nimbin in Australia; small rural eco-villages such as Gaia Asociación in Argentina and Huehuecoyotl in Mexico; urban rejuvenation projects, including Los Angeles EcoVillage and Christiania in Copenhagen; perma-culture design sites such as Crystal Waters in Australia, Cochabamba in Bolivia and Barus in Brazil; and educational centres such as Findhorn in Scotland, the Centre for Alternative Technology in Wales, and Earthlands in Massachusetts.

Immediately following the Findhorn conference, I joined my fellow Master's students in Lauriston Hall, an old manor house in south-west Scotland, near Dumfries. This is home to an intentional community of 23 years' standing, and host to Reforesting Scotland's annual conference. As a pre-event to the conference, a group of us went on a 'buildings in the forest' study tour, visiting a Kilqubanity thatched hut, the Lothlorien log house retreat centre (the largest log house in Britain), the Torthorwald cruck-frame barn and the Chencairn (15 m high) tree house – a most fas-cinating excursion indeed.

To give some idea of what these sustainable community experiments are like, let me describe Lauriston Hall. When I visited, it was home to about 30 residents, who appeared to have found a healthy balance between liv-ing in a community and giving sufficient autonomy for pursuing individ-ual interests. They collected their own firewood for heating, and raised sheep and cows for slaughter, but also relied on products and services from 'outside'. Most found employment in the nearby village, although some worked on organising events hosted on the premises.

As with many of these eco-villages, Lauriston Hall is located in exqui-site natural surroundings. I wrote in my diary at the time:

> A walk through the mostly native forest adjacent can only be
> described as magical and enchanting: bright red-and-white spot-
> ted faerie mushrooms, orange and yellow lichen, sparkling rain-
> drops suspended from sun-showered trees like a fantastical web
> of light, velvet moss cushioning tree bark, and torrents of water
> gushing down on its way to the rippled expanse of loch.

I must confess that, despite these eco-villages being all about going 'back to nature' and practising 'brotherly or sisterly love' – or maybe because of this – I have always been slightly cynical about their value. They seem to me somewhat isolationist, a throwback to the hippie generation, not engaging with the real challenges of urban living, widespread poverty and mainstream careers. Apart from Findhorn and Lauriston Hall, I had previously also visited the Centre for Alternative Technology in Wales, so my opinions were not formed entirely in ignorance. However, during my year in Edinburgh, I challenged myself to study these intentional communities, in search of lessons to be learned. In the end, I came to the conclusion that these eco-villages were vital experiments in what I started thinking of as community-centred economics.

Emergence of 'new' economics

In a paper I wrote on community-centred economics for my Master's degree, I explored the writings of former World Bank economist Herman Daly and community activist Helena Norberg-Hodge. They claimed that there was a direct link between the advancement of industrial development based on neo-classical economics thinking and the erosion of communities. While Daly argued convincingly from a theoretical perspective, Norberg-Hodge took an anthropological approach, telling the story of how modernization and economic 'development' had taken its toll on the cultural integrity of the Ladakhi people in northern India, bordering on Tibet.

This erosion of community, they argued, exacerbated numerous other social problems and created negative effects such as economic dependence, community disempowerment, cultural breakdown, social diseases and environmental destruction. A more community-centred economics, by contrast, would embrace concepts such as 'person-in-community' (rather than 'free, rational, utility-maximising individuals'), self-reliance, counter-development and eco-communitarianism. On a more practical level, the establishment and support of community businesses and local currencies or exchange systems would be encouraged. The benefits of this community approach, it was said, included wealth creation, empowerment, social cohesion, ethical conduct, sustainability and fulfilment of human needs.

While I remain unconvinced that we should all seek out a pastoral, community enclave in the wilderness, I was persuaded during my year in Edinburgh that the Western economic system and the process of trade liberalisation has serious shortcomings. What is more, a powerful new vision of economics seemed to be emerging. Its founding fathers were E.F. Schumacher (*Small is Beautiful*) and Herman Daly (*Steady-State Economics*), while a new generation of leaders had taken up the cause – people such as James Robertson (*Future Wealth*), Hazel Henderson (*Redefining Wealth and Progress*), Manfred Max-Neef (*Real-Life Economics*) and Paul Ekins (*Wealth Beyond Measure*). In 1984, Ekins and others (Jonathan Porritt, David Flemming, Alison Pritchard and Jakob von Uexkull), had set up TOES – The Other Economic Summit, which later became the New Economics Foundation (NEF) – to offer an alternative perspective to the neoliberal agenda of the G7 Summits.

There was a real buzz of revolution in the air, and I wanted to be part of it. I was convinced that this approach – changing the economic rules of the game – had far more potential to change the world than hiding away in eco-village experiments (although, of course, they also have their place as innovation hubs). Some of the ideas of what came to be known as the 'new economics movement' never gained traction – such as proposals for a guaranteed citizens' income and a Tobin tax on speculative currency trading. Other ideas, however, offered practical tools and viable policy alternatives that resulted in far-reaching changes.

Social accounting and responsible investment

For example, at the New Economics Foundation, Simon Zadek (who I met at the time) had been working with the fair trade organisation, Traidcraft, to develop new social audit methods. He recalls that:

> we discovered and grew a community of like-minded folks, especially Peter Pruzan from Denmark, who was working on ethical accounting, the folks from Body Shop and Ben & Jerry's who likewise were experimenting with social auditing, but also Alice Tepper Marlin, John Elkington, Jane Nelson and others

focused on social accounting to promote ethical consumerism and improved labour standards, notably in the emblematic apparel and footwear sector.

This led to the establishment of AccountAbility, nurtured within NEF and then spun out on its own, with a mission to advance the noble art of 'social and ethical accounting, auditing and reporting', advanced in theory by people such as Rob Gray, but only marginally in practice by mainstream business at that time. As Zadek later reflected:

> whether AccountAbility catalysed change or rode on its skirts is a moot point often hard to deal with scientifically. But what we do know is that huge strides have been made over the intervening period in advancing the practice of what we might today call 'sustainability accountability, auditing and reporting', with methods, standards, professional qualifications and in some areas the rule of law all driving the volume of practice, and in some respects the quality and its impacts. In less than two decades, the pottering side-events of Traidcraft, Body Shop and a few other unusual institutions have transformed into a global industry and practice, supported by new institutions.

These new institutions included the likes of the GRI (with its Sustainability Reporting Guidelines), Social Accountability International (with its SA 8000 standard), Transparency International (Corruption Perceptions Index), EITI, the UN Global Compact and the Carbon Disclosure Project, to mention but a few.

Another field that was rapidly advancing in the mid-1990s was SRI, due in no small part to the efforts of indefatigable pioneers such as Amy Domini, Tessa Tennant and Steven Lydenberg. In 1980, when Amy Domini was working as an American stockbroker, she began to notice that some of her clients weren't happy to invest in certain companies, such as large defence contractors and tobacco companies, whose policies they disagreed with. They questioned whether it was possible to pursue their investment objectives without violating their conscience. As a result, in 1990, she set up Domini Social Investments and established the Domini 400 Social Index, which tracked companies that had been screened using ethical criteria.

Tessa Tennant, who *The Independent* described as 'the mother of green investment', has a similar story. She founded Britain's first green equity fund back in 1988 and went on to establish the UK Social Investment Forum, and similar initiatives in Europe and Asia, as well as heading up SRI Strategy for Henderson Investors and serving on advisory boards for the UK Government, HRH The Prince of Wales, the Calvert World Values Fund, and the UNEP Finance Initiative. Steven Lydenberg's focus has been on the SRI data needed to support sustainable investment screening. He was a founder of KLD Research & Analytics and provided some intellectual guidance for the movement in his books, *Investing for Good* and *Corporations and the Public Interest*.

By the time I finished my year in Edinburgh, having completed my Master's in Human Ecology, I was determined to take the new economics and human ecology revolutions to South Africa. This led to the establishment of the South African New Economics (SANE) Foundation, and then to setting up and running KPMG's Sustainability Services, both of which I wrote about in earlier chapters. Certainly, I made some progress in placing some of these issues more firmly on the South African map, but maybe it was the lack of my hoped-for 'revolution' that eventually brought me to the United Kingdom, to start a PhD – which is where we hop to in the next chapter.

Meaning and change
Making a difference
(United Kingdom: 2003–2006)

Existential searching

My move from South Africa to the United Kingdom to begin a new phase of my career really began in August 2002, at the World Summit on Sustainable Development (WSSD, or Rio+5) in Johannesburg. I used the event as a climax for launching my new book: *Beyond Reasonable Greed: Why Sustainable Business is a Much Better Idea!* It was also where I officially told my team at KPMG that I would be leaving to do a PhD. And it was, by chance, where I met Polly Courtice, Director of the Cambridge Programme for Sustainability Leadership, who became (and remains) such a significant catalyst for my work in sustainable business.

In February 2003, I had made the big leap, moving to Nottingham to start my PhD at the International Centre for Corporate Social Responsibility (ICCSR) at Nottingham University Business School, under the expert supervision of Professors Jeremy Moon (Director of ICCSR) and Andrew Crane (now at Schulich Business School, York University in Toronto, Canada). It was a period of tremendous personal growth and my intellectual horizons expanded daily. Having planned to do a comparative study of sustainable business in Africa, four months into the process, I changed tack and decided to focus on 'meaning in the life and work of South

African sustainability managers'. Essentially, I wanted to understand what motivates us to work in sustainability, and what are the personal satisfactions and frustrations that come with the territory. This combined my two enduring passions – sustainability (or CSR) and existential psychology (meaning in life).

My findings are written up in detail in my book *Making a Difference*, so here I will simply summarise some of these findings and insights. Although the research focused on South African managers, I believe the model of purpose-inspired leadership that I derived is globally applicable. Indeed, I have since tested it on many audiences around the world and it seems to resonate true for all of them.

My first challenge was to understand the link between work and meaning or satisfaction in life. I quickly found that this was a subject that had intrigued management scholars, economists and psychiatrists alike for many years – from Abraham Maslow, E.F. Schumacher and Richard Layard to Viktor Frankl, Irvin Yalom and Paul Wong. Maslow's basic theory of motivation is well known, namely that people are seeking to fulfil a hierarchy of needs – from physiological and safety (lower-order) needs to social, esteem and self-actualisation (higher-order) needs. Applying his theory to an organisational context, as many have sought to do, implies that, once employees' lower-order needs have been met, they will be more motivated to do work which is interesting, challenging and oriented towards personal development. So far, so good.

What many do not know is that, in Maslow's later life, he wrote extensively on 'the farther reaches of human nature' and introduced numerous self-actualisation-related concepts such as Theory Z organisations, eupsychian management, B-values (being values), meta-motivation and meta-needs. Maslow claimed that 'self-actualising people are not primarily motivated (i.e. by basic needs); they are primarily meta-motivated (i.e. by meta-needs, or B-values)'. Of relevance here is that he identified 'meaningfulness' as one of the 15 core B-values, along with its antithetical meta-pathologies (when the need becomes frustrated) of meaningless, despair and senselessness of life.

Someone who was more concerned about the latter, namely the dehumanisation of work, was radical economist, E.F. Schumacher. In his now classic book *Small is Beautiful: A Study of Economics as if People Mattered*, he observed that Western economics tends to reward work that is essentially self-centred, while undervaluing work that is of genuine service to society. As an alternative, he coined the term 'Buddhist economics', to reflect the idea that greater incentives should be attached to work that is self-transcending, such as the teaching and care-giving occupations.

More recently, Daniel Khaneman, the winner of the 2003 Nobel Prize for Economic Sciences, added scientific evidence to the debate through his research on hedonic psychology. What the data shows is that happiness has not risen in Western nations in the last 50 years, despite significant increases in wealth. Professor (and Lord) Richard Layard, Director of the London School of Economics' Centre for Economic Performance, agrees that today's economic goals do not address or result in improved levels of wellbeing. In the pursuit of money, working ever harder, he says, we are on a 'hedonic treadmill'.

Meaning in work

Viktor Frankl, the Viennese psychiatrist and survivor of four Nazi concentration camps, expressed this idea eloquently when he said: 'This spreading meaning vacuum is especially evident in affluent industrial countries. People have the means for living, but not the meanings.' Having said that, Frankl believed that work was, as a rule, a highly potent vessel for the experience of meaning. But he was at pains to make clear that the occupation or job itself was less important than the extent to which it allowed for the expression of what he called 'creative values'. In other words, the meaning and value is attached to the person's work as a contribution to society, not to the actual occupation as such.

Frankl's notion of the meaning of work is similar to Abraham Maslow's 'meta-motivation theory', according to which self-actualising people are 'devoted to some task, "outside themselves", some vocation or duty or beloved job'. In other words, their work tends to coincide with their 'calling or mission', which is by its very nature personally meaningful. Maslow regarded this conclusion as one of the:

> truly revolutionary consequences of the discovery that … man has a higher nature which is just as 'instinctoid' as his lower nature and that his higher nature includes the needs for meaningful work, for responsibility, for being fair and just, for doing what is worthwhile and for preferring to do it well.

As you can imagine, it was not very difficult to hear the echo of sustainable business bells ringing behind these words, and the confirmations kept on coming. For example, included in Maslow's list of the motivations and gratifications of self-actualising people was 'delight in bringing about justice; delight in stopping cruelty and exploitation; they enjoy doing good; they manage somehow simultaneously to love the world as it is and to try to improve it; and pleasure in philanthropy'. Furthermore, research in the 1990s by existential psychology academic Paul Wong found that three of the drivers of personal meaning highlighted the importance of community: 'relationship' emphasised the skills and attitudes necessary for working together and community building; 'self-transcendence' focused on the value of serving others; and 'fairness/respect' indicated the need for individuals to receive fair treatment and respect from society.

As I began linking these ideas of deep motivation to sustainable business, the first rich vein of research I started to mine was the concept of 'champions' within an organisation. This goes back to the emergence of HR champions in the 1980s, but in the 1990s we saw the idea starting to be applied to environmental management and corporate social performance, as well. What is a sustainable business champion? Essentially, it is an individual who has the ability to translate a set of personal beliefs about creating a just and sustainable future into an attractive vision for their organisation or sector. Or put another way, a master at identifying, packaging and selling sustainable business issues to those who have power and influence.

Sustainable business champions – who are not always those with formal CSR roles – are often described as being action-oriented, enthusiasts, inspirers, experts, volunteers, communicators, networkers, sponsors, implementers and catalysts. They find that, contrary to popular belief, individuals have considerable discretion within organisations to pursue and promote agendas that they are passionate about. Crucially, however, they need a combination of knowledge and skills to be successful. For example, they need to be able to gather sufficient credible information to make a rational case for change. They need the ability to tell an emotionally compelling story about a more sustainable future; and they need enough political savvy and interpersonal skills to persuade others, especially leaders, to listen and take action.

We know, therefore, that many sustainable business professionals are effective change agents when they act as champions. But this still does not tell us what motivates them to engage with the agenda in the first place. This is the question I set out to answer in my doctoral research. And in the process, I found that, while change echoed as a consistent theme among all the sustainable business professionals I interviewed, the way in which they make change happen, and the satisfaction they derive as a result, differs considerably.

Purpose-inspired leadership

For some sustainable business professionals, as one might have guessed, values play an important role. In particular, sustainable business is seen as a way to align their work with their personal values. For example, one said: 'It's the inner drive, it's the way I am put together, my value system, my belief system ... it's my Christian belief, my ethical approach.' Another explained that it is important to have 'inspirational leadership and people who align with your value sets'.

For many sustainable business professionals, their motivation derives from the 'nature of the beast', the fact that sustainability is such a dynamic, complex and challenging concept. 'The satisfaction is huge', said one CSR manager. 'Because there is no day that is the same when you get into your office. It's always changing, it's always different.' Another reflected that sustainable business 'painted a much bigger picture' and is 'just as holistic as you want it to be. It requires a far broader vision.'

These two factors – values alignment and the sustainability concept – were fairly cross-cutting. However, after analysing all the interviews, I also found that I could distinguish four fairly distinctive types of sustainable business professional, based on how they derived satisfaction from their work. In practice, every individual draws on all four types, but the centre of gravity rests with one, representing the mode of operating in which that individual feels most comfortable, fulfilled or satisfied.

The first type of sustainable business change agent is the expert. Experts find their motivation though engaging with projects or systems, giving expert input, focusing on technical excellence, seeking uniqueness through specialisation, and pride in problem solving abilities. To illustrate, one expert-type sustainable business professional explained: 'There were a couple of projects that I did find very exciting ... It was very exciting to get all the bits and pieces in place, then commission them and see them starting to work.' Another said: 'I usually get that sense of meaning in work when I've finished a product, say like an environmental report and you see, I've really put in a lot and here it is. Or you have had a series of community consultations and you now have the results.'

The second type of sustainable business change agent is the facilitator. Common themes among facilitators are the derivation of motivation from transferring knowledge and skills, focusing on people development, creating opportunities for staff, changing the attitudes or perceptions of individuals, and paying attention to team building. For example, one facilitator-type sustainable business professional said: 'If you enjoy working with people ... [working in sustainability] is a sort of functional role ... you have direct interaction; you can see people being empowered, having increased knowledge, and you can see what that eventually leads to.' Another explained:

> The part of my work that I've enjoyed most is training, where I get the opportunity to work with a group of people – to interact with people at a very personal level. You can see how things start to get clear for them, in terms of understanding issues and how that applies to what they do.

The third type of sustainable business change agent is the catalyst. For catalysts, motivation is associated with initiating change, giving strategic direction, influencing leadership, tracking organisational performance, and having a big picture perspective. One catalyst-type sustainable business professional I interviewed claimed:

> The type of work that I'm doing is ... giving direction in terms of where the company is going. So it can become almost a life purpose to try and steer the company in a direction that you believe personally is right as well.

Another reflected:

> I like getting things changed. My time is spent trying to influence people. The real interesting thing is to try and get managing directors, plant managers, business leaders, and sales guys to think differently and to change what they do.

That is quite different from the fourth type of sustainable business change agent, which is the activist. For activists, motivation comes from being aware of broader social and environmental issues, feeling part of the community, making a contribution to social upliftment, fighting for a just cause, and leaving a legacy of improved conditions in society. For instance, one activist-type sustainable business professional said:

> It's also about the issue of being poor. It actually touches you. You see these people have been living in appalling conditions, the shacks, the drinking water is so dirty, or there's no running water at all, you see those kind of things, it hits you, and you think: What can you do?

Another confessed:

> I think my purpose here is to help others in some way and leave a legacy for my kids to follow. I could leave a legacy behind where I actually set up a school, a kids' school, or a campus for disadvantaged people, taking street kids out and doing something, building homes for single parents.

Dynamics of meaning

It is important to note that the typology is dynamic. In the same way that people's sources of meaning can vary over their life-cycle or other changing circumstances, there is ample evidence to suggest that sustainable business professionals' default types can change as well. For example, one sustainable business manager I interviewed seemed to have shifted from being an activist to being a facilitator (moving from political activism to business training and lecturing); another, from expert to catalyst (from laboratory work to strategic policy advice); and yet another, from expert to facilitator (from a technical scientist to a team unit manager).

For some (but not all) sustainable business change agents, their formal roles and their types are aligned, as in the examples cited above. Hence, there is a suggestion that either people are naturally attracted to roles that fit with their change-agent types, or that their roles shape the meaning they derive as certain types, or perhaps both. As one manager reminded me, 'In your career or in your work, the manager must be able to swing from the one type to the other.'

Another important influence is organisational context. For instance, one sustainable business professional observed that the 'organisation dynamics of corporates require conformism to the organisational culture, which to a large degree requires maintenance of the status quo … this makes it difficult for activists'. Career stage or life-cycle is another important context. One sustainable business manager said:

> I think that one of the things that you have to bear in mind is how much individual flexibility you get in working environments. I think at an earlier stage in someone's career, no matter what their typology might be, they don't necessarily yet have the luxury of finding themselves in the position that gives expression to their preference.

Beyond simply improving our understanding of sustainable business change agents, there are several practical uses for the typology. The most obvious potential applications occur at an individual and team level, with benefits for sustainable business managers, managers of CSR teams and HR managers. For sustainable business managers, the typology acts as a prompt for individuals to reflect on their most natural type, or mix of types. This allows them to think about what sorts of role they derive the most satisfaction from, and to consciously compare this to their formal role. If there isn't a natural fit between their type and their formal role, it may help to explain work frustrations or lack of motivation. As one sustainable business manager testified: 'It immediately helps me to understand some of the frustrations that I have with some of the areas.'

For managers of a sustainable business team, the typology helps to cast light on the mix of team members, from the perspective of their different sources of motivation. This can influence the way in which individuals are managed and allocated tasks, as well as the general management style adopted. For example, if there is a predominance of experts, incentives that recognise quality may be far more effective than for a catalyst-dominated team, where tracking of strategic goals may be more motivational.

The greater hunger

If the typology is used as a team-building exercise (where each individual's self-classification is shared among the group), mutual understanding, sensitivity and team dynamics may improve. The manager of a sustainable business team may decide that there is merit in having a balance of all four types represented, which will in turn affect recruitment decisions. HR managers may also use the typology to assist in recruitment, either for targeting a particular type to fit the corporate culture, or a specific role or need in the organisation, or as a way to ensure a balanced distribution of types in the organisation or the sustainability team. It could also be invaluable in designing targeted recruitment campaigns and incentive packages for this niche of professionals. For example, an appeal to values and expertise may be more successful on average than promises of financial reward and job status.

Another link to HR management is the potential of employee volunteering. Numerous surveys and studies show that there is a compelling business case for involvement in CSR issues generally and employee volunteering more specifically. The basic rationale is that engagement with sustainability improves employee satisfaction and motivation, which in turn enhances loyalty, commitment and productivity, and reduces turnover. However, my research suggests that companies also stand to gain a lot by going beyond the business case, in other words by justifying their corporate sustainability activities on the basis of values – what some call the 'moral case'. My findings suggest that taking this position (in addition to, rather than instead of, the business case) would tap into a powerful source of motivation, namely the life satisfaction that sustainable business managers (and in all likelihood many other employees) derive from values alignment.

To conclude this story about my PhD research on sustainable business motivations, there is a saying in Africa that there are two hungers – the lesser hunger and the greater hunger. The lesser hunger is for the things that sustain life – goods and services and the money to pay for them. The greater hunger is for an answer to the question 'why?', for some understanding of what life is for. It is my contention that sustainable business change agents have a fantastic opportunity to feed the greater hunger, by making a constructive difference and leaving a positive legacy. As Victor Frankl said, 'each person is questioned by life; and they can only answer to life by answering for their own life'.

23
Research and reading
Landmarks for Sustainability
(United Kingdom: 2007–2009)

Sustainable economy principles

After getting my PhD, my focus shifted to working with the University of Cambridge's Programme for Sustainability Leadership (CPSL), where I held various positions over the ensuing years, including Development Advisor, Research Director and Senior Associate. CPSL was established in 1989 and has become globally recognised for its executive learning programmes, especially the Business and Sustainability Programme and the Corporate Leaders Group on Climate Change (both of which it runs on behalf of HRH The Prince of Wales) and more recently, its Master's in Sustainability Leadership, which I helped to design and provide on-going support for.

During my time with CPSL, I have been involved in producing some fascinating publications, including papers (such as 'Sustainability and the individual'; 'Sustainability innovation'; 'A new model of business–government policy dialogue on sustainability'; and 'Cross-sector partnership as an approach to inclusive development'), reports (such as the Sustainable Economy Dialogue; the Sustainable Consumption and Production Business Primer; the Climate Leaders' Reference Guide; and the State of

Sustainability Leadership Report 2011), and two books (*Landmarks for Sustainability*; and *The Top 50 Sustainability Books*).

Most of these publications are still available, either for download or purchase, so here I simply want to shine a spotlight on some of the most interesting findings. For example, in the *Sustainable Economy Dialogue* report, we summarised the views of more than 400 senior leaders, which had been captured during 161 dialogues run in five countries (Austria, Kenya, South Africa, the United Kingdom and United States) between 2003 and 2006. Participants were asked to respond to the three questions: (1) What is the fundamental goal or purpose of a good economy? (2) Why do current economies fail to achieve this fundamental goal? and (3) What can business do to help eliminate these failings?

Out of this consultative process, a consensus emerged that the fundamental goal or purpose of a good economy is 'to steadily improve the well-being of all people, now and in the future, with due regard to equity, within the constraints of nature, through the active engagement of all its participants.' Furthermore, that the ten principles of a good economy are that it should be:

1. *Fulfilling.* Focusing on well-being and quality of life

2. *Inclusive.* Focusing on sharing and global benefits

3. *Farsighted.* Focusing on consequences and future generations

4. *Developing.* Focusing on progress and improvement over time

5. *Equitable.* Focusing on fairness and even distribution

6. *Sustainable.* Focusing on nature and life support systems

7. *Participatory.* Focusing on engagement and stakeholder democracy

8. *Innovative.* Focusing on creativity and rewarding achievement

9. *Diverse.* Focusing on variety and equal opportunities; and

10. *Accessible.* Focusing on openness and providing opportunity

In the *Sustainable Consumption and Production* report, we explored how to de-link economic development from environmental degradation using techniques such as technology, innovation and design; resource productivity and efficiency; life-cycle assessment; closed-loop production;

sustainable procurement; and customer engagement. I remember one startling statistic in the report, namely that if you factored in the waste materials generated in the production cycle, a gold wedding ring would weigh 6,000 kilograms.

The report included many case studies, including BT, adidas, ICI, Nokia, Marine Stewardship Council, Round Table on Sustainable Palm Oil, Fonebak and the City of London. I found Fonebak particularly interesting. It was launched in 2002 to deal with the growing mobile phone 'mountain' created by consumers disposing of obsolete phones every 18 months, while leaving the lithium, platinum, gold, silver, copper and reusable plastics in every phone. Fonebak takes the returned old phones and extracts these material for reuse and recycling, as well as refurbishing the phones for on-sale. In its first three years, the company had already prevented 1,800 tonnes of electrical waste from 18 million mobile phones going to landfill, and increased overseas sales by 127% in three years. This is a great example of a social enterprise that is closing the loop on production, or practising C2C principles.

In the *Cambridge Climate Reference Guide*, we identified and summarised 12 publications on climate change that every senior leader should be familiar with. Even today I would argue this makes for a solid and relevant essential reading list. Another report I worked on is *A Journey of a Thousand Miles: The State of Sustainability Leadership 2011*, which includes some of the fruits of my most recent research for Cambridge University. Working with Polly Courtice, Director of CPSL, our first step in understanding sustainability leadership was to go back to the basics and ask: 'What is leadership?' The definition we developed is that *a leader is someone who can craft a vision and inspire people to act collectively to make it happen, responding to whatever changes and challenges arise along the way.*

Are sustainability leaders different?

There are also various theories on leadership and while it was not our intention to provide an exhaustive review of these, they do set a frame for sustainability leadership. Hence, we distinguished three main approaches to understanding leadership: (1) The trait/style school, which focuses on the characteristics or approaches of individual leaders; (2) The situational/context school, which focuses on how the external environment shapes leadership action; and (3) The contingency/interactionist school, which is about the interaction between the individual leaders and their framing context.

These general perspectives on leadership established the foundation for our more specific enquiry into the nature of sustainability leadership. Based on our review of the academic literature, together with CPSL's experience working with senior leaders over the past 20 years, we distilled the following simple definition: *a sustainable business leader is someone who inspires and supports action towards a better world.*

Looking at the theories of leadership that inform this definition, our conclusion was that sustainability leadership is not a separate school of leadership, but rather a particular blend of individual leadership characteristics applied within a definitive context. Put another way, the context – comprising the sustainability challenges facing the world and our aspirations for a better future – calls for particular types of leadership.

This approach aligns most closely with the contingency/interactionist school, although our emphasis is as much on the actions of leaders as the context that shapes their behaviour. Hence, our model of sustainability leadership has three basic elements: context, characteristics and actions. The model was tested and refined through interviews with selected sustainability leaders, some of whose thoughts and insights are shared below.

The sustainability context has become 'mission critical' for many businesses. According to a survey of 766 United Nations Global Compact (UNGC) member CEOs conducted by Accenture, 93% of CEOs globally see sustainability as important to their company's future success, especially tackling issues such as education, climate change, resource scarcity and health. Seventy-three per cent of CEOs see this as a way of strengthening their brand, trust and reputation.

Jeffrey Immelt, CEO of General Electric, agrees, saying, 'The most important thing I've learned since becoming CEO is context. It's how your company fits in with the world and how you respond to it.' Similarly, Sandy Ogg, Chief HR Officer for Unilever, told us that CEO Paul Polman stands out as a sustainability leader 'because he understands the context and he understands leading with empathy in a multi-stakeholder environment'.

There are many characteristics (traits, styles, skills and knowledge) that are associated with sustainability leaders. Our research suggests that the following seven are key among the most important elements in distinguishing the leadership approach taken by individuals tackling sustainability issues: systemic understanding, emotional intelligence, values orientation, compelling vision, inclusive style, innovative approach and long-term perspective. Although it is unlikely that any individual will embody all seven characteristics, they are illustrated in our report by observations from a selection of leaders, many of whom we have worked with and who demonstrate some of these qualities themselves, in order to give a flavour for each characteristic.

Paradoxes of sustainability leadership

One of our most compelling and persistent findings was that sustainability leadership is fraught with paradoxes. As the competitive landscape shifts and global challenges evolve, companies that were lauded in the past as sustainability leaders may be discredited in the present. Similarly, today's targeted villains may end up being tomorrow's sustainability heroes and vice versa. There are a number of reasons for this state of flux in sustainability leadership.

First, sustainability is aspirational. No company, or society, has achieved sustainability. The goal of sustainable development is an ideal state that we are striving for. By definition, companies will fall short of the mark and be exposed for their inadequacies. Second, the context is dynamic – our global challenges are part of a complex, living system, which is constantly changing. Companies that do not innovate and adapt to match the evolving context will be left behind, while others will emerge as new leaders.

Third, perceptions can change. The sustainability agenda is driven as much by emotions and perceptions as by factual realities. Society's views on issues – such as the use of nuclear technology and GMOs – can change, and with it the perceived sustainability performance of companies. And finally, sustainability is a learning process. As our understanding of sustainability challenges and solutions improves, so do our expectations of companies. In their turn, companies need to constantly renew their sustainability learning, or be left wanting.

Ultimately, given the scale and urgency of the challenges, sustainability leadership needs to be bold leadership. It also needs to be collaborative – leaders acting together at all levels of organisation and society. Many of the sustainability leaders whom we spoke to emphasised the importance of collective action. James Smith, Chairman of Shell UK, told us that his view of leadership is not based on a hierarchical model but on the notion of a network – that leadership is not invested in one person. Smith concedes that many CEOs do base their leadership on the cult of personality and cause things to happen, but their success is short lived. Sustainability leadership, by contrast, 'is about cultivating good people for sustainability to be delivered'.

Hence, while individual leaders at the apex of organisations are critical change agents for sustainability, finding sustainable business leaders or champions throughout our communities, government departments and companies, is also essential. Some call this approach 'distributed leadership', which MIT Professor Deborah Ancona says is 'where junior leaders act when local needs arise and as organizational imperatives demand'.

We all have the potential to be sustainability leaders, whatever our area of practice, our role and level of seniority. We also conclude from our research that – given the paradox of sustainability leadership – the success or otherwise of the sustainability leader (whether individual or organisational, hierarchical or distributed) must rest with the performance of the company. Ultimately, sustainability leadership must be judged by the success of our actions and the extent to which we inspire and support others to follow our vision and passion for a better world.

Landmarks for Sustainability

Apart from the research reports, one of the book projects I researched (together with Oliver Dudok van Heel) and wrote for Cambridge University was *Landmarks for Sustainability*. As the subtitle indicated, we set out to map the 'events and initiatives that have changed the world'. In fact, we identified more than 220 such events and initiatives, dating back to 1919. This book was in part an answer to the question: how did we come so far in such a short time (20 years), and is it still a case of 'too little, too late'?

Back in 1988, the Brundtland Commission had only just introduced its touchstone definition of sustainable development and all the talk was of the ozone hole, with climate change still something that most people didn't know or care too much about, despite the International Panel on Climate Change (IPCC) being set up by the UN that same year.

Fast-forward to 2008 and we were awash with codes of conduct, certifiable standards, corporate programmes, industry initiatives, green politicians, triple-bottom-line reports and Oscar-winning documentaries about sustainability. At the same time, many of our global challenges – be they climate change, water depletion, biodiversity loss, bribery and corruption or income inequality – seem if anything to have become worse rather than better.

This leads to the second question that served as a catalyst for the book, namely: how can we deepen our understanding of the processes of change – at a societal, sector, organisational and individual level – and how have these processes acted either in support of, or in opposition to, sustainability? The book illustrates a number of trends. First, it is clear that many of the issues highlighted in its 20 chapters have moved from the marginal fringes into the mainstream. For example, although the UK Soil Association introduced its organic label in 1967, it took until 2004 before Walmart converted to organic cotton supplies and changed the market irrevocably.

Second, we have seen a move from general problems to specific solutions. For example, we now talk less about environment, poverty and sustainable development, and more about ISO 14001, the MDGs and emissions trading. Twenty years ago, the call was for more data and debate; today, it is for more policy and action.

Third, business and government has changed from being largely reactive to being more proactive. For example, the reaction by the chemicals industry to Rachel Carson's *Silent Spring* in the 1960s, Greenpeace's activism in the 1970s and the spate of industrial disasters in the 1980s stands in stark contrast to the approach taken by the FSC in the 1990s and the Corporate Leaders Group on Climate Change in the 2000s.

Fourth, we have shifted from high-level cross-sector principles to more detailed industry sector responses. For example, the Sullivan Principles in 1977, the Valdez Principles (now the Ceres Principles) in 1989 and the

International Chamber of Commerce (ICC) Business Charter for Sustainable Development in 1991 have given way to such initiatives as the Marine Stewardship Council (MSC) certification scheme, the Equator Principles for project finance and EITI.

Fifth, we have seen a growing consensus on principles and standards. The initial flurry of codes and guidelines seem to have settled around a few core standards, such as the GRI's Sustainability Reporting Guidelines, UN Global Compact and MDGs, the World Resources Institute's Greenhouse Gas Protocol and the UN Principles for Responsible Investment.

Catalysts for change

Looking at the events thematically, we can conclude that change is a long-term process, but sustained momentum is important to reach the necessary tipping points in public opinion, policy response and business action. For example, the global warming greenhouse effect was first discovered by Jean-Baptiste Fourier in 1824, but it is only really since 2005 that climate change has become a top agenda item for the news desks, parliaments and boardrooms of the world.

Likewise, the process of institutionalising globalisation may have begun with the formation of the League of Nations in 1919 and marched behemoth-like onward with Bretton Woods in 1944 and GATT (General Agreement on Tariffs and Trade) and WTO into the 1990s, but it took the 'Battle of Seattle' in 1999 and subsequent 'anti-globalisation' protests to reopen the debate on what kinds of globalisation and capitalism will create a just and sustainable world.

The *Landmarks for Sustainability* book helped tell the story of gathering momentum and shifting agendas. Its message in many ways is simple: the last 20 years have been critical, with significant and increasing responses by business, government and civil society. But all the signs are that our social and environmental problems continue to get worse. Therefore, the next 20 years will be even more important – especially with the narrow 'window of opportunity' on climate change, poverty alleviation and sustainable development paths for China, India and other developing countries. The quality of the leadership that we experience and that we offer will determine whether we take the right path as a species – the path to breakdown, or the path to breakthrough.

In *The Top 50 Sustainability Books*, we had a similar objective – summarising key sources of thought leadership – but in this case extended to the whole of sustainability, reaching back over a century of writing, and focusing on seminal books. The top 50 list was based on a poll conducted among the CPSL alumni, as well as the recommendations of the CPSL faculty, senior associates and directors.

For those who are curious, the Top 10 rankings from the poll (conducted at the end of 2007) were:

1. *An Inconvenient Truth* by Al Gore, 2006

2. *Silent Spring* by Rachel Carson, 1962

3. *The Economics of Climate Change* by Nicholas Stern, 2007

4. *Small is Beautiful* by E.F. Schumacher, 1973

5. *Capitalism as if the World Matters* by Jonathon Porritt, 2005

6. *Collapse* by Jared Diamond, 2005

7. *Natural Capitalism* by Amory Lovins, L. Hunter Lovins & Paul Hawken, 2000

8. *Gaia* by James Lovelock, 2000

9. *Our Common Future* by WCED, 1987

10. *Cannibals with Forks* by John Elkington, 1999

This book project also gave me the extraordinary privilege and opportunity to interview around 30 of the authors, visiting Canada, the United States, Switzerland and Austria to track them down. I included illustrative quotes from the interviews in the book itself, and 21 videos of the interviews are featured on the CPSL website, together with the full transcripts. I have already dipped into many of these conversations over the course of this book, so in the next chapter it only remains for me to add the voices of a few of the UK-based luminaries who have not yet been highlighted, namely John Elkington, Jonathan Porritt, Charles Handy and James Lovelock.

24

Pioneers and paradoxes
In search of sustainable business
(United Kingdom: 2004, 2008–2011)

The Hungry Spirit

When I was starting out on my business career over 20 years ago, one of the management 'gurus' who most inspired me was Charles Handy. In fact, when I was studying for my Bachelor of Business Science degree at the University of Cape Town, I remember photocopying and devouring his entire *Gods of Management* book and being fascinated by others, such as *The Age of Unreason*, *Waiting for the Mountain to Move* and *The Empty Raincoat*.

In 2004, I finally had the chance to meet him for breakfast at his Putney flat in London. He struck me as extremely humble, with a quietly engaging manner. I was honoured that he had read my book, *Beyond Reasonable Greed*, and equally delighted with the comment that he wrote in the front cover of one of his books, *The Elephant and the Flea*, which I asked him to autograph: 'Wayne, I like the way you think – and the way you write. I hope that you can help to change the world. Good luck and good writing.'

I met Handy again in 2008, as part of the Cambridge *Top 50 Sustainability Books* project. *The Hungry Spirit* had been particularly relevant for my PhD, which looked at meaning in life and work, and I also thoroughly enjoyed his biographical memoirs, *Myself and Other More Important Matters*. As I put it in a letter I wrote to him after the interview:

> I especially appreciate your skill in weaving together business stories, conceptual ideas, personal stories and philosophical insights. This, in my mind, makes you not only unique as a social philosopher and management writer, but also a wonderful role model for me.

The first meaty topic we got our teeth into in the interview was about shareholder-driven capitalism, since the subtitle of *The Hungry Spirit* is *Beyond Capitalism*. Handy confessed:

> I've always had my doubts about shareholder capitalism because we keep talking about the shareholders as being owners of the business, but most of them haven't a clue what business they're in. They deal through agents of one sort or another ... and they are basically punters with no particular interest in the horse that they're backing, as long as it wins.

'So I've been very sceptical about this as a responsible model for capitalism', he continued. 'It's the way it's emerged; it's not the way it started, where owners really did have a personal stake and often managed the operations.' Reflecting on the global financial crisis, he admitted, '[It] gives me a rather rueful satisfaction – I think it's over-reached itself and maybe this correction that we're going through at the moment and the credit crunch is quite a healthy correction.'

I asked Handy whether SRI was a useful counter-balance to the short-termism of mainstream shareholders – a way of using their own power against them. Handy is unconvinced. Rather, he says:

> I want to reduce the power of shareholders. I think they've got too much power and too little responsibility. And everybody else says, 'Well give them more responsibility. Let them exercise their power responsibly.' I think that's a myth. I think we've got to give them less power. And so how do you reduce the power? By actually giving other people more power. Give the people who actually create the wealth – the workers – more rights. Don't give the workers shares because then they become shareholders and they get just as greedy as the shareholders. But give them rights, because after all, they're creating the wealth. The other people have only financed the possibility of creating wealth.

But don't directors have a legal, primary duty to the shareholders? According to Handy:

> Shareholders have only one duty and that is to elect the board of directors. What the board of directors then do is entirely up to them. They have been elected by the shareholders to do what they think is right for the company – not for the shareholders, for the company. The effective power of the shareholders in legal terms is really very small, and so it's a bit of a myth that seems to have grown up, that somehow everything that they do is for the shareholders.

When I asked for an example of a company that is bucking the slave-to-shareholders trend, Handy cited Camelia, an agricultural products business where 40% of its shares are traded publicly, but 60% are held by a trust – a trust that is dedicated to reinvesting its dividends in the countries where it makes its products. Handy explained:

> So that there's a sort of discipline on the managers to meet the will of the 40% shareholders who want a decent return on their investment and so they can't just idle their time away. But on the other hand they do realise that they're not just working for the shareholders, they're working for the countries and the homelands of the workers that are there.

I wondered what Handy thought about sustainable business. It seems he characterises most of what passes for CSR as 'jester social responsibility' – 'things that you can put in your annual report and say "look what a good citizen we are".' He explains that:

> being a good employer, being a good producer, just behaving yourself in your communities, that's obviously a good thing, but it's not attacking the heart of the problem as I see it, which is that companies' purposes are skewed inevitably towards the shareholder rather than the customer.

For Handy, proper sustainable business means looking after your workers and 'producing wonderful products that do their job properly; that are user-friendly and not harmful in any way'.

I concluded the interview by returning to Handy's main theme, which is 'the quest for purpose' in business. Reflecting on this, he said,

> I don't think it's easy to find your meaning in the big corpora-
> tions these days. I sometimes say that, without meaning to, they
> become prisons for the human soul because they force you to be
> somebody you are not really, to work to their commands. And
> because they pay you a lot, you do it, but you despise yourself
> for doing this thing which you don't think is necessary or par-
> ticularly useful or done particularly well. We need more emo-
> tion in our organisations. We need more stories. We need more
> passion. We need more love actually and care of people. In the
> end, we'll need to make a reality of this phrase that 'people are
> our assets'. You should cherish your assets, not bleed them to
> death.

Ah, such words of wisdom! Let's move on to the next British thought leader.

Cannibals with Forks

Once I began focusing my career more on issues of social responsibility and sustainable development, it was inevitable that I would encounter the seminal thinking of John Elkington, who coined and popularised the idea of 'green consumerism' and introduced the 'triple bottom line' concept as shorthand for sustainable business. Happily, our paths have crossed many times over the past decade. When I interviewed him in 2008, our conversation ranged far and wide, from the influence of Quakerism and LSD to the power of social entrepreneurs and creative destruction.

Speaking about one of his most popular books, *Cannibals with Forks*, he recalled:

> I'd spent 18 months trying to work through why I was so uneasy
> with the eco-efficiency agenda that the World Business Coun-
> cil for Sustainable Development was promoting. What I felt that
> lacked on the financial dimension was the economic impacts
> that companies have. The other piece was the social agenda.
> Companies were just beginning to get comfortable with some
> bits of the environmental agenda, but the social piece was very,
> very much more complex and painful for them. Taken together,
> those elements became 'the triple bottom line'. It was for cor-

porate leaders like popping a pill where you suddenly saw the world slightly differently.

Elkington credits three books with having a major influence on his thinking: Nikolai Kondratiev's work on what are called Kondratiev cycles (economic cycles or waves lasting 50–60 years in which an economy is built up, then suddenly taken apart and the ground prepared for something new); Joseph Schumpeter's work on creative destruction, very much in the same territory; and Thomas Kuhn's *The Structure of Scientific Revolutions*, which introduced the notion of a 'paradigm shift'.

Elkington recalled an experiment cited by Kuhn in which its subjects were fitted with distorting lenses that flip the visual field so that they see the world upside down. 'I think that's what happened when the environmental revolution came through, when the Apollo images started to flow back', reflected Elkington. 'The world was changing in front of people's eyes and the older generations, or the more rigidly wired minds, found this quite difficult.'

In the experiment, initially the individuals started to feel quite nauseous. Then, their visual fields started to oscillate – to wobble between the world as they should have seen it through the lenses and the world as it was, the reality. Finally, their perception flipped and they actually saw the world as it should be (right way up), rather than the way that the lenses were telling them to see. Elkington told me:

> I think that over the last 40 or 50 years, that's what we've been going through. And I think it has still got quite some time to run. An established economic model – and everything that goes with it, the politics and the way you think – is coming under profound challenge, and the 'captains of industry' have found this really deeply upsetting. I've often said that our greatest allies in environmental and sustainability worlds are death and retirement. I mean they just weed out people who can't change and then a younger generation comes through and they do increasingly think differently.

Elkington believes that our crises will get worse – or at least more turbulent – before they get better.

> I think, in some ways, key parts of our economies and societies are on a doomed path really, and I think that's unavoidable. I think we're heading into a period of creative destruction on a

scale that really we haven't seen for a very long time. There are all sorts of factors that feed into it – the entry of the Chinese and Indians into the global market, quite apart from things like climate change and new technology.

When I caught up with Elkington again in 2010, when we shared a speaking platform at an event in Greece, his views had become, if anything, more extreme. 'What happens in an earthquake?' he asked rhetorically. 'The land becomes thixotropic; what was solid suddenly becomes almost semi-liquid. I think we are headed towards a period where the global economy goes into a sort of thixotropic state.'

As to what this means for business, Elkington believes that:

> all of these pressures are going to mobilise a set of dynamics which are unpredictable and profoundly disruptive to incumbent companies, so some companies will disappear. I think most companies that we currently know will not be around in 15–20 years, which is almost an inconceivable statement. But periodically this happens and there's a radical bleeding of the landscape. We'll find this sort of reassembly going on. Over a period of time we're going to have some fairly different products, technologies and business models coming back into the West, and I think it's going to be quite exciting, but very disruptive.

Smart versus dumb growth

Another voice on sustainability that has been 'shouting in the wilderness' of British politics and business circles for many years is that of Jonathon Porritt, co-founder of the UK Green Party in the 1980s and Forum for the Future a few decades later. Porritt is also very involved in the sustainability programmes that Cambridge University runs on behalf of HRH The Prince of Wales, so our orbits have overlapped fairly frequently over the past five years or so.

When I interviewed him in 2008, I asked Porritt if his last book, *Capitalism as if the World Matters* – in contrast with his first, *Seeing Green* – was something of a compromise, as he is talking more about reformation than revolution. He explained that:

It is a pragmatic acceptance. Looking at people all over the world today, rich and poor, they are not remotely close to a state of mind that would call for anything revolutionary. There's no vast upheaval of people across the world saying, 'This system is completely and utterly flawed and must be overturned and we must move towards a different system.' There isn't even that, let alone an identification of what the other system would look like.

So the idea that there's a kind of great revolutionary ferment going on in the world today, sort of a Naomi Klein-type proposition, that there is a very clear, articulated, anti-globalisation revolution – I don't see the evidence for that. So pragmatically, if this is not the time for revolution, what do we do? The dominant system is capitalism. It seems to me the choice therefore – if you're not going to erect barricades and overthrow capitalism – is to firstly explore what sustainable capitalism would look like, and then commit wholeheartedly to a set of radical reform processes which would convert today's capitalism into a kind of capitalism which would deliver a sustainable world.

Part of this reformation, according to Porritt, is to opt for 'smart growth' over 'dumb growth'. He explains that:

If you pursue the concept of economic growth within environmental limits and economic growth that is generating real outcomes for societal inclusion and social justice, you can go a long way towards something that makes growth look pretty intelligent, pretty smart. [We need to] eliminate these insane externalities associated with economic growth today – to de-couple the economic growth from the physical material throughput in the economy, to de-couple it from the impacts on the biosphere. Having done the de-coupling, then you have to do the coupling with outcomes for society, so real improvements in well-being. If you can do these two things – do the de-coupling on the environmental footprint and the re-coupling on the social outcomes, then you can see how you'd get to a point where growth makes sense. It is so different from what we have now that some people would say, 'That's not really growth as we know it; that's a completely different measure of progress.' Well yes, that's precisely the point. It has to be a completely different measure of progress.

Lessons from Gaia

Another thought leader who has been questioning the wisdom of our 'dumb growth' over the years is the scientist and creator of the Gaia Theory, James Lovelock. In a nutshell, the theory is based on the observation that the earth is a self-regulating system – that the climate and the atmospheric composition, the ocean composition, the surface soils, all stay more or less at a state which favours habitability, or sustainability.

When I interviewed Lovelock in 2008, he talked about the main challenges to the earth's self-regulatory balance. The first is our population – he believes that 'we can't possibly support seven billion, and it's only just a matter of time before massive famine and other problems begin to cull the numbers.' The second, related challenge is climate change, which he warns in the *Revenge of Gaia* may already be beyond our control. As he put it to me:

> Living things, when threatened or stressed, at first resist – and the [Earth] system's been doing that for quite a while now ... But somewhere around about 1900 we began to go beyond the limit. So now the system is doing the other thing that living things do and fleeing to a safe place that it knows. And the safe place which it's been at many times before is the hot regime where the global temperature is 5 or 6 degrees planet-wide hotter than now.

So is Lovelock a fatalist? Is there nothing we can do about climate change? Lovelock admitted:

> I think that there is a lot of promise in harvesting algae in the oceans. But the only chance we've got of reversing global heating, really getting to it, is to take on Gaia as an ally. You see, every year the great earth system pumps down 550 gigatonnes of carbon dioxide by photosynthesis from all the plants. That's huge compared with the emissions that we are making, which are 30 gigatonnes. And so how can we ask the system to just help out a bit?
>
> Well actually it's not too hard. All that you have to do is to, for example, take all agricultural waste and convert it to charcoal. It could be done on every farm using a small charcoal producer – from straw, dung, everything that the farmer produces. And all the farmer has to do is to plough the charcoal back into his

fields. There's good evidence that this does not interfere with productivity; in fact it can be beneficial in some places – and the charcoal will stay there forever; it doesn't oxidise. That way you've got the photosynthesis to really pull massive quantities of carbon dioxide out of the air.

I reckon that if we could just take 20% of the total photosynthate and bury it as charcoal in the land, and at the ocean bottom with algal farms, then we would be taking out something in the order of 110 gigatonnes of CO_2 per year. Now this is far more than our emissions and enough to start pumping down the greenhouse to more reasonable levels. So there is a way out. There is something we can do.

Lovelock's slightly ominous, yet strangely positive message seems a good segue to the final chapter, in which I will conclude my 'epic journey' with how my thinking on sustainable business has evolved towards the concept of CSR 2.0 and the 'triple-S' future agenda for business.

Death and rebirth
From CSR 1.0 to CSR 2.0
(United Kingdom: 2008–2012)

Internet inspirations

By May 2008, it was clear to me that this evolutionary concept of Web 2.0 held many lessons for sustainable business. I published my initial thoughts in a short article online entitled 'CSR 2.0: The new era of corporate sustainability and responsibility', in which I said that:

> the field of what is variously known as CSR, sustainability, corporate citizenship and business ethics is ushering in a new era in the relationship between business and society. Simply put, we are shifting from the old concept of CSR – the classic notion of Corporate Social Responsibility, which I call CSR 1.0 – to a new, integrated conception – CSR 2.0, which can be more accurately labelled Corporate Sustainability and Responsibility.

The allusion to Web 1.0 and Web 2.0 is no coincidence. The transformation of the internet through the emergence of social media networks, user-generated content and open source approaches is a fitting metaphor for the changes business is experiencing as it begins to redefine its role in society. So let us look at some of the similarities (Tables 1 and 2).

Table 1 **Similarities between Web 1.0 and CSR 1.0**

Web 1.0	CSR 1.0
A flat world just beginning to connect itself and finding a new medium to push out information and plug advertising	A vehicle for companies to establish relationships with communities, channel philanthropic contributions and manage their image
Saw the rise to prominence of innovators such as Netscape, but these were quickly out-muscled by giants such as Microsoft with its Internet Explorer	Included many start-up pioneers such as Traidcraft, but has ultimately turned into a 'product' for large multinationals such as Walmart
Focused largely on the standardised hardware and software of the PC as its delivery platform, rather than multi-level applications	Travelled down the road of 'one size fits all' standardisation, through codes, standards and guidelines to shape its offering

Table 2 **Similarities between Web 2.0 and CSR 2.0**

Web 2.0	CSR 2.0
Defined by watchwords such as 'collective intelligence', 'collaborative networks' and 'user participation'	Defined by concepts such as 'global commons', 'innovative partnerships' and 'stakeholder involvement'
Tools include social media, knowledge syndication and beta testing	Mechanisms include diverse stakeholder panels, real-time transparent reporting and new-wave social entrepreneurship
Is as much a state of being as a technical advance – it is a new philosophy or way of seeing the world differently	Is recognising a shift in power from centralised to decentralised; a change in scale from few and big to many and small; and a change in application from single and exclusive to multiple and shared

As our world becomes more connected, and global challenges such as climate change and poverty loom ever larger, businesses that still practise CSR 1.0 will (in common with their Web 1.0 counterparts) be rapidly left behind. Highly conscientious and networked stakeholders will expose them and gradually withdraw their social licence to operate. By contrast, companies that embrace the CSR 2.0 era will be those that collaboratively find innovative ways tackle our global challenges and be rewarded in the marketplace as a result.

The ages and stages of CSR

Building on these ideas, and in order to make sense everything I have seen in the 50 countries I have travelled to over the past 20 years, I devised a model that depicts the evolution of business responsibility in terms of five overlapping periods – the ages of greed, philanthropy, marketing, management and responsibility – each of which typically manifests a different stage of sustainable business, namely: defensive, charitable, promotional, strategic (all CSR 1.0 approaches) and transformative CSR (CSR 2.0) (Table 3). My contention is that companies tend to move through these ages and stages (although they may have activities in several ages and stages at once), and that we should be encouraging business to make the transition to transformative CSR in the dawning age of responsibility. If companies remain stuck in any of the first four stages, I do not believe we will turn the tide on the environmental, social and ethical crises that we face. Simply put, sustainable business will continue to fail.

Let me introduce briefly the ages and stages of sustainable business. The age of greed is characterized by *defensive CSR* in which all corporate sustainability and responsibility practices – which are typically limited – are undertaken only if and when it can be shown that shareholder value will be protected as a result. Hence, employee volunteer programmes (which show evidence of improved staff motivation, commitment and productivity) are not uncommon, nor are targeted expenditures (for example, on pollution controls), which are seen to fend off regulation or avoid fines and penalties.

Charitable CSR in the age of philanthropy is where a company supports various social and environmental causes through donations and sponsorships, typically administered through a foundation, trust or chairman's fund and which are aimed at empowering community groups or civil society organisations (CSOs).

Table 3 **The ages and stages of CSR**

Economic age	Stage of CSR	Modus operandi	Key enabler	Stakeholder target
Greed	Defensive	Ad hoc interventions	Investments	Shareholders, government and employees
Philanthropy	Charitable	Charitable programmes	Projects	Communities
Marketing	Promotional	Public relations	Media	General public
Management	Strategic	Management systems	Codes	Shareholders & NGOs/CSOs*
Responsibility	Systemic	Business models	Products	Regulators and customers

* CSOs, civil society organisations

Promotional CSR in the age of marketing is what happens when corporate sustainability and responsibility is seen mainly as a public relations opportunity to enhance the brand, image and reputation of the company. Promotional CSR may draw on the practices of charitable and strategic CSR and turn them into PR spin, which is often characterized as 'greenwash'.

Strategic CSR, emerging from the age of management, means relating sustainable business activities to the company's core business (such as Coca-Cola's focus on water management), often through adherence to sustainable business codes and implementation of social and environmental management systems, which typically involve cycles of sustainable business policy development, goal and target setting, programme implementation, auditing and reporting.

Transformative CSR in the age of responsibility focuses its activities on identifying and tackling the root causes of our present unsustainability and irresponsibility, typically through innovating business models; revolutionizing their processes, products and services; and lobbying for progressive national and international policies. Hence, while strategic CSR is focused at the micro-level system – supporting social or environmental issues that happen to align with its strategy (but without necessarily changing that strategy) – transformative CSR focuses on understanding the interconnections of the macro-level system (society and ecosystems) and changing its strategy to optimise the outcomes for this larger human and ecological system.

The failure of CSR 1.0

Why has CSR 1.0 – those approaches from the ages of greed, philanthropy, marketing and management – failed so spectacularly to address the very issues it claims to be most concerned about? In my view, this comes down to three factors – which I call the triple curse of modern CSR (Table 4).

Table 4 **The failures of modern CSR**

Curses	Nature of the failing
Peripheral CSR	CSR has remained largely restricted to the largest companies, and mostly confined to PR, or other departments, rather than being integrated across the business
Incremental CSR	CSR has adopted the TQM* model, which results in incremental improvements that do not match the scale and urgency of the problems
Uneconomic CSR	CSR does not always make economic sense, as the short-term markets still reward companies that externalise their impacts to society

*TQM, total quality management

Peripheral CSR is evident when you ask any sustainable business managers what their greatest frustrations are and they tell you: lack of top-management commitment. This is 'code' for saying that sustainable business is, at best, a peripheral function in most companies. There may be a sustainable business manager, a CSR department even, a CSR report and a public commitment to any number of sustainable business codes and standards. But these do little to mask the underlying truth that shareholder-driven capitalism is rampant and its obsession with short-term financial measures of progress is contradictory in almost every way to the long-term, stakeholder approach needed for high-impact sustainable business.

The reason Enron collapsed, and indeed why our current financial crisis was allowed to spiral out of control, was not because of a few rogue executives or creative accounting practices, it was because of a culture of greed embedded in the DNA of the company and the financial markets. Whether you agree or not, and despite the emerging research on 'responsible competitiveness', it is hard to find any substantive examples in which the financial markets consistently reward responsible behaviour.

Incremental CSR occurs as a result of one of the great revolutions of the 1970s, namely total quality management (TQM), conceived by American statistician W. Edwards Deming and perfected by the Japanese before being exported around the world as ISO 9001. At the very core of Deming's TQM model and the ISO standard is continual improvement, a principle that has now become ubiquitous in all management system approaches to performance. It is no surprise, therefore, that the most popular environmental management standard, ISO 14001, is built on the same principle.

There is nothing wrong with continuous improvement per se. On the contrary, it has brought safety and reliability to the very products and services that we associate with our modern quality of life. But when we use it as the primary approach to tackling our social, environmental and ethical challenges, it fails on two critical counts: speed and scale. The incremental approach to sustainable business, while replete with evidence of micro-scale, gradual improvements, has completely and utterly failed to make any impact on the massive sustainability crises that we face, many of which are worsening at a pace that far outstrips any futile sustainable business-led attempts at amelioration.

Which brings us to Curse 3, *uneconomic CSR*. If there was ever a monotonously repetitive, stuck record in sustainable business debates, it is the one about the so-called 'business case' for CSR. That is because CSR managers and consultants, and even the occasional saintly CEO, are desperate to find compelling evidence that 'doing good is good for business'; in other words, that sustainable business pays. The lack of corroborative research seems to be no impediment for these desperados endlessly incanting the motto of the business case, as if it were an entirely self-evident fact.

The rather more 'inconvenient truth' is that sustainable business sometimes pays, in specific circumstances, but more often does not. Of course
there are low-hanging fruit – such as eco-efficiencies around waste and
energy – but these only go so far. Most of the hard-core sustainable business changes that are needed to reverse the misery of poverty and the
sixth mass extinction of species currently under way require strategic
change and massive investment. They may very well be lucrative in the
long term, economically rational over a generation or two, but we have
already established that the financial markets do not work like that: at
least, not yet.

The principles of CSR 2.0

Initial responses to my framing of CSR 2.0 were largely positive and confirmed that I was onto something – perhaps a new language or conceptu-
alisation of responsibility, or at the very least a nexus for talking about the
radical changes needed in sustainable business. However, I felt it needed
an institutional vehicle if it was going to have any chance of success, and
so CSR International was born, with the express mission to be an incuba-
tor for CSR 2.0. The think-tank was launched on 3 March 2010 in London,
complete with the theatrical burial of the old CSR and its rebirth as CSR
2.0.

It quickly became clear, however, that a metaphor can only take you so
far. What was needed was a set of principles against which we could test
sustainable business. These went through a few iterations, but I eventually settled on five, which form a kind of mnemonic for CSR 2.0: creativity (C), scalability (S), responsiveness (R), glocality (2) and circularity (0).
These principles, which are explored in detail *The Age of Responsibility*,
can be described briefly as follows:

- *Creativity.* The problem with our current obsession with sustainable
  business codes and standards (including the ISO 26000 standard) is
  that it encourages a tick-box approach to sustainable business. But
  our social and environmental problems are complex and intractable;
  they need creative solutions, such as Freeplay's wind-up technology
  or Vodafone's M-Pesa money-transfer scheme

- *Scalability.* The sustainable business literature is liberally sprinkled with charming case studies of truly responsible and sustainable projects. The problem is that so few of them ever go to scale. We need more examples like Walmart 'choice editing' by converting to organic cotton, Tata creating the affordable eco-efficient Nano car or Muhammad Yunus's Grameen microfinance model

- *Responsiveness.* More cross-sector partnerships and stakeholder-driven approaches are needed at every level, as well as more uncomfortable, transformative responsiveness, which questions whether particular industries, or business models, are part of the solution or part of the problem. A good example of responsiveness is the Corporate Leaders Group on Climate Change

- *Glocality.* This means 'think global, act local'. In a complex, interconnected, globalising world, companies (and their critics) will have to become far more sophisticated in combining international norms with local contexts, finding local solutions that are culturally appropriate, without forsaking universal principles. We are moving from an 'either–or' one-size-fits-all world to a 'both–and' strength-in-diversity world

- *Circularity.* Our global economic and commercial system is based on a fundamentally flawed design, which acts as if there are no limits on resource consumption or waste disposal. Instead, we need a C2C approach, closing the loop on production, as Shaw Carpets does, and designing products and processes to be inherently 'good', rather than 'less bad'

Shifting from CSR 1.0 to CSR 2.0

These principles are the acid test for future sustainable business practices. If they are applied, what kind of shifts will we see? In my view, they will happen at two levels. At a meta-level, there will be a change in sustainable business's ontological assumptions or ways of seeing the world. At a micro-level, there will be a change in sustainable business's methodological practices or ways of being in the world.

The meta-level changes can be described as follows: paternalistic relationships between companies and the community, based on philanthropy, will give way to more equal partnerships. Defensive, minimalist responses to social and environmental issues will be replaced by proactive strategies and investment in growing responsibility markets, such as clean technology. Reputation-conscious public-relations approaches to sustainable business will no longer be credible, and so companies will be judged on actual social, environmental and ethical performance, which illustrates whether things getting better on the ground in absolute, cumulative terms.

Although sustainable business specialists still have a role to play, each dimension of CSR 2.0 performance will be embedded and integrated into the core operations of companies. Standardised approaches will remain useful as guides to consensus, but sustainable business will find diversified expression and implementation at very local levels. CSR solutions, including responsible products and services, will go from niche 'nice-to-haves' to mass-market 'must-haves'. And the whole concept of sustainable business will lose its Western conceptual and operational dominance, giving way to a more culturally diverse and internationally applied concept. These shifts are summarised in Table 5 below.

Table 5 **CSR 1.0 to CSR 2.0 – meta-level ontological shifts**

CSR 1.0	CSR 2.0
Philanthropic	Collaborative
Risk-based	Reward-based
Image-driven	Performance-driven
Specialised	Integrated
Standardised	Diversified
Marginal	Scalable
Western	Global

How might these shifting principles manifest as sustainable business practices? Supporting these meta-level changes, the anticipated micro-level changes can be described as follows: sustainable business will no longer manifest as luxury products and services (as with current green and fair trade options), but as affordable solutions for those who most need quality of life improvements. Investment in self-sustaining social enterprises will be favoured over cheque-book charity. Sustainable business indexes, which rank the same large companies over and over (often revealing contradictions between indexes) will make way for sustainable business rating systems, which turn social, environmental, ethical and economic performance into corporate scores (A+, B−, etc., not dissimilar to credit ratings) and which analysts and others can usefully employ in their decision-making.

Reliance on sustainable business departments will disappear or disperse, as performance across responsibility and sustainability dimensions are increasingly built into corporate performance appraisal and market incentive systems. Self-selecting ethical consumers will become irrelevant, as CSR 2.0 companies begin to choice-edit, that is, cease to offer implicitly 'less ethical' product ranges, thus allowing guilt-free shopping. Post-use liability for products will become obsolete, as the service-lease and take-back economy goes mainstream. Annual CSR reporting will be replaced by online, real-time sustainable business performance data flows. Feeding into these live communications will be Web 2.0-connected social networks that allow 'crowdsourcing', instead of periodic meetings with cumbersome and biased stakeholder panels. And typical CSR 1.0 management systems standards such as ISO 14001 will be less credible than new performance standards, such as those emerging in climate change that set absolute limits and thresholds. These practical shifts are summarised in Table 6 below.

Table 6 **CSR 1.0 to CSR 2.0 – micro-level methodological shifts**

CSR 1.0	CSR 2.0
CSR premium	Base of the pyramid
Charity projects	Social enterprise
CSR indexes	CSR ratings
CSR departments	CSR incentives
Product liability	Choice editing
Ethical consumerism	Service agreements
CSR reporting cycles	CSR data streams
Stakeholder groups	Social networks
Process standards	Performance standards

The DNA model of CSR 2.0

Pulling it all together, I believe that CSR 2.0 – or transformative CSR (I also sometimes call it systemic CSR, radical CSR or holistic CSR, so use whichever you prefer) – represents a new model of sustainable business. In one sense, it is not so different from other models we have seen before. We can recognise echoes of Archie Carroll's CSR pyramid, Ed Freeman's stakeholder theory, Donna Wood's corporate social performance, John Elkington's triple bottom line, Stuart Hart and C.K. Prahalad's BOP, Mark Kramer and Michael Porter's shared value and the ESG approach of SRI, to mention but a few. But that is really the point – it integrates what we have learned to date. It presents a holistic model of sustainable business.

The essence of the CSR 2.0 DNA model (Table 7) are the four DNA responsibility bases, which are like the four nitrogenous bases of biological DNA (guanine, cytosine, thymine and adenine), sometimes abbreviated to the four letters GCTA (which was the inspiration for the 1997 science fiction film GATTACA). In the case of CSR 2.0, the DNA responsibility bases are value creation, environmental integrity, good governance and societal contribution, or VEGS if you like. Each DNA base has a primary goal and each goal has key indicators. The goals and key indicators, summarised in the table below, are what begin to show the qualitative and quantitative differences between other models of sustainable business and the CSR 2.0 DNA model.

Hence, if we look at *value creation*, it is clear we are talking about more than financial profitability. The goal is economic development, which means not only contributing to the enrichment of shareholders and executives, but improving the economic context in which a company operates, including investing in infrastructure, creating jobs, providing skills development and so on. There can be any number of key performance indicators (KPIs), but I want to highlight two that I believe are essential: beneficial products and inclusive business. Do the company's products and services really improve our quality of life, or do they cause harm or add to the low-quality junk of what Charles Handy calls the '*chindogu* society'? And how are the economic benefits shared? Does wealth trickle up or down? Are employees and SMEs in the supply chain, and are poor communities genuinely empowered?

Good governance is another area that is not new, but in my view has failed to be properly recognised or integrated in sustainable business circles. The goal of institutional effectiveness is as important as more lofty social and environmental ideals. After all, if the institution fails, or is not transparent and fair, this undermines everything else that sustainable business is trying to accomplish. Trends in reporting, but also other forms of transparency like social media and brand- or product-linked public databases of sustainable business performance, will be increasingly important indicators of success, alongside embedding ethical conduct in the culture of companies. Transparency tools – such as Goodguide, KPMG's integrity thermometer and Covalence's EthicalQuote ranking – will become more prevalent.

Societal contribution is an area that sustainable business is traditionally more used to addressing, with its goal of stakeholder orientation. This gives philanthropy its rightful place in CSR – as one tile in a larger mosaic – while also providing a spotlight for the importance of fair labour practices. It is simply unacceptable that there are more people in slavery today than there were before it was officially abolished in the 1800s, just as the use of child labour by high-brand companies is despicable. This area of stakeholder engagement, community participation and supply chain integrity remains one of the most vexing and critical elements of sustainable business.

Finally, *environmental integrity* sets the bar much higher than minimising damage; rather, it aims at maintaining and improving ecosystem sustainability. The KPIs give some sense of the ambition required here – 100% renewable energy and zero waste. We cannot continue the same practices that have, according to WWF's Living Planet Index, caused us to lose one-third of the biodiversity on the planet since 1970. Nor can we continue to gamble with the prospect of dangerous – and perhaps catastrophic and irreversible – climate change.

A final point to make is that CSR 2.0 also proposes a new interpretation for the terms 'sustainability' and 'responsibility'. Like two intertwined strands of DNA, sustainability and responsibility can be thought of as different, yet complementary elements of CSR. Hence, sustainability can be conceived as the destination – the challenges, vision, strategy and goals, in other words, what we are aiming for – while responsibility is more about the journey – our solutions, responses, management and actions, that is, how we get there.

Table 7 **DNA model of CSR 2.0**

DNA code	Strategic goals	Key indicators
Value creation	Economic development	• Capital investment (financial, manufacturing, social, human and natural capital) • Beneficial products (sustainable and responsible goods and services • Inclusive business (wealth distribution, bottom of the pyramid markets)
Good governance	Institutional effectiveness	• Leadership (strategic commitment to sustainability and responsibility) • Transparency (sustainability and responsibility reporting, government payments) • Ethical practices (bribery and corruption prevention, values in business)
Societal contribution	Stakeholder orientation	• Philanthropy (charitable donations, provision of public goods and services) • Fair labour practices (working conditions, employee rights, health & safety) • Supply chain integrity (SME* empowerment, labour and environmental standards)
Environmental integrity	Sustainable ecosystems	• Ecosystem protection (biodiversity conservation and ecosystem restoration) • Renewable resources (tackling climate change, renewable energy and materials) • Zero waste production (cradle-to-cradle processes, waste elimination)

* SMEs, small and medium-sized enterprises

Smart, shared and sustainable
The alchemical quest (2012 and beyond)

The next ten years

This book has been about an epic journey over the past 20 years – a journey of the sustainable business profession emerging and seeking to define itself; a journey of the sustainability and responsibility movement as it matures and goes mainstream; and a journey of a single individual, myself, through the profession, swept along by the movement, and carried on the wings of curiosity around the world.

In the last chapter on CSR 2.0, I presented a vision of a purpose-driven, principle-based approach, in which business seeks to identify and tackle the root causes of our present unsustainability and irresponsibility, typically through innovating business models; revolutionising their processes, products and services; and lobbying for progressive national and international policies. Based on this vision – and the evolution of sustainable business over the past 20 years, I have created ten forecasts for the next ten years.

> *Forecast 1.* By 2022, we will see most large, international companies having moved through the first four types or stages of CSR (defensive, charitable, promotional and strategic) and practising, to varying degrees, transformative CSR, or CSR 2.0

Forecast 2. By 2022, reliance on sustainable business codes, standards and guidelines such as the UN Global Compact, ISO 14001and SA 8000, will be seen as a necessary but insufficient way to practise CSR. Instead, companies will be judged on how innovative they are in using their products and processes to tackle social and environmental problems

Forecast 3. By 2022, self-selecting 'ethical consumers' will become less relevant as a force for change. Companies – strongly encouraged by government policies and incentives – will scale up their choice-editing and cease offering 'less ethical' product ranges, thus allowing guilt-free shopping

Forecast 4. By 2022, cross-sector partnerships will be at the heart of all CSR approaches. These will increasingly be defined by business bringing its core competencies and skills (rather than just its financial resources) to the party

Forecast 5. By 2022, companies practising sustainable business will be expected to comply with global best-practice principles, such as those in the UN Global Compact or the Ruggie Human Rights Framework, but simultaneously demonstrate sensitivity to local issues and priorities

Forecast 6. By 2022, progressive companies will be required to demonstrate full life-cycle management of their products, from cradle to cradle. We will see most large companies committing to the goal of zero-waste, carbon-neutral and water-neutral production, with mandated take-back schemes for most products

Forecast 7. By 2022, some form of Generally Accepted Sustainability Practices (GASP) will be agreed, much like the Generally Accepted Accounting Practices (GAAP), including consensus principles, methods, approaches and rules for measuring and disclosing sustainable business. Furthermore, a set of credible CSR rating agencies will have emerged

Forecast 8. By 2022, many of today's sustainable business practices will be mandatory requirements. However, CSR will remain a voluntary practice – an innovation and differentiation frontier – for those companies that are either willing and able, or pushed and prodded through non-governmental means, to go ahead of the legislation to improve quality of life around the world

Forecast 9. By 2022, corporate transparency will take the form of publicly available sets of mandatory disclosed social, environmental and governance data – available down to a product life-cycle impact level – as well as Web 2.0 collaborative sustainable business feedback platforms, WikiLeaks-type whistle-blowing sites and product-rating applications

Forecast 10. By 2022, CSR will have diversified back into its specialist disciplines and functions, leaving little or no sustainable business departments behind, yet having more specialists in particular areas (climate, biodiversity, human rights, community involvement, etc.), and more employees with knowledge of how to integrate CSR issues into their functional areas (HR, marketing, finance, etc.)

Collectively, these forecasts reflect a scenario of widespread adoption of CSR 2.0 by 2022, a future in which companies become a significant part of the solution to our sustainability crisis, rather than complicit contributors to the problem, as they are today. Given the current global crises and mounting system pressures, and knowing business's ability to adapt and change rapidly, I regard this as a highly likely prediction sketched out by a concerned pragmatist, rather than the wish-list of a sustainable business 'true believer'.

A triple-S future for business

I will end by sharing where I plan to focus my energies over the coming years. For me, it all comes back to redefining the purpose of business. Charles Handy calls this 'the capitalist dilemma':

> Money, and profit, is essential to the survival and growth of any enterprise, but if it is the only or even the main purpose, it will be seen as selfish and may lead to a neglect of the wider responsibilities that business owes to society.

I like to talk about the challenge in terms of purpose-inspired businesses – companies that can synergise the 5 Ps of purpose, principles, passion, partnership and prosperity. *Purpose* is about business recapturing its original mission of serving society. *Principles* relates to companies that make hard strategic decisions based on higher values, not simply financial returns. *Passion* is about creating a work environment where people can be proud of their company and inspired by their jobs. *Partnership* means seeing the world as a kaleidoscope of stakeholder relationships and solving the world's biggest challenges in collaboration with government and civil society. *Prosperity*, finally, is about improving our qualitative well-being, so that nature and society flourish.

I believe that over the next ten years or so, we will see the emergence of a new triple bottom line – a 'triple-S' focus on business strategies that are smart, shared and sustainable. *Smart* strategies will see the confluence of technologies that connect and empower even the remotest communities, thereby addressing the 'digital divide' and making access to knowledge virtually free and universal. *Shared* strategies will see the maturing of models of inclusive business and shared value creation, placing far more emphasis on how wealth is distributed by business. *Sustainable* strategies will see the circular economy of C2C design, and what John Elkington calls the 'zeronauts', becoming the new foundation on which all business is conducted. These triple-S strategies are the topic for my next book – *The Future of Business: Smart, Shared and Sustainable* – so watch this space.

As for this book, we have reached the end of our journey together. If you have made it to the end, hearty congratulations. My quest for sustainable business over the past 20 years has indeed been epic. When people ask me why I travel so much – and indeed why I have written 15 books – my answer is that I am an eternal student. I am intrigued and fascinated by business and its potential for good. I hope that the lessons I have learned and the insights I have gained will inspire you to continue the quest in your own endeavours.

I often end my presentations with a cartoon, in which a member of the audience at a sustainable business conference asks the keynote speaker a question: 'What if it's all a big hoax and we create a better world for nothing!?' I use this to remind myself – and my audiences – that we are all trying to create a better world. But let us not fool ourselves. We have made amazing progress, but we are still very early on our collective quest for sustainable business. We must be clear and honest with ourselves and each other: so far, our experiment with voluntary CSR and sustainable enterprise has failed to deliver on its promise.

That is no reason to give up, quite the opposite in fact. We live in exciting times – a true period of bifurcation. We live on the cusp of the post-industrial revolution, and for the first time, we can finally glimpse what a new model of sustainable business and purpose-inspired capitalism could look like. As with so many things in life, the quest for a sustainable future is like a wheelbarrow. The only way we will make progress is if we pick it up and push forward. And the only way we will motivate people to join us in this effort is if they believe in what we are building. And what are we building? We are building nothing less than a new civilization.

For me, the quest has always been for a new way of doing business – a kind of alchemy in which we symbolically transform the base elements of moneymaking into the valuable gold of meaning-creation. The path to a smart, shared and sustainable future lies ahead. I look forward to our wheelbarrows crossing along the way.

If this book has moved or inspired you in any way, you are welcome to contact me on wayne@waynevisser.com.

Dr Wayne Visser
London, June 2012

About the author

Dr Wayne Visser is Founder and Director of the think-tank CSR International and research company Kaleidoscope Futures. He is the author of 15 books and over 180 publications (chapters, articles, etc.), and has delivered more than 170 professional speeches in over 50 countries in the last 20 years. In addition, Wayne is Senior Associate at the University of Cambridge Programme for Sustainability Leadership, and Adjunct Professor of CSR at Warwick Business School, United Kingdom.

Before gaining his PhD in Corporate Social Responsibility (Nottingham University, United Kingdom), Wayne was Director of Sustainability Services for KPMG, and strategy analyst for Capgemini in South Africa. His other qualifications include an MSc in Human Ecology (Edinburgh University, United Kingdom) and a Bachelor of Business Science with Honours in Marketing (Cape Town University, South Africa).

In 2011, Wayne was listed in the *Top 100 Global Sustain Ability Leaders* (ranking by ABC Carbon) and the *Top 100 Thought Leaders in Europe and the Middle East 2011* (ranking by Centre for Sustainability and Excellence, and Trust Across America). He was also winner of the *Outstanding Author Contribution Award at the Emerald Literati Network Awards for Excellence 2011* and recipient of the *Outstanding Teacher Award of The Warwick MBA 2010/11*.

Wayne's work has taken him to more than 50 countries in the last 20 years. In the past two years alone, he has travelled to more than 25 countries to share best practices in corporate sustainability and responsibility. Wayne lives in London, United Kingdom, and enjoys art, nature, writing poetry and travelling around the world. A full biography and much of his writing and art is on www.waynevisser.com

Other books by Wayne Visser

Non-fiction

South Africa: Reasons to Believe (with G. Lundy; Cape Town, South Africa: Aardvark Press, 2003).

Business Frontiers: Social Responsibility, Sustainable Development and Economic Justice (Hyderabad, India: ICFAI Books, 2005).

Making a Difference: Purpose-Inspired Leadership for Corporate Sustainability and Responsibility (CSR) (Saarbrücken, Germany: VDM, 2008).

The Top 50 Sustainability Books (on behalf of the University of Cambridge Programme for Sustainability Leadership; Sheffield, UK: Greenleaf Publishing, 2009; www.greenleaf-publishing.com/top50).

Landmarks for Sustainability: Events and Initiatives that have Changed Our World (on behalf of the University of Cambridge Programme for Sustainability Leadership; Sheffield, UK: Greenleaf Publishing, 2009; www.greenleaf-publishing.com/landmarks).

The Age of Responsibility: CSR 2.0 and the New DNA of Business (Chichester, UK: John Wiley & Sons, 2011).

Corporate Sustainability and Responsibility: An Introductory Text on CSR Theory and Practice – Past, Present and Future (London, UK: Kaleidoscope Futures, 2012).

The A to Z of Corporate Social Responsibility (with D. Matten, M. Pohl and N. Tolhurst; Chichester, UK: John Wiley & Sons, 2007).

Corporate Citizenship in Africa (edited with M. McIntosh and C. Middleton; Sheffield, UK: Greenleaf Publishing, 2006; www.greenleaf-publishing.com/africa).

Beyond Reasonable Greed: Why Sustainable Business is a Much Better Idea! (with C. Sunter; Cape Town, South Africa: Human & Rousseau and Tafelberg Publishers, 2002).

The World Guide to CSR: A Country-by-Country Analysis of Corporate Sustainability and Responsibility (edited with N. Tolhurst; Sheffield, UK: Greenleaf Publishing, 2010; www.greenleaf-publishing.com/worldguide).

Fiction

Seize the Day: Favourite Inspirational Poems (London, UK: Kaleidoscope Futures, 2011).

Wishing Leaves: Favourite Nature Poems (London, UK: Kaleidoscope Futures, 2011).

I Am An African: Favourite Africa Poems (London, UK: Kaleidoscope Futures, 2011).

Index

Note: Page numbers in *italic figures* refer to tables.

For Product Safety Concerns and Information please contact our EU
representative GPSR@taylorandfrancis.com
Taylor & Francis Verlag GmbH, Kaufingerstraße 24, 80331 München, Germany